The Revelations of Saint Birgitta

EDITED FROM THE GARRETT MS.
PRINCETON UNIVERSITY LIBRARY
DEPOSIT 1397

EARLY ENGLISH TEXT SOCIETY

Original Series, No. 178

1929 (for 1928)

PRICE 10s.

The Revelations of Saint Birgitta

EDITED FROM THE FIFTEENTH-CENTURY MS. IN
THE GARRETT COLLECTION IN THE LIBRARY OF
PRINCETON UNIVERSITY

BY

WILLIAM PATTERSON CUMMING, Ph.D.

LONDON:
PUBLISHED FOR THE EARLY ENGLISH TEXT SOCIETY
BY HUMPHREY MILFORD, OXFORD UNIVERSITY PRESS
AMEN HOUSE, E.C.
1929

Printed in Great Britain

TO MY PARENTS

PREFACE

I wish to express my grateful appreciation for the invaluable advice and encouragement of Professor Gordon Hall Gerould of Princeton University throughout the editing of this manuscript. My thanks are also due to Dr. E. C. Richardson, Director of Princeton University Library, and to Mr. S. H. Leach, former Reference Librarian of Princeton University Library, who first called my attention to the Garrett manuscript. This work was originally submitted to the English Department of Princeton University in fulfilment of the partial requirement for the Doctor of Philosophy degree; certain sections of the original work have been omitted and the Introduction has been re-written.

The especial acknowledgement of the Early English Text Society, as well as of the editor, is due to Mr. Walter Roesler of New York City for his generous gift to the Society of a sum to assist in the cost of publishing this work.

W. P. C.

DAVIDSON,

NORTH CAROLINA,

February, 1929.

CONTENTS

TABLE OF ABBREVIATIONS

A.S. = *Acta Sanctorum*, quotquot toto coluntur, Bruxellis & Parisiis, October, tom. iv, Birgitta.

Durantus = *Revelationes Sanctae Birgittae*, Olim a Card. Turrecremata recognitae & approbatae, & a Consaluo Duranto Ep*iscopo* Ferettrano notis illustratae, & in duos Tomos distributae. Romae, apud Ludouicum Grignanum, 1628.

Klemming = *Heliga Birgittas Uppenbarelser*, G. E. Klemming, Svenska Fornskrift-Sällskapet, vols. i–v, Stockholm, 1857–64.

S.R.S. = *Scriptores Rerum Suecicarum Medii Aevi*, vols. i–iii, edited by E. M. Fant, E. G. Geijer, I. H. Schröder, and C. Annerstedt, Upsala, 1818–76.

Westman = *Birgitta-Studier*, K. B. Westman, *Uppsala Universitets Årsskrift*, Bd. i, Upsala, 1911, pp. 1–304.

Wyld = *A History of Modern Colloquial English*, H. C. Wyld, London, 1920.

INTRODUCTION

PART I. MANUSCRIPT

A. *Description of the Manuscript*

Princeton University Library Deposit 1397, a M.E. manuscript containing translations from the revelations of Saint Birgitta, is the property of Mr. Robert Garrett, Baltimore, Maryland, U.S.A.

The manuscript has a cover of dark leather bound on boards. The dimensions of the binding are 23·7 cm. × 17·0 cm. The leather is gold tooled, with a gold line border, and with an oval-shaped medallion (on each cover) between the initials B and S. The medallions have the same design ; each represents the crucifixion, with two figures standing on either side of the cross, and the sun, moon, and stars above. On the back of the binding, printed in later type, is the erroneous title, *Life of S. Brigit.*

There are four paper fly-leaves at the beginning, and six at the end, of the volume, which are probably contemporary with the binding. On the inside of the front cover are pencilled in different hands ' Revelations of St. Bridgitt ', ' 7313 ', and ' R. G. Oct. 1905 '.[1] The first and second fly-leaves are mutilated ; the third has ' Old No. 894 ' in pencil. The fourth fly-leaf, recto, has the stamp of a lion rampant above ' Sir T[homas] P[hillips], Middle Hill ', with ' 1366 ' written below in pencil. The fourth fly-leaf, verso, has 'Saint Brigitt' and 'Phillipps MS. 1366' in ink ; the first vellum leaf also has 'Phillipps MS. 1366' in ink.

The manuscript has seventy-seven vellum leaves, 22·7 cm. × 16·5 cm.[2] The nine gatherings vary in length ; the first gathering has nine leaves, the next three ten leaves, the next

---

[1] Bought by Robert Garrett in October 1905.

[2] The vellum used in the manuscript is not of very good quality. There are six holes within the text columns, and some leaves have been made by pasting together pieces of vellum.

three eight leaves, and the last two only seven leaves.[1] Most of the signatures were lost when the manuscript was bound. The remaining signatures, as well as all the catchwords, are noted in the text.

The text, which usually runs over the four marginal lines that are drawn on every page, averages 17·3 cm. × 11·5 cm. The text shows the handwriting of two scribes, both of whom wrote in the cursive bookhand of the middle of the fifteenth century. The first hand runs to leaf 63a, most of which, as well as all of leaf 63b, is left vacant. The second hand begins at the top of leaf 64a and continues to the end. The chapter headings and quotations from the Vulgate are rubricated ; the marginal glosses and capitals in the text of the second scribe are also frequently rubricated. The initial letters of each revelation throughout the manuscript are two lines in height and coloured in blue. The lines average thirty-one to the page.

There are no colophons or marginal notes to give a clue as to the names of the scribes or the early history of the manuscript. The manuscript is not listed in the Syon Monastery catalogue.[2] However, the catalogue is for the men's library, and this manuscript may have been a copy of a translation for the nuns.[3] The binding is of the late sixteenth or early seventeenth century ;[4] I have been unable to identify the medal-

---

[1] Originally, the last gathering had eight leaves ; see the note to line 123/3o of the text.

[2] Mary Bateson, *Catalogue of the Library of Syon Monastery*, Cambridge University Press, 1898, pp. 107–8, 115. Syon Monastery is the only monastery of the Birgittine order in England of which we have record. There are seven volumes of Birgitta's works listed in the catalogue, apparently all in Latin (Bateson, *op. cit.*, p. ix).

[3] It is probable that the nuns' library had a translation of the revelations. *The Myroure of Our Lady* (E.E.T.S., E.S.; xix) and the *Martilogue* (*ibid.*, p. xlvi) were both Englished for the nuns ; and we know that they had other books translated for them because of their inability to understand Latin (Bateson, *op. cit.*, p. ix, note 1, and p. xiv).

[4] The water-marks in the fly-leaves put an *a quo* limit to the binding of 1578. The water-mark is a double cross with two opposed C's under a crown. There is a rather complicated countermark. C. M. Briquet (*Les Filigranes*, Hiersemann, Leipzig, 1923, vol. ii, p. 493 and water marks 9320 ff.) says that the opposed C embracing the crowned cross of Lorraine originated in 1578 ; this mark became very common, and countermarks were used for more complete identification.

lion.[1] The manuscript was finally acquired by Sir Thomas
Phillipps; it was sold at the auction of part of his library in
June, 1896.[2] In October, 1905, Mr. Robert Garrett, the pre-
sent owner, bought the volume, and later placed it in the
Princeton University Library as a loan deposit.[3]

B. *Date.*

1. *Language.* Both scribes write in the London dialect of
the fifteenth century. The frequent use by the scribes of *her,
hyr, hir,* for the third person plural possessive pronoun indicates that the manuscript was written before 1475.[4] The first
scribe has a very few scattered forms in *ther*; the second scribe
uses *her,* but also *their, thair,* and especially *thaire.* Both
scribes use *hem,* but the second also writes *thaym, them,* and
especially *thaim.* The regular use of the plural form *schulle(n)*
by the second scribe points to a date some years before 1475.[5]
The use of personal pronouns and verbal endings coincides
in many important respects with the language of Gregory's
Chronicle. William Gregory, who died in 1467, wrote the
genuine London English of his day.[6] The similarity in

---

[1] The late date of the binding seems to preclude the possibility of the
B S standing for Bibliotheca Syonis, nor do the seals of the monastery
which I have seen bear the device (G. M. Aungier, *History and Antiquities
of Syon Monastery,* 1840, plate opposite p. 106).

[2] Phillipps Sales Catalogue, 10–17 June 1896, p. 24. The description is
an amusing combination of fact and misinformation:

'(No.) 141 BRIGIT. THE LYFE AND REVELATIONS OF SEYNTE
BRIGITTE, *fine manuscript of the fourteenth century, written in old English*
ON VELLUM, *with capitals coloured and titles rubricated, in first-rate pre-
servation, calf* 154 pages, 4to, XIV CENT. The binding on both sides
of the volume is impressed with a representation of the Crucifixion, gilt,
with the initials B.S. on either side. A very valuable and probably
unique manuscript.'

In the Princeton University Library copy of the catalogue, which has a
list of the purchasers and the auction prices, the hand has here written
'Quaritch, 88.—.—.' in the margin.

[3] Mr. G. M. Peck of the Princeton University Library informs me that
the date of accession was 12 February 1906.

[4] H. C. Wyld, *A History of Modern Colloquial English,* London, 1920,
p. 327.

[5] *Ibid.,* p. 357. [6] *Ibid.,* pp. 92–5.

language extends to other forms and spellings common in the
London dialect of the period. The interchange of *w* and *v*, of
which there are several examples in the Garrett MS., is found
in the writings of Gregory and other London writers.[1] By
the middle of the fifteenth century the prefix of the past participle is chiefly confined to texts showing a Southern provincial influence. However, Gregory and the scribes of the
Garrett MS. both use the past participle prefix.[2] The first
scribe has a number of Northern or North-Eastern forms;[3]

[1] Wyld, p. 292. The Garrett MS. has the interchange of *w* for *v* in
wessell 72/24, *woyce* 62/30, *wery* 98/4, and of *v* for *w* in *vykked* 21/25, *videw*
38/14. A few other examples of similarities in language may be noted.
Gregory and the Garrett MS. have comparatively few *e*-forms for O.E. *y, i*,
and these are all known to have been in use in genuine London English: Gregory has *steryd, besely, levyd* (*ibid.*, pp. 92–3); the Garrett
MS. has *besyly* 68/5, *besy* 61/29, *besily* 101/18, *steryth* 3/10, *leving* 115/23,
beld 9/10. The combination *-an* is often written *-on* not only in *londe,
stonde, honde*, but also in the unlengthened combination *thonke* (*ibid.*, p. 93).
The relative pronoun *who* is occasionally written *ho, hoo, hos*, showing
that the *w* was not pronounced (*ibid.*, p. 95). The third person singular
present ending of the verb is usually *-eth*, although the first scribe of the
Garrett MS. has exceptions in *-es*, and *strenght* 14/17, *plesyt* 23/1, *hat* 30/25,
and *punishet* 59/10. In the third person plural the first scribe has the
Southern *-eth*, a very few endings in the more typical E.Midl. *-en*, a few
-es endings, and no ending (cf. *ibid.*, p. 76). With the second scribe *-en*
is more frequent. The present part. is regularly *yng(e), ing(e)*, but the
second scribe occasionally has *eng* (cf. *ibid.*, p. 76). The past part. of weak
verbs is usually *-ed(e), id*; but the first scribe occasionally has no ending;
wesh 17/36, *kepe* 26/15, *translate* 51/32, *devote* 52/8.

[2] Wyld, pp. 95, 342. All occurrences of the prefix in the Garrett
MS. are given here: the first scribe, *y-ʒoue* 4/27, *I-gote* 30/18, *I-comme*
38/25, *ishamed* 41/21 (O.E. *gesceomod*), *I-gotte* 50/25, *I-gott* 79/9, *I-yeve* 86/38,
97/31, *I-do* 92/25; the second scribe, *I-done* 121/23, *I-write* 123/4.

[3] *Awn* 36/22, *aune* 87/2, 'own'; *worching* 29/31, 'working' (H. M.
Flasdieck, *Forschungen zur Frühzeit der Neuenglischen Schriftsprache*, Teil ii,
Studien zur Englischen Philologie, Heft lxv, p. 32, ' O dringt in London erst
sehr spät und spärlich ein'); *whenched* 8/24, 'quenched', *qwhik* 68/28,
whykke 20/22, *whyke* 77/1, 'quick'; *whiter* 47/8, 'quitter', 'pus'. At
26/105, 48/183, 65/27, is a Northern form of 'that'. The third person
singular present indicative occasionally ends in *es, -ys*, which is unusual
at this time (Wyld, pp. 332–7): *spekys* 1/19, *callys* 36/19, *stondes* 10/7,
thynkes 16/3, *betokenes* 18/3, *spekes* 64/22, *despices* 96/35. The *-es* ending
for the third person plural present indicative is a Northern form of
which there are no contemporary examples found in the genuine London
writings (*ibid.*, p. 340); *stondes* 5/7, *sees* 7/21, *profettes* 23/14, *beholdes* 57/13,

whether these were in the original translation or are due to
the present scribe it is very difficult to determine. Northern
forms are the exception rather than the rule, and it seems
more probable that a Midland translation was copied by a
scribe in or from the Northern dialect area.[1]

2. *Scribes.* The first scribe expected the manuscript to end
with his *Assint laudes deo.* The heading of the last chapter
(see text, 98/1–5) and the discoloration of leaf 63b, which
indicates that for a time it was the end of the manuscript,
show this. The second scribe, on the other hand, with his
more frequent use of the pronominal *their* and *them* forms, the
more pointed style in his handwriting, and the increase in
flourishes,[2] has characteristics which naturally place him a few
years later than the first scribe. The first scribe was probably
a transcriber; the frequent omission of single words, the
repetition of words and phrases, and other errors bear strong
evidence for this view.[3] The second scribe may have translated directly from the Latin. He makes several corrections,
and has repetition of a word once.[4] However, the second

---

abydes 62/34, *towches* 63/28. Other unusual or interesting forms which
occur in the manuscript will be found in the Glossary.

[1] From the list of brethren in Syon Monastery we know that a few were
from Yorkshire; and two of the three bequests of translations of the
Revelations which are mentioned in contemporary wills are from Cecily,
Duchess of York, and Elizabeth Sywardby of Sywardby in Yorkshire
(p. xxxviii, notes 1, 2).

[2] Maunde Thompson, *Introduction to Greek and Latin Palaeography*, Oxford,
1912, p. 554.

[3] A list of passages in the first hand where words or phrases have been
omitted, with the corresponding words in the Latin text, follows : *te*
16/36, *ventus* 33/22, *Deum* 36/12, *cogitauit* 39/24, *consilio* 41/2, & *Filii mei*
41/12, *non* 46/16, *Benedictum* 53/10, *quia sentiunt* 55/5, *bitumen* 58/34, *nullum*
60/9, *non* 61/4, *per* 70/31, *Deo* 73/2, & *post* 74/20, *animae* 78/15, *facere*
80/37, the preposition *of* in *Angelum Dei* 84/12, a complete clause 87/34, *me*
89/6, *veniet* 97/33. The scribe seems to have misrendered *maly*[t]*e* as
malyce 77/28, [f]*rosses* as *throsses* 82/18, and Latin *praedicabam* as *purchesed*
91/2 ; his eye probably skipped from the first to the second *hauyn* . .
hauyn 33/26–27, an error which he later rectified. I have not included
the repetition of letters made when beginning a new page in the following
list of words and phrases which have been repeated : 12/14, 18/9, 21/17,
21/37, 29/26, 30/29, 32/7, 44/5, 66/8, 69/31, 75/21, 80/30, 88/34, 90/1,
94/34.

[4] He repeats *I* 115/35, and makes three corrections : see 99/31, 100/27,

scribe is a much more careful writer than the first, and he may have made an unusually clean copy.

Since the date of the manuscript has to be determined entirely on internal evidence, no exact dating is possible. The first scribe wrote shortly before 1450, while the second scribe probably wrote towards the end of the third quarter of the century.

C. *Other English Manuscripts*

I

1. *British Museum MS. Julius F. II.* 'The Revelations of S. Bridget, princess of Nerike in Sweden', Bks. I–VII, translated into English ; with the Prologue of Matthias, canon of Lincöping. The Prologue begins : 'Wondyr and marvelys are herd in owre cuntre and [*erased* or] in owre land. yt was a mervelous thinge.' A leaf is missing after f. 92, containing Bk. III, middle of ch. 20 to middle of ch. 23 ; Bk. IV ends at ch. 130 ; Bk. V includes the Prologue and the 'Expositio et Declaratio' at the end ; Bk. VI ends with ch. 109 ; Bk. VII is complete and ends with ch. 31 on f. 246 b. It is followed immediately by the Epistola Solitarii ad Reges Domini Alphonsi, beginning 'O ȝe cler and bright kynges and wold to god' and includes the Recapitulation [ch. 7] which ends 'as it schewis breffly in all thinges before seid. And of the seyinges of al doctours and holy fadris vpon this matur diffusely and manyfold wise speking'. This is followed on f. 254 by an Epilogue beginning 'yt shewys euydently to all cristen pepil þat in þe yere fro thincarnacion of our lord ihesu crist Mlo CCCo LXXII the 10o Kalend of August þat is the day aftir mary mawdeleyn blissid lady Brigid of Swecy died in the cety of Rome'. This Epilogue (part of which has been printed by G. M. Aungier, *History and Antiquities of Syon Monastery*, 1840, p. 19) gives a brief account of her death, writings, and canonization. On the last page (f. 254 b) are two Latin prayers to St. Birgitta.

Paper : ff. 254. 12″ × 8½″. Fifteenth century.

105/15. He writes *bys[p]renglith* as *bystrenglith* 108/32. The haplography on 102/5 may have been made either by the scribe or in the Latin.

2. *British Museum MS. Claudius B. I.* 'The Revelation of sainct Bridgitte', translated into English ; preceded by a life of St. Birgitta, imperfect at beginning and end (ff. 2–4), which differs from the other extant English lives. Many chapters are abbreviated throughout the text. The Revelations are imperfect at the beginning, commencing in the middle of ch. 1 (f. 5): 'of man þat I have boght with mine owen blode bot he dose noght þat as mightier þan I '. Bk. I, chs. 15 and 18 are reversed ; Bk. I, end of ch. 38, chs. 39–40, and beginning of ch. 41 missing through loss of two leaves after f. 42 ; Bk. II, end of ch. 10 and beginning of ch. 11 are missing through loss of a leaf after f. 84 ; Bk. III, end of ch. 28 and beginning of ch. 29 are missing through loss of a leaf after f. 144 ; Bk. IV, end of ch. 16 to end of ch. 31 missing through loss of several leaves after f. 167 ; Bk. IV, end of ch. 111 to beginning of ch. 115 missing through loss of leaf after f. 203 ; end of ch. 129 and ch. 130 (where Bk. IV ended) missing through loss of leaf after f. 211 ; Bk. V is complete with the Prologue, except for the short introductory paragraph at the beginning of the book (beginning in the Latin 'Vidi thronum ') ; Bk. VI has 107 chapters which correspond to chs. 1–109 of the Latin printed edition with the omission of ch. 65, as ch. 64 includes chs. 64 and 66 of the printed edition ; Bk. VII, chs. 1–29 (last chapter imperfect) correspond to chs. 1–28 of the Latin printed edition, as ch. 13 is divided into two parts ; the manuscript ends in the middle of ch. 28 of the printed edition, and chs. 29–31, which are the last three chapters of Bk. VII, are missing.

Vellum : ff. 281. $13\frac{1}{4}'' \times 9''$. Gatherings of 8 leaves (first[6], II[9], V[7], VI[6], IX[9], XI[7], XXII[7], XXVIII[7], last[2]). Fifteenth century.

3. *British Museum MS. Harley 4800.* An English translation of Bk. IV and the beginning of Bk. V of the Revelations of St. Birgitta. The end of ch. 6 and the beginning of ch. 7 of Bk. IV are missing through loss of a leaf after f. 8 ; two gatherings (e–f) are missing after f. 38 containing chs. 40–72, which are wanting ; one leaf is also missing after f. 67, containing middle of ch. 89. Begins : 'A persone appered to þe spouse semynge to her þat he was cutted about as yn maner of repref'. Ends in the middle of Bk. V, ch. 2 : 'Therfor ho

þat forsaketh hys propre wyl and ys obedient to me he schal have hevyn wythoute peyne'. There are traces of several leaves having been torn out at the end. Pages from f. 1 to f. 106 are headed 'liber quartus', but from ff. 1–28 'liber primus' was originally written and cancelled in the same hand. Paper: ff. 109. $11\frac{1}{4}'' \times 8\frac{1}{4}''$. Gatherings of 10 leaves, letters a–d, g–o (first[8], VI[9], and last[2] imperfect). Fifteenth century. Chapters numbered. Headings in black, initials in red. The name Edward South is written on f. 1, probably as a former owner. On f. 53 b is written : 'Luke vnto Mr Syr James Parson of no church and vycare of the same', and on f. 54 'I lent my mony vnto my frend as many men dothe in land I axed my mony of my frend by-cause yt was so longe. I loste my mony and my frend me thought it was great wrong. J. Bray'; both in the same seventeenth-century hand.

4. *Bodleian MS. Rawlinson C. 41.* Selections from the revelations. The manuscript is imperfect ; the first leaf is numbered f. 97. There are two parts. I. The first part contains the life of the Blessed Virgin Mary, and begins in the middle of Bk. I, ch. 9 : 'Shew to the how moche my son hath honourde my name, my body, & my soule. [Chapter heading follows.] Of the most excellent dignite of the holy name of this vergin mary. Capitulum primum. I am gwen to hevyn'. Chapter 9 is followed by selections from different books, rather loosely translated. Each leaf is headed with the running title 'Vita beate Marie'. Ends on f. 43 b: 'Here have I shewyd to the how much god wyche ys my sonne hath lovyd and honourd my soule & my body. Amen. Deo gratias'. II. The second part contains 'The wordis of Christ to hys spowse of the artyclys of the very trewe feyth & what be the ornamentes & tokyns & the wyll that a spowse ought to have to her spowse'. There are three chapters (ff. 44 a–52 a). The first revelation is Bk. I, ch. 2, and begins : 'I am maker of hevyn, of erth, of the see, and of all thyngs that be in them'. The second part ends with Bk. II, ch. 26 on f. 52 a : 'then for to covete and have a wyll allway to synne'.

Paper : ff. 91 4to. End of fifteenth century.

Bound in with the same volume is a poem written about the

end of the seventeenth century by Th. Robinson, and dedicated by him to W. Taylor, B.D., his former tutor : 'The life and Death of Mary Magdalene, or, Her Life in Sin and Death to Sin '. ff. 54–91.

5. *British Museum MS. Arundel 197.* A small volume containing mystical and religious pieces ; on ff. 38 b–47 b two chapters 'drawy*n*ne out of the revelati*oun* of se*n*t Bryde'. On f. 38 b begins a treatise on active and contemplative life (Bk. VI, ch. 65) : 'I finde as Y rede bi doctoris and holimennis wretinge'. This is followed on f. 46 b by a short revelation (Bk. II, ch. 16) in which God admonishes St. Birgitta to love him above all things and to eschew pride and the lusts of the flesh. It ends : 'This bethe the wordis that oure lorde speke to Sent Bryde, his owne spouse and derelynge'.

Vellum : ff. 73. $8\frac{3}{4}'' \times 5\frac{1}{4}''$. 4to. The last half of fifteenth century.

6. *Lambeth Palace Library MS. 432.* For a description of all the items in the manuscript see C. Horstmann, *Anglia*, iii, p. 319. The manuscript is a miscellaneous collection, written about the middle of the fifteenth century ; it has several revelations and a prayer of Birgitta, which are scattered through the work. A revelation on ff. 36 a–36 b has the following chapter heading : 'how our lady seint marie comendith seint Jerom to þe reuelecion of seint Burgitt'. Another short revelation (ff. 36 b–7 a) continues Mary's praise of Jerome to Birgitta. A translation of Bk. I, ch. 10, is found on ff. 76 a–83 a, with the chapter heading : 'wordys of the Blessed virgyne our lady seint marye to Seint Burgitt of the incarnacion and passion of our lord Ihesu Crist'. F. 83 a–b has a translation of Bk. VI, ch. 6 : 'Ihesu Crist Blamythe Seint Brygytt for vnpaciens, and techith hir Sonne to with-stonde hitt'. A prayer of Birgitta in Latin follows on ff. 83 b–84 a. The first two revelations (ff. 36 a–37 a) have been edited by C. Horstmann, *Anglia*, iii, pp. 359–60.

Paper : ff. 99. $8\frac{3}{4}'' \times 6''$. 4to. Fifteenth century.

II

The seven extant manuscripts vary greatly in size, content, and literary value. They bear no apparent relationship to each other. Rawlinson C. 41 differs in method of translation and in style from all the others. It expands the Latin text and adds ideas not in the original. Arundel 197 and Lambeth Palace Library 432 contain a few extracts from the revelations. Claudius B. I abbreviates and omits passages in the Latin text frequently. It differs both in style and wording from the other manuscripts, and has many Northern forms (*kyrke, ilk, ane, awn, wald, swylke*). Harley 4800 has only the fourth book and part of the fifth book; the translation is a poor one. Julius F. 2, which has a translation of the first seven books of the revelations, is the most complete of the manuscripts. The forms are slightly later than those of the Garrett MS.; it uses *seis, them, ther, shall*, where the Garrett MS. has *seyth, hem, her, schullen*. There is a tendency in Julius F. 2, as in Harley 4800, to abbreviate by the excision of words or phrases; the method of abbreviation is not as pronounced as that of Claudius B. I, which omits long sections or paragraphs. Julius F. 2 is the fullest of the manuscripts, and for this reason ranks next in interest to the Garrett MS., a collection of the revelations which, in care of translation and in literary style, stands apart from all the others. The Garrett MS. has passages of excellent prose and gives evidence of care in the selection of the revelations; the other manuscripts vary from businesslike translations to mere rough jottings which show the general content of the work. It is only natural that straightforward translations from the Latin, even when entirely independent, should have frequent similarities; the translators of most of the manuscripts, when they follow the Latin at all, hold as nearly as possible to the Latin order in the sentence, and frequently use the Latin word in translation. The individual words, phrases, and methods of translations continually differ. The chapter headings of each of the manuscripts differ from each other, as well as from the standard Latin text. The Syon Monastery Library, because of its great resources, was a 'lending library',[1] and may have sent its copies of the revelations to the other libraries to be transcribed.[2] Since

---

[1] Bateson, *Catalogue of the Library of Syon Monastery*, Cambridge, 1898, p. x.

[2] Latin MSS. in English Libraries are fairly numerous : Harley 612

there was apparently no English translation of the revelations in the library,[1] this may account for separate translations by those who wished to have the revelations Englished.

D. *The Text of the Garrett MS.*

The Garrett MS. is the logical choice for an edition under the circumstances. There is no question of the earliest text, since the manuscripts are independent. For practical purposes, Julius F. II and Claudius B. I are both too long to edit. Hundreds of chapters in the full text are occasional, repetitive, and uninteresting. The Garrett MS. is a selection of the best revelations,[2] and has by far the most studied and interesting prose. The translation was probably made from a manuscript in the library of Syon Monastery which, in turn, was derived from the original Latin manuscript at Vadstena. A manuscript which was carefully transcribed from this original in Sweden for the English chapter is still extant.[3]

The sequence of chapters in the Garrett MS. is independent of the order which is followed in the Latin manuscripts. A

(transcribed for Syon Monastery in 1427 from the original in Vadstena), St. John (Cambr.) 69, Merton (Oxf.) 215, Bodley 346, Bodley 169, Royal 7. C. IX, Canon. (Bodl.) 475, Sloane 982, Magd. Coll. (Oxf.) 77, Trinity Coll. (Camb.) 0. 9. 28, Brit. Mus. 982, Arundel 66, Royal 13. E.X., Royal 8. B.X., Royal 11. A.I., Vespasian E. VII. Emmanuel Coll. (Cambr.) II. 2. 17 and III. 3. 8. Some of the manuscripts have only short extracts from the revelations.

[1] There are seven Latin MSS. listed (Bateson, *op. cit.*, p. xiii). The nuns had a library distinct from the monastery library.

[2] It contains, for example, Bk. VIII, ch. 48, one of the most powerful of Birgitta's revelations, which is in no other extant English manuscript.

[3] British Museum MS. Harley 612 can be identified as M. 64 of the Syon Monastery Library (Mary Bateson, *op. cit.*, p. 107). The manuscript is a huge volume of 1,202 columns which contains fourteen books of the revelations (including prologues, &c.), attestations, various lives, and other matters. At the end one Peter, notary public of Lincöping, Sweden, certifies that the book is an accurate transcription from the true original, made at the request of John Hartman 'pro parte Roberti Belle et Thome Sterinton, Professorum in Monasterio de Syone'. Dated May 1427.

The arrival of the brothers and the cause for their mission is noted in the *Diarium Wazstenense* for 18 April 1427 (E. M. Fant, *Scriptores Rerum Suecicarum*, tom. i, p. 146) : 'In die Parasceves venerunt de Anglia duo fratres ordinis nostri petentes & reportantes raciones super aliquis chapter from the second book follows one from the fourth ; a chapter from the sixth book precedes one from the first. Chapters relating to the same general subject-matter are often placed together ; this grouping, however, is not systematically carried out. Some of these groups are gathered together from two or three different books, while others are connected by position and subject-matter in the Latin also. The chapters included in 100/20–117/23 (Bk. II, ch. 23 ; Bk. IV, ch. 9, Bk. VI, ch. 52) deal with humility and its opposite, pride. In Bk. VIII, ch. 48 (63/14–87/4) and Bk. VIII, ch. 56 (87/5–97/32), the translator has brought together two visions of judgement on unjust rulers. Bk. II, chs. 24–7 (19. 12/13–25/13), Bk. IV, ch. 7–9 (43/7–53/6), and Bk. I, chs. 50–9 (53/7–59/34) are groups of chapters with a common theme in the Latin ; the translator has recognized and preserved their unity. The revelations which have been selected are those which deal with general subjects. Birgitta wrote many of her revelations for particular persons, and these naturally have a local application which would not be suitable in a translation for English readers.

The translation follows the Latin closely. Occasional passages which are awkward and unidiomatic are so because of this strict adherence to the Latin order. The sentences are sometimes long and involved. But in general both scribes write with a directness and simplicity which admirably bring out the pictorial qualities of the revelations. Neither scribe adds anything to the original. The omissions of phrases, which are made occasionally by the first scribe are probably accidental.

---

punctis regule.' On 30 September 1428 Robert Belle was appointed confessor-general of Syon Monastery on the death of Thomas Fishbourne, the first confessor-general. At that time John Hartman was a lay brother ; Thomas Sterinton is not mentioned. (G. J. Aungier, *History and Antiquities of Syon Monastery*, 1840, pp. 51–2.)

PART II. SAINT BIRGITTA

A. *The Life of Saint Birgitta*[1]

In the year 1302 or 1303[2] Birgitta[3] was born at Finstad, a town a few miles from Upsala in the province of Upland. Her father was Birger, the lagman or governor of Upland.

Birgitta began to have visions at the age of seven;[4] in these visions an angel, the Blessed Virgin Mary, or Christ, usually appeared and talked to her. When she was 10 years of age she heard a sermon on the passion of Christ. That night Christ appeared to her as if he had just been crucified, and said, 'Thus am I tortured'. Birgitta, thinking that the wounds were fresh, asked, ' O Lord, who has done this to Thee? ' Christ replied, ' Whoever despises Me and spurns My love does this to Me '. From that day on, the passion of Christ affected her so much that she seldom could think of it without tears.[5] It is a constantly recurring theme in her revelations.

---

[1] The main authorities for the life of Birgitta are the *Vita Sanctae Birgittae* (edited in S.R.S. iii, pp. 185-206, by C. M. Annerstedt), which was written within four months after her death by her two confessors, Peter, prior of Alvastra, and Peter Olafson, the first confessor of Vadstena ; and the later *Vita Sanctae Birgittae* (A.S., pp. 485-93), by Birger, archbishop of Upsala. The *Vita Abbreviata*, published in the first printed edition of her revelations, and also printed in Durantus's edition, uses the revelations themselves as a chief source. C. M. Annerstedt (S.R.S. iii, pp. 186-88) has a full list and critical discussion of the *Vitae*. Klemming (v, pp. 244-58) gives a list of manuscript lives and printed biographies up to 1884. The best modern critical biographies are by Fr. Hammerich, *Den hellige Birgitta og Kirken i Norden*, Copenhagen, 1863 ; Comtesse de Flavigny, *Sainte Brigitte*, Paris, 1892 ; and K. Krogh-Tonnung, *Die heilige Birgitta*, *Sammlung illustrierter Heiligenleben*, Band v, Kempten und München, 1907.

[2] The earliest authorities differ (S.R.S. iii, p. 189, note *k*).

[3] Birgitta is her correct name, and not Brigitte, Brigida, or Bridget. Birgitta is probably from Brighitta (cf. A. Noreen, *Altschwedische Grammatik*, § 339. 2), borrowed from Irish ⴁⱃⰻⰾⱅⰻⰾ (Brighid), which is from ⴁⱃⰻⰾⱅ (brigh), virtue, strength, an extension of ⴁⱃⰻ, which has the same sense. Cf. Fr. Stark, *Sitzungsber. d. Kais. Akad. v. Wissenschaften*, Phil.-hist. Classe, Wien, lix. 2. 196-7, 1868.

[4] S.R.S. iii, p. 190.

[5] Durantus, ii, p. 476 (*Vita Abbreviata*).

At thirteen years of age her father, much against her wishes,[1] married her to the eighteen-year-old Ulf Gudmarson, a youth of noble family and fine personal character. They lived together continently for a year,[2] and Birgitta was especially fervent in her prayers and ascetic devotions.   Ulf eventually became the lagman of the province of Nericia,[3] and Birgitta bore him four sons and four daughters.[4] St. Catherine, who later accompanied her mother on many of her journeys, was the most famous of her children.[5] During this period of Birgitta's life, the learned Matthias, canon of the cathedral of Lincöping, was her father confessor and constant adviser.[6]   Ulf, her husband, died in 1344, after they had lived for some years in continence and pious study.[7]

A few days [8] after her husband had died, Christ appeared to Birgitta and told her that he had chosen her to be his bride.[9] From this time on Birgitta's life was changed ; she turned over the management of her estate to others and devoted herself to a religious life.   She greatly increased her self-discipline ; she fasted often, dressed poorly, and underwent severe penances.   In 1346 she received a revelation bidding her to go to Rome.[10]   But it was no easy undertaking to leave her affairs

[1] S.R.S. iii, p. 225, *De Processu Canonizationis Birgittae*, depositio Katerinae filiae Birgittae, super quarto articulo.

[2] S.R.S. iii, pp. 191, 225. Their continency was probably due as much to their youth as to piety, which is the reason given by her biographers.

[3] The title ' Princess ' of Nericia or Sweden was often given to Birgitta. C. M. Annerstedt has shown conclusively that she had no real claim to the title (S.R.S. iii, p. 188, notes *c, d, e*).

[4] S.R.S. iii, p. 209, *Chronicon de Genere et Nepotibus Sanctae Birgittae*, auctore Margareta Clausdotter, abbatissa Vadstenensi.

[5] Durantus, ii, pp. 530–53, *Vitae Divae Catherinae.*

[6] S.R.S. iii, pp. 191–2.   [7] S.R.S. iii, p. 193.

[8] A.S., p. 404, no. 151. Some of the early accounts say that it was a year or two after Ulf's death, but the weight of evidence seems to be that Christ chose her to be ' sponsa mea et canale meum ' within a few days.

[9] S.R.S. iii, p. 194, note *k*. This revelation forms the first chapter of the Garrett MS.

[10] *Revelationes Extravagantes*, ch. 8 : 'Christus loquitur Sponsae existenti in Monasterio Aluastri, dicens : Vade Romam, & manebis ibi, donec videas Papam, & Imperatorem, & illis loqueris ex parte mea verba, quae tibi dicturus sum. Venit igitur Sponsa Christi Romam, anno aetatis suae xxxxii, & mansit ibi iuxta diuinum praeceptum xv annis, antequam veniret Papa, videlicet Vrbanus V & Imperator Carolus Boemus. Quibus

and arrange for her children ; two or three years elapsed before her journey began.[1] With a small retinue, including her two confessors, Peter, prior of Alvastra, and Peter Olafson, first confessor of the Vadstena monastery, she finally left Sweden, never more to return alive. On the way to Rome Peter of Alvastra began to teach her the use of Latin. However, she continued to write down her revelations in Swedish, and her confessors translated them into Latin.[2]

Long before leaving Sweden Birgitta had shown a fearless nature in her denunciations of the king and his court.[3] During the years of her stay in Rome she waged ceaseless war against the widespread corruptions in the Church. She unhesitatingly condemned the prelates, forced the abbots to improve the standard of living at their monasteries, and frequently sent letters of advice or denunciation to the pope himself.[4]

She was especially anxious that the papal seat, which had long been at Avignon, should be re-established at Rome. But the popes did not wish to leave the quiet of Avignon for the turmoil of a rebellious city. It was not until 1367 that Urban V brought the long absent court back to Rome. The conditions prevalent in Rome at that time were unendurable to the pope, and he decided to abandon Rome in 1370. This aroused in Birgitta great anger and grief ; she warned him, upon penalty of God's severe displeasure and punishment, not to leave Rome.[5] This revelation was delivered to him by

obtulit Reuelationes pro reformatione Ecclesiae, & Regulam.' Birgitta did not see Urban V until 1367, over twenty years later ; see A.S., p. 444, nos. 317-18, for an attempt to explain this chronological discrepancy.

[1] S.R.S. iii, p. 202, notes *m, n, o.*

[2] A.S., p. 406, ch. xi.

[3] In *Revelationes Extravagantes*, chs. 74 and 77, Birgitta flays Magnus Erikson, the king of Sweden, and his court for their worldliness ; she also visited and rebuked the king personally. Book VIII, called *Liber Celestis Imperatoris ad Reges*, has denunciatory revelations which were sent to many kings and queens. Although the revelations seemed to have but little effect on their lives, Birgitta must have instilled a wholesome fear in the hearts of those to whom she wrote, for she was received with the greatest consideration and respect wherever she went.

[4] See 5/20-6/12 of the text for an outspoken statement concerning the condition of the Church.

[5] Bk. IV, ch. 33.

Alphonso,[1] one of Birgitta's devoted friends, but did not change the pope's decision. He left the city, and died the same year, in less than a month after returning to Avignon.

Another desire of Birgitta was to have her Order, the Order of St. Saviour or the Birgittine Order, officially approved. She firmly believed that she had received and had written down the rules of the Order exactly as they were given to her by the Mother of God. This Order, the founding of which is Birgitta's chief religious accomplishment, was to consist of sixty sisters and twenty-five monks. The monks and nuns were to live in separate houses, communicating with the church; the nuns' choir was to be placed above in such a position as to enable them to listen to the offices of the monks in the lower choir. The monastery was so arranged that the monks and nuns could not see each other, even at confession. Severe, chaste, and abstemious living were strictly prescribed.[2] After many years of command and entreaty by Birgitta, the Order was approved by Urban in 1370.[3] The monastery at Vadstena had been in existence for some time,[4] and after this date the Order rapidly expanded.[5]

In 1372, in obedience to the divine command,[6] Birgitta went to Jerusalem.[7] While in Palestine she had many visions revealing to her incidents in the life of Christ and the Blessed Virgin Mary; these revelations form the major part of Bk. VII. Birgitta returned to Rome the same year, very much enfeebled. On 23 July 1373, surrounded by a group of her

---

[1] Alphonso the hermit, formerly bishop of Jaën, wrote the *Prologus* of Book VIII and edited Birgitta's revelations in 1377.

[2] Durantus, ii, pp. 351–70, *Regula Sancti Salvatoris*.

[3] A.S., p. 445, no. 322.

[4] S.R.S. i, pp. 1–224, *Diarium Wazstenense ab anno 1344 ad annum 1545*, edited by E. M. Fant.

[5] The monastery of Syon House, of the Birgittine Order, was founded by Henry V in the manor of Isleworth, in Middlesex, in 1414–16. It became one of the richest monasteries in England. See William Dugdale, *Monasticon Anglicanum*, London, 1830, pp. 540–4 ; G. J. Aungier, *History and Antiquities of Syon Monastery*, London, 1840 ; J. H. Blunt, the preface to *The Myroure of Oure Ladye*, E.E.T.S., E.S. xix, pp. xi–xix.

[6] Bk. VII, ch. 1.

[7] On the death of her son Charles at Naples see note on 117/37–118/1 of the text.

followers, she died. Her bones were carried to Vadstena,[1] where they may still be seen.[2]

Her two confessors, and Catherine, her daughter, soon returned to Rome to inaugurate the proceedings for her canonization. Gregory XI appointed a commission to investigate the life and writings of Birgitta. The commission was headed by Cardinal Johannes de Turrecremata, who made a very careful study of the revelations. After some delay the canonization, performed by Boniface IX, took place with great pomp on 8 October 1391. On account of the great schism which had split the Church at that time, the validity of the canonization was questioned. The bull of canonization of Birgitta and her Order were confirmed by John XXIII in 1414; and after the schism had ceased, Martin V, after another investigation, signed a confirmation in 1419.[3]

B. *The Revelations of St. Birgitta*[4]

The works of many mystics show careful revision and study. Their writings are the result of a conscious reconstruction, caused either by the advice of a confessor or produced out of their own theological knowledge. Birgitta, on the other hand, immediately after beholding a vision, wrote down the revelation, or dictated it to an amanuensis if she were too ill to write it herself. She wrote in Swedish, and one of her confessors translated the revelation into Latin. This translation was then read to her that no word might be omitted or changed. The original was often destroyed, but Peter of Alvastra wrote the Latin in a book which developed into the *Revelationes Celestes*.[5]

It is this lack of supplementation and literary revision which differentiates Birgitta's visions from others of their type.[6] Her revelations were usually the result of some particular situation

---

[1] Durantus, ii, p. 480; A.S., p. 462, no. 389.

[2] Sven Gronberger, *St. Bridget of Sweden*, *American Catholic Quarterly Review*, vol. xlii, 1917, p. 145.

[3] A.S., pp. 409–18, chs. xii–xiv.

[4] Birgitta's revelations reach a total of over 650.

[5] Klemming (iv, pp. 177–85) has edited the only two fragments of Birgitta's handwriting which have been preserved.

[6] In the *Sermo Angelicus* and the fifth book of the revelations (*Liber Questionum*) there is evidence of a re-ordering of the material.

or occasion. A friend would inquire about the condition of
a dead relative ; shortly afterward, Birgitta would not only
have a revelation which showed the condition of the soul of
the dead person, but could also inform the anxious relative
what alms or prayers would shorten the stay of the deceased in
purgatory or alleviate his sufferings while there.[1] Or if the
wickedness of a king or the worldliness of a prelate needed
correction, Birgitta would receive a revelation in which Christ
or the Mother of God denounced his sin in no uncertain words.
After such a vision had been revealed and written down, a
copy of it was made and immediately sent to the inquiring
friend or offending sinner.[2] The lack of revision in the revelations shows itself in repetitions, useless elaboration, and frequent lack of cohesion and unity of thought.

If the revelations show lack of conscious literary style, they
are strong in imaginative versatility. Birgitta had an unusually
active imagination, and her descriptions of hell and purgatory,
of Christ's crucifixion, and of incidents in the life of the
Blessed Virgin Mary, stand out vividly. She prefers concrete
representations to abstract theological discussions. She does
not propound universal dogmas, as does Hildegard of Bingen ;
her visions are not rationally and consciously constructed as
are those of Elizabeth of Schönau.[3] However, her fifth book
(*Liber Questionum*) could (with very little rearrangement) be
turned into a popular theological tract. These defects, however, do not obscure the positive literary qualities which the
revelations possess. Through her visions Birgitta exercised a
remarkable authority over the laity as well as over the kings
and prelates of her time. The drastic strength of her warnings
and the profuse wealth of images which her visions contain
explain the popularity which they have enjoyed. The revelations are given a high place in Swedish literature of the
Middle Ages by literary historians of the present day.

[1] See note on 116/27.
[2] S.R.S. iii, pp. 196-7.
[3] Westman (pp. 151-259) compares Birgitta with the other mystics of
her time. See also the letter of Westman, reprinted in Notes, p. 125.

C. The Revelations of St. Birgitta in England in the Fifteenth Century

Birgitta died in Rome, 23 July 1373. Even before her death, Latin copies of the revelations found their way into England and aroused great interest in Oxford and London.[1] Bale writes in his *Scriptorum Illustrium Maioris Brytanniae* : ' Huius Dianae tenebrosa somnia, seu, ut ipsi uocant, Revelationes, in scholis Oxoniensibus & in cathedris publicis, magistraliter exposuerunt magni sua aetate doctores, Thomas Stubbes Dominicanus, Ricardus Lauynham Carmelita, & adhuc alii eius generis multi, circa Domini 1370, ut talibus muliercularum delirationibus sole clariorem Dei veritatem sophistae obnubilarent.' [2]

With the marriage of Philippa, daughter of Henry IV, to Eric XIII of Sweden in 1406, the knowledge of St. Birgitta became more general in England. Henry V decided to establish a foundation of the Birgittine Order, and on 22 February 1415 laid the corner-stone of Syon Monastery in the presence of Richard Clifford, Bishop of London. The new monastery, which at the time of the dissolution ranked eighth in wealth in England, had an uninterrupted career of prosperity for a hundred and twenty years. Bequests of books to the library were frequent and generous, as the still existing catalogue

---

[1] Pits (John Pits, *De Illustribus Angliae Scriptoribus*, Paris, 1616, p. 512) enumerating the works of Thomas Stubbes, a Dominican, who he says died in 1373, mentions : *In revelationes S. Brigidae, Librum vnum* [beginning] *Beata & venerabilis Domina*. Recording the works of Richard Lavenham (*d.* 1381), confessor to Richard II and Professor of Theology at Oxford, Pits (*ibid.*, pp. 532–5) lists : *Determinationes notabiles Oxoniae & Londoni publice lectas pro libro revelationum S. Birgittae, Libros septem*, [beginning] *Stupor & mirabilia audita sunt*. But *Stupor & mirabilia audita sunt* is the beginning of the Prologue to the revelations written by Matthias, father confessor to St. Birgitta, and it may be that these ' notable public lectures in seven books' are merely seven books of the revelations with the usual Prologue. The volume attributed to Lavenham in the Bodleian (Bodl. MS. 169), which I have examined, has nothing but the Prologue and the first four books of the revelations.

[2] John Bale, *Scriptorum Illustrium maioris Brytanniȩ*, Basileae, 1557, *Pars Posterior*, p. 188. Bale confuses St. Birgitta with St. Bridget of Ireland.

shows.[1] One of the most famous donors to the library was Thomas Gascoigne, Vice-Chancellor (1434–9) and Chancellor (1442–5) of Oxford, who seems to have taken an especial interest in Syon Monastery. He wrote a life of St. Birgitta, which he translated into English for the sisters and monks of Syon.[2] In his *Dictionarium Theologicum*, Gascoigne records examples of miracles performed by St. Birgitta at Oxford, where a man 'possessed of an evil spirit' was saved by prayers to the saint from onlookers.[3]

---

[1] M. Bateson, *Catalogue of the Library of Syon Monastery*, Cambridge, 1898, Appendix I.

[2] There are three English prose lives of St. Birgitta extant, none of which seems to be that written by Gascoigne. One is *The Life of St. Bridget*, printed by Pynson in 1516 (ed. J. H. Blunt, E.E.T.S., E.S. xix, pp. xlvii–lix). Pynson's *Life* is usually ascribed to Thomas Gascoigne (*ibid.*, p. ix) ; but the miracle which Gascoigne says he included ('quam historiam scripsi latius in vita ejusdem Sanctae Brigittae' : see next note) is not found in the printed *Life*. The revelations in Claudius B.I, are preceded by a life of Birgitta, imperfect at the beginning and end (ff. 2–4), which differs from and is fuller than the printed *Life*. The revelations in Julius F. II are followed on the last leaf of the manuscript (f. 254) by a description of Birgitta's writings and the circumstances of her death.

[3] 'Sicut nuper novi Oxoniae, circa annum Domini m°cccc°l°, et circa annum Domini m°cccc°lij°, quando hominibus orantibus ad Sanctam Brigittam viduam quondam, et principissam Sueciae, novi virum graviter mentaliter vexatum horrore et timore per Sathanam immisso, quem novi tunc subito liberatum ab illa magna vexatione mentali, beata Brigitta sibi in mentali visione aut specie fulgente apparenti et cum verbis mentalibus eum consolante. Item, novi tunc Oxoniae quendam magistrum Ricardum Tenant, qui horribiliter et saepissime vexatus est, possessus a maligno spiritu vel a malignis spiritibus, quia semper longo tempore clamavit, "Ego sum dampnatus ! et sententia est data. Ite, maledicta, in ignem aeternum !" "Nullus est Deus nisi dyabolus !" et hoc saepissime dixit publice coram pluribus, et me dicente sibi, " In nomine Jesu Xti, dicatis, Jesu Xte. Deus et homo ! miserere mei !" Ipse michi saepe respondebat dicens, "Non possum hoc dicere " ; et tunc, clausis labiis suis, similiter statim iterum verba praedicta horribiliter clamavit, dicens, " Ego sum dampnatus, ego sum dampnatus, non est Deus nisi dyabolus !" et circumstantibus diversis hominibus, et ex motione unius ad sanctam Brigittam sponsam Xti orantibus, praedictus magister Ricardus Tenant liberatus fuit de manibus daemonum, et dixit saepe, " O Domine Jesu Xte, miserere mei ". " Ego ", inquit, "fui male vexatas " ; et postea saepe osculatus est ymaginem Xti Jesu crucifixi pro nobis ; et postea saepe, me audiente, " Sancta Brigitta, ora pro nobis " ; et receptis sacramentis ecclesiae infra biduum post suam liberationem mortuus est, in die Veneris et in vigilia

Hoccleve (*Regement of Princes*, E.E.T.S., E.S. lxii, p. 194) has a paraphrase of Revelations, Bk. IV, ch. 105, in which St. Birgitta advises the kings of France and England to obtain peace by an alliance of marriage. In Arundel MS. 66 (f. 291), a beautifully ornamented manuscript for the use of Henry VII, are *Visiones de Regibus Angliae et Franciae*, which are extracts from the revelations in Latin.

The blind and deaf poet John Audelay, chaplain in the monastery of Haghmon(d), which lay four miles north-east of Shrewsbury, in Shropshire, wrote a *Salutacio Sancte Brigitte*. It is found in the only extant copy of Audelay's poems, Douce 302 (Bodl.), and was written shortly after 1426. The poem, which has not been printed, is on ff. 25 a (col. 1)–26 a (col. 2).[1]

[A Salutation to St. Birgitta.]

Hic incipit salutacio Sanctę Birgittę virginis & q*uomodo* domin*u*s I*h*esu*s* Ch*ristu*s apparuit illi corporalite*r* & ded*it* illi sua*m* benedictionem suam.   quo*þ* Awdelay.

1 Hayle! maydyn & wyfe. *hayle*! wedow brygytt.
    Hayle! þu chese to be chast & kepe charyte,
    Hayle! þu special spouse, kyndle to þe knyt;
    Hayle! he consentyd to þe same by concel of the
    To be relegyous.
    Hayle! fore þe loue of I*h*esu*s* C*r*ist
    ʒe foresake ʒo*ur* fleschele lust ;
    Þer-fore be ʒe boþ eblest
    In þe name of swete I*h*esu*s*.

Pentecostis Oxoniae sepultus in ecclesia sanctissimae Mariae semper virginis ; quam historiam scripsi latius in vita ejusdem Sanctae Brigittae, quam vitam ego transtuli de Latino in Anglicum sororibus et monialibus de ordine Sancti Salvatoris in monasterio Syon, Londiniensis dioceseos. Haec ergo mulier, sancta sponsa Xti Brigitta, magnam fecit confusionem in domo principis tenebrarum.'—J. E. Thorold Rogers, *Loci e Libro Veritatum*, 1881, pp. 139-40.

[1] J. E. Wülfing, *Der Dichter John Audelay und sein Werk*, Anglia, xviii, 1896, pp. 175–217, gives a description of the contents of the manuscript. J. K. Rasmussen, *Die Sprache John Audelay's*, Bonn, 1914, has a study of the Salopian dialect of the manuscript. On f. 22b (col. 2) of the manuscript is a short colophon, dated 1426, which tells us all we know about the life of John Audelay. Since the *Salutacio Sancte Brigitte* is written only a few pages later, it was composed not long after 1426.
l. 3. *knyt* : Ulf Gudmarson, her husband.

10 Haile! þe mod*e*r of god to þe con apere.
Haile! he told þe of h*is* passion & of his spetus payne.
Hayle! ȝe wepit fore wo to-ged*e*r whe*n* ȝe were,
Hayle! fore h*is* dolful deþ þat so was eslayne,
Oure lade to þe ga*n* say:
Hayle! blessed bregit, let be þe chere
& þo*n*ke my su*n* fore his deþ dere
Þ*a*t has cȝcuc*n* þo powcro
To be wyfe, wedow, ond may.

19 Haile! seche a kyndle coupil ca*n* no mo*n* here kyn.
Hayle! ȝe fore-soke reches & ryal aray.
Hayle! ȝe hopid hile i*n* ȝo*ur* hert þe*n*.
Hay[le]! al þe worchip of þis word wol sone wynd away
W*ith*-i*n* a lytil stownd.
Haile! þis wordle hono*ur*
H*i*t fallis & fadis as a flo*ur*
To-day is fresche i*n* h*is* colo*ur*
To-morrow he gyrdis to grownd.

28 Hayle! ȝe be-toke ȝo*ur* tresou*ur* to þe tr*i*nete
Fore he is truste & trew w*ith*-out treynyng.
Hayle! he dissayuyd no soule w*ith* no sotelte.
Hayle! fayþfully þat ȝe fond at ȝo*ur* endyng,
Þe soþe fore to say.
Hayle! oþer tresoure haue we noȝt
Out of þis word whe*n* we be broȝt
Bot good word, wil, dede, & þoȝt,
Whe*n* we schuld wynd away.

37 Hayle! w*ith* þese iiij feyþfully ȝe [b]oȝt ȝoue heue*n* blis,
W*ith* good word, will, dede, & þoȝt, To obey godis bidyng.
Hayle! w*ith* þe werkis of me*r*ce ȝe gete*n* ȝou mede, I wis.
Haile! ȝe fore-soken flesschele lust, þe fend, false couetyng,
Þ*a*t were ȝo*ur* iij enmys.
Haile! þai sett yn al her sotelte
Houe mo*n*s soule þai mow distre
W*ith* pride, lechory, & glotonye
& cursid couetyse.

l. 11. *spetus*: despitous, cruel.
l. 22. MS. *hay*.
l. 29. *treynyng*: training, deceit.
l. 37. MS. *hoȝt*.
l. 38. This line is incorrectly divided in the manuscript; a new line begins with *To obey* in the manuscript.

46 Haile! blessid bregid fore þi benyngnete,
   Haile! þe perles prince to þe con apere.
   Haile! he grownded þe in [g]race in þi vergenete,
   Hayle! specially he speke with þe oft in þi prayere
   Hayle! to þe pope þe send
   Fore to grawnt þe his special [g]race
   & to al þat vesid þi holy place
   To assoyle ham of here trespas
   Þat here mysdedis wol amend.   fol. 25 b.

55 Haile! he bed þe bild a plas o relygion.
   Haile! blessid bregid, fore fro][one place
   Haile! to pope Urban, to Rome, þu shalt goon,
   Þat is my veker in erþ to grawnt þe his grace
   To have þe same perdon
   Þat is in pet[e]rs cherche at Rome:
   To al þe pilgrems þat to þe cum,
   Þat vesid þe in Cristis name,
   To have playn remyssion.

64 Haile! he said: if þat pope wil grawnt þe no grace
   With-out mone or mede be-cause of couetys,
   Haile! þe fader of heuen schal preuelege þi place
   Haile! & schal conferme þi bul, þat above him is.
   Þat schal he, y know.
   Haile! my moder my sele schall be;
   My witnes, al þe sayntis of heuen on hye;
   My blessyng, þe hole gost I be-take to þe.
   Þe pope schal lout ful low.

73 Haile! to þat perles prelat, to þe pope, when þu come,
   Haile! þu mendist þi mesage in a meke manere.
   Haile! fayþfulli þat fader ful reverenly at Rome,
   Haile! he welcumd þe worþele with a wonder chere
   Into þat hole place.
   Haile! he said with myld steuen:
   Welcum be ȝe fro þe kyng of heuen
   Now blessid be þai þat in þe leuen,
   Þat ever þu borne was.

82 Haile! meruelus maide ful of mekenes,
   Haile! hele þe hole gostis lyȝt þe with-in.
   Haile! god haþ grouned þe gracfulli in his goodnes

1. 51. MS. *crace.*   1. 55. MS. *o* : of.   1. 60. MS. *petrs.*

c

Haile! to be sauer of soulis & seser of syn
Be his ordenans.
Haile! i grawnt to al remyssion
Þat chryue hem clene with contrichon
& wil do here satisfaccion ;
I reles here penans.

91 Haile! to al þat worþely veset yn þe hole place.
Haile! þat sechen þi socor schal have saluacion,
Haile! fore sake of þat sofren þat þe to me send had
Haile! in reuerenc of þat lord I grawnt hem remyssion
Of al here trespace.
Haile! to þi pilgrems perpetualy
Þat worchipen þi place graciously
With prayers, siluer, gold, lond of fe,
I grawnt ham þis special grace.

100 Now gramarce, gracious fader, of your blessyng I ȝou pray ;
Mi blessid suster bregit, my blessyng ȝif I þe.
Here I grawnt þe þis grace specialy I say,
With-outen mone or mede I make hit to þe fre,
Þis special perdon.
To al þe pilgrems fer & nere
Þat veset yn þi place in good manere
To here gostele fader I grawnt pouere
To asoyle ham everchon.

109 Haile! to þat pereles priynce, bregit, fore me pray,
Þat haþ groundid þe in grace & is þi [g]ouernoure.
Haile! my blessid doȝter, þi blessidnes hit may
At þe day of my deþ my soule þen socour
& ȝif me wil & wit
Mi misdedis here to amend
Out of þis word or þat I wynd.
To þe trenite I þe recommend ;
Fare wel, blessid breget.

118 Þus þe pope preueleged here place & haloud hit to Christis
entent.
Anon hure hole husbond a couennt to him con take,
& Bregit mad here of maydyns anoþer blest couent
Þat fore-soke here fleschle lust for Ihesu Cristis sake
In þe name of þe trenete.

l. 110. **MS.** *couernoure.*

Þer þai disceuerd hem to.
Hure husbond to his bredern con go,
& to hure susteres heo whent him fro
To leue in chastite.

127 Haile! þus þis perles prelet fro þe passid away
When he with his benyngnete had ȝeuen þe his blessyng.
Haile! at þe day of our deþ þat settis no day,
Haile! þen, blessid Bregit, our soulis to blis bryng
& graunt vs þi special grace
In erþ, þat we mowe werchip þe.
After in heuen we may þe se
In [i]oi & blis perpetualy
With-in þat blisful place.

136 Beside þe chene soþly seuen myle fro Lundun,—
Our gracious kyng Herre þe V. wes founder of þat place,—
Haile! he let preuelege þat hole place & callid hit Bregit Sion.
Þe pope conferme þerto his bul þroȝ his special grace
In þe worchip of S. Bregit,
To al here pilgrems on Lammesday
& also Mydlentyn Sunday;
Þis perdon to last fore ȝeuer & ay.
God graunt vs a pert of hit!

144 Mekil is al Ynglan, I hold, to pray for kyng Herre,
Þat so worþele our worchip in eueroche place,
Boþ in Fraunce & in Breten & in Normandy,
Þat oure faders had lost before he get aȝayn be grace;
& more-ouer speciali
To make soche a house of relegioun,
& to preueleche þerto þat gracious perdon,—
Al Ynglond to haue remyssioune.
Now Crist on his soule haue merce.

fol. 26 a.

153 Was neuer a holeer order preueleged in no plas
Fore to red al þe rollis of relegyown.
Fore þai schal neuer schew chappe ny fygure of face;
Ne with-out lycence or leue speche speke þai non,
Bot [þ]e warden be present.
Noþer fader ne moder ne no mon leuyng
Schal speke to hom no erþle þyng
With-out þer warden be þer hereng
& know boþ here entent.

l. 134. MS. oi.   l. 157. MS. he.

XXXVI

162 Redle þei rysun with gret reuerens oneþtes out of hure rest,
    Devoutele with deuocion here seruys to syng & say,
    & crucefyen here caren & slen here fleschele lust
    With priue prayers & penans þe priynce of heuen to pay.
    Deuotle day & niȝt
    Þai prayn to god specialy
    Fore al þat þai here leuyng be
    In masse, in matyns, in memore,
    To þat lord of myȝt.

171 Fore hit fars noȝt be gotele goodis as doþ be temperal;
    Þe men þat han pert þer of so lasse is vche dole.
    Bot he þat delis gostle goodis hit is so spiritual
    Þat vche mon þat haþ his pert haþ fulle þe hole.
    Ensampil chul ȝe se:
    Alse mone men as may here a mas,
    Vche mon his perte hole he has.
    & ȝet þe masse is neuer þe lasce,
    Bo[t] so more of dyngnete.

180 Pray we to god specialy to saue þat spiritual plas,
    Þat þai obey obedyens þat þay be bound to.
    Fore þai may þroȝ here precious prayoure purches her our
        grace,
    Have we neuer in þis word wroȝt so muche wo,
    Þai han þat pouere.
    Fore al þat here wele done
    Crist wil graunt hem here bone.
    Þai wot neuer hou sone
    He hers here prayere.

189 Crist þat was crucefid on cros & cround with þorne
    & ched his blesful blod fore oure syns sake
    Let neuer þis worþ lond, lord, be forelorne.
    Bot puttis doune here pouere þat werris wil awake
    & sese al males.
    Fore ȝong kyng Herre now we pray,
    Þat Crist him kepe boþ niȝt & day
    & let neuer traytor him betray,
    & send vs rest & pes.

198 Al þat redis reuerenly þis remyssioune
    Prays to blisful Bregit, þat merceful may,

l. 162. *oneþtes*: uneaths, not easily.
l. 164. *caren*: carrion, the fleshly nature of man.
        l. 179. MS. *Bo.*

Fore he*m* þat med þis mate*r* w*ith* dewo*c*ion,
Þ*at* is boþ blynd & def, þe synful Audelay.
I p*ray* ȝoue specialy,
Fore I mad þis w*ith* g*o*od entent
In þe reue*r*[en]s of þis v*er*gyn v*er*ement,
Heo gr*a*unt ȝoue gr*a*ce þat beþ p*re*sent
To haue ioy & blis p*er*petualy.

Ame*n*.

The *O's of St. Bridget* or *Fifteen O's* are fifteen orisons on
the Passion of Christ, attributed to St. Birgitta, which became
very popular in England. Each prayer begins with *O Jesu* or
a similar invocation.[1] At the time of the Reformation, these
Fifteen O's were fiercely denounced as 'papistical supersti-
tions'.[2] There is a short poem in Sloane MS. 3548, a fifteenth-
century paper commonplace-book, which possibly refers to the
orisons. It is written on a blank leaf in a word-list of Latin
synonyms, and may have been copied from a manuscript containing the *Fifteen O's*, to which it served as the introduction.

l. 204. MS. *reuers.*

[1] There are several copies of a translation of the *Fifteen O's* printed by
Caxton which are extant: *O Jhesu, endeles swetnes of louyng soules,* etc. 4°.
[Westminster] W. Caxton. [1491.] Of this book there is a modern
reproduction: *The Fifteen O's and other Prayers,* Reproduced in Photo-
lithography by Stephen Ayling, Griffith and Farran, 1869. A discussion
of the Bristol fragment (at the Baptist College) of Caxton's edition is found
in Henry Bradshaw's *Collected Papers,* Cambridge University Press, Cambridge, 1889, pp. 341-4. At Blair's College, Aberdeen, is a copy of
The XV Oos in Englysshe with other prayers. 16°. R. Copláde, 1529.
The *Hore beate marie virginis,* according to the Salisbury use, 1531, has
the Latin *Quindecem Orationes* with an English heading: Thys be the
.xv. oos the whych to (i. e., the) vyrgyn saint brigitta was woi*n*te (i. e.,
wonte) to say dayly before the holy roode i*n* saint paules church at
Rome / who so sayth thys a hole yere he schall delyuer .xv. soules oute of
purgatory of hys next kynred : a*n*d co*n*uerte other .xv. synners to good
lyf & other .xv. ryghtuose men of hys kynrede shall perseuer in good lyf.
And what he desireth of god he sal haue yt yf it be to the saluacion of hys
soule.

[2] *Certain Sermons or Homilies* (by T. Cranmer?), 1547, ch. v, *Of Good
Works* : And briefly to pa*s*s over the vngodly & counterfete religions, let
vs reherse some other kindes of papistical superstiti*o*ns and abuses, as of
beades, of lady psalters and rosaries, of .xv. Oos . . . which were so
esteemed & abused to þe great preiuduce of Gods glorye and commaundementes, that they were made most high & most holy thinges, whereby to
attaine to the eternal life, or remissi*o*n of synne.

Sloane 3548, f. 118, *b*.

A holy wooman that hight seynt Bryde
Couetid to knowe the woundys wyde
Of Ihesu Cryste, howe fell thei woor,
And often prayed hem therfor.
Ihesu, that all goodnes be-gan,
Apperid and bad this whoman than :
Saye every daye vppon thi knees
XV pater nosters and XV aues
Vnto a ꝫere fulli endid bee ;
So many woundis had I for thee
Wherefore I graunte wyth memory
XV soules out of purgatorye
And XV men that have dissesse
Of there old synne I am relesse,
Iff thei thise XV Orysyuns say
Or ellis XV pater nosters day be day.
More-over my body in fourme of brede
They shall receyve or thei be dede,
Whiche shall there saluacion bee.
In the blisse of heven therfor saye wee
This orysyuns with goode ententt
To Ihesu Cryste omnipotent,
That of this worlde when we shall misse
He vs induce vnto his blis. Amen.

The revelations of St. Birgitta, translated into English, are
mentioned in several fifteenth-century wills. The earliest
occurrence is in the will of Elizabeth Sywardby proved in
1468 : De libro compilato in lingua Anglica de Revelationibus
Sanctae Brigidae, inferius legato, lxvjs. viij*d*.[1] In 1481 Margaret Purdawnce of Norwich left 'to the Nunnery of Thet-
ford, an English book of St. Bridget'.[2] Of especial interest is
the bequest of Cecily, Duchess of York, to her daughter Anne
de la Pole in 1495 : 'Also I geve to my daughter Anne, priores
of Sion, a boke of Bonaventure and Hilton in the same in Eng-
lishe, and a boke of the Revelations of Saint Burgitte.'[3]

[1] *Testamenta Eboracensia*, Surtees Society, vol. iii, p. 163.
[2] *Norfolk and Norwich Arch. Soc.*, vol. iv, p. 335.
[3] *Wills from the Doctors' Commons*, ed. J. G. Nichols and John Bruce,
Camden Society, 1863, p. 3.

There are seven extant manuscripts containing translations of the revelations, which are discussed in another part of the Introduction.

PART III. METHOD OF TRANSCRIPTION

The manuscript has been followed as closely as possible and I have amended the text only in cases of obvious error. The reading from the Latin text, where this is at all necessary, has been given also.

I have modernized the punctuation, as that of the manuscript is confusing. Where in-to, to-for, ther-for, neuer-the-less, a-boue, o-lyue, in-stede, for-getting, over-come, be-hold, I-nogh, I-write, &c. are separated in the manuscript, they have been hyphenated in the text. Proper names, and among divine names God and Jesus Christ, have been uniformly capitalized ; where nouns have capitals in the manuscript they remain ; elsewhere, capitalization at the beginning of the sentence has been normalized. Ff in the manuscript has been normalized to F or f according to the general rules of capitalization. The crossed ll, th, and bl, the m- and n- macron, and the r- and d- flourish, which are used without meaning through-out the manuscript, are not preserved except where an expansion is obviously intended by the scribe. With a few exceptions, the first scribe does not differentiate between þ and y ; in the text, y has been changed to þ when it stands for th. Where the first scribe has written yᵉ and yᵘ, I have normalized to þe and þu. All abbreviations are expanded.

THE REVELATIONS OF SAINT BIRGITTA

Owr[1] lorde Ihesu Cryst tellyth seynte Birgitte why he
chesyth hyr to be hys spovse, and how as a spowse she
awyth to aray hyr and be redy to hym.

fol. 1 a
Revela-
tions,
Book I,
Chap. 2[5].

I am maker of heuen and erth and see and of all thynges
5 that bene in hem. I am on wyth the fader and the holy goste,
nott as goddys of stones or of[2] golde, as some tyme was seyde,
ne mony goddys, as then was wende ; bott on God, fader and
sone & holy goste, iij in persones and on in substance, maker
of all thynges and made of none, vnchangeble and almyghty
10 lestyng with-out begynnyng & wyth-out ende. I am he that was
borne of the vyrgyne, notte leuyng the godhed bott knytting itt
to the manhode, þat I shuld be in on person þe verry sonne of
God and the sonne of the virgyne. I am he that honge one
the crosse and dyede and was beryed, þe godhed abydynge vn-
15 hurte. For þough[3] the manhode and body whych I, sonne,
alone toke wer dede, yett ine[4] þe godhede in whych I was oo
God wyth þe fader and þe holy goste I lyuede all way. I am
also þe same þat roose frome deth and styede in-to heuyn that
nowe spekys wyth þe wyth my spiryte. I haue chosse & take
20 the to me to be my spowse for to shewe the my privey con-
celles, for so itt lykyth me. And also thow arte myne be all
maner of ryght, when in the deth of thyne hossebond thowe
yeuyste þi wylle jne to myn hondes, and also after hys deth
whan thowe thoughteste and praydeste how þow myght be-com
25 poor for me and for me for-sake all thynges. And ther-for of
ryght þow arte myne and for so mych cheryte me byhouyth to
orden for the ; ther-for I take the to my spowse and to myn

---

[1] The chapter headings are rubricated throughout, and the initial letter of each of
the revelations is in blue.

[2] MS. of inserted above line. All insertions and corrections are in the same
hand, unless otherwise stated.

[3] MS. of cancelled after þough.

[4] MS. ine marked through as if for cancellation.

[5] The corresponding chapters in the complete Latin text of the Revelations are given
in the side-notes at the beginning of each chapter in the text.

B

owne pro̜pur delyte, sych as semyth goode to haue with a
chaste sowle.

To the spovse þer-for it longyth to be redye when hyr spowse
wyll make hys weddyng, that she be semely arayde and clene.
Then arte thow well made clene, yf thy thowght be al-way 5
a-bowte þi synnes; how I clensed the frome the synne of
fol. 1 b Adam yne þy baptym & howe often I | haue suffered the and
supportede the when þow haste fallen into synne. The spovse
also owyth to haue tokenes of hyr spovse on hyr breste; that
ys, to [1] take kepe of the benefettez and werkys that I haue 10
done for the ; that is to sey, how nobley I made the, yeuyng
the body and sovle, and howe nobley I haue endewede the,
yeuynge the helth and tempe̜rall goodes, and how swetely
I bowght the ayeyne when I dyed for the and restorede the
thyn herytage, yf thu wyll haue ytt. The spovse owyth also 15
to do the wyll of hyr spovse. What is my wyll, bott that þow
wyll love me above all thynges and to wyll non other thynge
bott me ? I haue made all thynge for man, and all hem soiette
to hym ; bott he louyth all þyng̜es saue me, and hatyth ryght
nott bott me. I bowght hym ayeyne hys herytage that he 20
lost. Bot he is so alyen̜de & turned from reson that he
desyryth mor thys tra̜nsytorye wyrshyp that is botte as froth
of the see, which sodenly rysyth vppe as a mounte and as sone
fallyth down to no3t, than eve̜rlastyng̜e wyrshyppe wher-in is
endeles goode.   25

Bot thow, my spowse, yf thu desyr no thing bott me, yf thu
dyspyse all þyng̜es for me, nott only thy chyldre̜n & kynne, bot
eke wyrshypes and rechesse, I shall yeve the moste precyos
and swettyste rewarde ; nott gold and sylue̜r, bot my-selfe, to
be thy spowse & endeles mede, that am kynge of blysse. And 30
yf þow be ashamed to be poor and dyspysed, be-hold that I thy
God goo to-for the,· whome seruauntez & frendes for-soke in
erthe ; for I sowght notte erthely frendes, botte heuynly.
And yf thow fere and drede the byrthen of labor and sykenes,
consyder how grevowse it is to brenne in the fyr whych thu 35
haddeste deseruede, yf þow hadde offended a tempe̜rall lorde as
thow hath offendede me. For thowgh I love the wyth all my
herte, yett I shall nott do ayenest ryghtwysnesse in þe leste

[1] MS. to *inserted above line.*

poynte, bott that as thu has trespased in all thy membres so
that in all þu do satysfaccion. Neuer-the-lesse yett for a good
wyll and purpose to amend, I chaunge ryghtwysnesse into
mercy, | foryeuyng grevouse tormentez for a lytell amende- fol. 2 a
5 mente. Ther-fore take to the gladely a lyttell labor, that þow
mayst þe sonner be made clene and come to grete rewarde.
For it is semely that the spowse labor wyth hyr spovse tyll
she be werye, that she may afterwarde the mor [1] sourely and
trystely take hyr reste wyth hym.

10 **Owr lorde Ihesu Cryste steryth Saynte Birgitt not to be** Revela-
a-ferde of hys spekynge wyth hyr, techyng hyr the dyffer- tions,
ence of the good spirite and the euyll. Book I,
Chap. 4.

I am maker of all thynges and ayane-byer : why dredyst þow
of my wordes and why thowghteste thu of what spyrite they
15 wer, of the goode or of the evyll ? Tell me what founde thu
in my wordes þat thyne owne conscyence told the noght to be
do ? Or bade y the any thynge ayanes reson ?

The spouse seynte Byrgitte answerde : No thynge, lorde,
bot all þat thu sayde ar trewe, and y erred euyll.

20 Then seyde our lorde : I bade thee iij thynges of whych thu
mayste knowe a goode spyrite. Fyrste, I bade the wyrshyp thy
God that made the and yaue the all þat þou haste ; and þys
thyn owne reson techyth the, to wyrshyp hym above all
thynges. Seconde, I bade the kepe and holde the ryght fayth ;
25 that is, to be-leve that nothynge ys doo nor may be doo with-
oute God. The iij, I bade the lofe resonable temperance and
continence of all þynges ; for the world ys made for mane that
he shulde vse it to hys nede.

So also be iij contrarie to these. Thu may knowe the vn-
30 clene spirite for he steryth the to seke thyn own wyrshyp and
praysyng and to be prowde of the yiftes þat God hath yeue
the ; and he steryth the to intemperance of all thy membres
and of all other þynges, and to þese he inflawmeth þy herte.
He dysseyuyth also some tyme vnder colowr of goode ; and
35 ther-for I haue bode the dyscusse thy conscyence and to open it
to spirituell wyssemen. Þer-fore dowte the notte bot that the
good spiritte of God ys than with the whan thu desyryste no

---

[1] MS. mor *inserted above line.*

fol. 2 b þing [1] | bot God, and of him thu art all inflamed. For that
may I alone do and it is inpossible the fende to negh vn-to the.
Ne he may nott neght to any euyll man, botte he be sufferede
of me, oþer for hys synnes or for some preuey doo[m] [2] knowe
to me. For the fende ys my creatur as all other thynges be ; 5
and of me he was well made, bot be hys own malysse he is
evyll, and therfor I am lorde ouer hym. And therfore they
that sey that they that serue me of grete deuocion wax madde
or hath a fende in hem, they putt a-pon me a wronge blame.
For they make me lyke to a manne that hadde a chaste wyffe 1
well tristyng in hyr hosbounde, and he putt hyr to a vowterer.
Sych on shulde y be, yf I sufferede a ryghtfull mane that hade
a lovyng herte to me to be take to the fende. Bot for I am
trusty & trew, the fende shall neuer haue lordeshippe in noo
sowle that deuotely seruyth me. For þough my fryndes seme 1
some tyme as madde, yett that is nott for passyon of the fende,
ne for they serue me of fervente deuocyon, bot for defaute of
her brayn or for some other priuey cause whych is to hem cause
of mor mekenes. It may also be some tyme that þe fende
takyth power of me opon the bodyes of goodemen to her 2
encrese of mede, and he that derkyth his conscience ; but in þe
sowles of hem that hath fayth and delyte in me may he [3] neuer
haue lordeshyp nor power.

Revela-
tions,
Book I,
Chap. 41. Her our lorde Ihesu Cryst enformyth saynt Birgytt how
the worlde stondeth anenste hym in all states and degrees 2
under lykenes of v men, wher comforth and helpe ys by-hote
to the goode and herde sentence y-ȝoue a-yeynes the euyll.

I am maker of all thynges. I am gote of the fader to-for
Lucifer. And I am vndepartable in the fader and the fader in
me, and oo spirite in both. Ther-for ther ys oo God, fader, 3
sonne and holy goste, and nott iij goddes. I am he that by-
hight to Abraham [4] endeles herytage, and by Moyses brought
my peple out of Egypte. I am also the same that spake in the
profettes. The fader sente me in-to the vyrgyns wombe, nott
dysseueryng hym fro me, bot abydyng vnseperably with me, 3

---

[1] a ij.

[2] MS. doon ; *Latin* iudicium.

[3] MS. he *inserted above line*.

[4] MS. ra *abbreviation written above final* m.

that manne whych was goo frome God shuld be my cherite turne
aȝeyn | to God.

Bot now to-fore yow, my heuynly Courte, þough ye see &
knowe all thing*es* in me, ȝett for knowleg*e* and instrucc*i*on of
thys my spouse that is presente and may nott p*er*ceyve
sp*ir*it*u*ell thyng*es*, I compleyne me apon these v men that
stondes to-fore me, that they offende me ine mony wyse. For
as some tyme by the name of Isr*ael* I vnderstonde all the men
ine the worlde, so now by these v men I vnderstonde all the
men ine þe worlde. The fyrst man is the gou*er*no*ur* of the
chyrch and hys clerkys. The ij is wykedde lay peple. The iij,
Ieweys. The iiij, paynems. The v, my frendys. Bot oute of
the Iewes I excepte all the Iewes that ar pryueley crysten men
and s*er*ue me p*ri*ualy in clene charite and ryght feyth and p*er*-
fyte werke. And oute of the paynems I excepte all thoo þat
wolde gladely goo by the way of my com*m*aundement*es* yf they
wyst how. And yf they wer enformyd and in dede they doo what
they kan or may, these shall in no wyse be demed wyth hem.

Bot now I compleyne on þe, thow hedde of my chyrch, that
syttest[1] in my sete, whych I take to Pet*er* & hys successours
to sytte ine iij fold dygnite and auctoryte. Fyrst, that they
shuld haue power to bynde and lowse sowles from synne.
Secunde, that they shulde opyn heuyn to heme that doth pennance. Thryde, that they shulde sparr heuyn to wyked and
cursede and dyspyse[r]s.[2] But thu that owest to vnbynd
sowles and p*re*sente hem to me, thu arte verely a sleer of
soules. For I ordenyd Pet*er* to be a shypperde and a keper of
my shepe; bot thu arte a dysp*er*peler and a reicett*er* of hem.
For thu arte wors and mor envyouse then Lucyfer. For he
hadde envye to me and desyride to flee non bot me, that he
myght be lorde in stede of me. Bot thu arte so mych wors
and mor envyouse then he, that thu nott only fleest me, puttyng
me frome the be thyn wyll & werk*es*, bot also thu sleste soules
by thin euyll ensample. I bowght sowles w*ith* my blode and
toke hem to the as to a trewe frende. Bot thu takeste hem
ayayne to the enmy from whom | I bowgh[t][3] hem. Thu art
mor vnryghtwosse then Pylate, that demed non to deth bott

[1] MS. syttsest.   [2] MS. dyspyses : *Latin*, contemnentibus.
[3] MS. bowgh.

me.   Bot thu not only demest me as lorde of non ne worthy
any goode, bot also thu demeste innocent soules, and lattes
gylty goo vnpunyshed.   Thu arte more enmy than Iudas, for
he solde non bot me.   Bot thu selleste notte me allone bot eke
the sowle of my chosen for thy sowle wynnyng and vayne
name.   Thu arte mor abhomynable then þe Iewes, for they
crucyfiede bot my body ; bot thu crucyfyes & punyshyth þe
sowles of my chosen, to whom thy malyce and trespace is
bitterer then any swerde.   And therfor, for thu art lyke to
Lucyfer in envye, more vnryghtfull than Pylate, mor enmy 1
than Iudas, and mor abhominable then the Iewes, therfor
worthely I compleyne a-pon the.

To the ij man, that is, to the lewed peple, our lorde sayde
thus : I haue made all thynges for thi profett, and thu haste
consented in me & I in the.   Thow hast yeuen thy fayth to 1
me and by-hight with thin oth to serue me, bot now art
gone from me as a man not knowyng hys God.   Thu counteste
my wordes bot lesynges and my werkes bot vanite ; thow seyst
that my wyll and commawndementes ar ou[er]¹ herde ; thu
haste broke the fayth that thu by-highest me and forsake my 2
name ;   thu haste dysseuerede the fro the novmbre of my
sayntes, and thu art comen to the novmbre of fendes and made
her felaw.   Þe semyth that none ys worthy to haue praysyng
and wyrshyp bott thu alone.   All my wyll and all that thow
art hold to do to me is herde to the, and all that pleysyth the 2
is esy.   Therfor worthely I compleyne apon the.   For thu
haste broke þi feyth that þu yaue me in thy baptim ; and seth
mor-ouer for my charite which I shewed the in worde & dede,
thow blameste me as a lyer.   And for my passion thu sayste
I am a fowle.   3

To the iij, that is, to the Iewes, our lorde seyde thus : I
bygan my cherite with yow and chose yow be my peple.
I bowght yow oute of thraldam and yafe yow my lawe and
fol. 4 a ledde yow into the londe that I by-hight your faderes. | I sente
yow profettes to yowr comforth, and after I chesse me a vyrgyn 3
of yow, of whom I toke manhod.   Bott now I compleyn me
apon yow now that ȝe wyll nott belefe, saying that Cryst come
not ȝett, bot he ² ys to come.

To the iiij, that is, to the hethen, our lorde sayde thus : I
haue made the and bought the as well as a cristenne man, and
done all godenesse for the. Bot thu art as a wode man, for
thu wott not wheþer thow gost. Thu wyrshipis creators for
5 thy maker and fals for throwth, and bowes thy kne to-for that
is lesse worthy than thu. And þer-for I compleyn apon the.

To the v our lorde seyde thus : Come ner, my frynde. Then
anon our lorde seyde vnto hys heuynly courte : my louyd
fryndes, I haue on frynde by whom I vnderstonde mony. He
10 is as a man closede amonge shrewes & prison de full herde. Yf
he sey treugth, they stoppe his mowth. Yf he do good, þey
put a sper in his breste. Loo, my fryndes and all my sayntes,
how longe shall I suffer all þese folke and sych contempte
of hem ?

15 Seynt Iohn þe Baptyst vnswerd : Thu, lorde, art as a myrrour moste clene ; for in the as in a myrrour we see and know
all thynges. With-out any worde or spech thu arte incom-
parable swettenes wher-in all goodenes sauoreth to vs. Thu
art as a swerde most sharpe that demeste in euynesse.

20 Than vnswerde our lorde to hym : forsoth, my frynde, thu
sayth trew. For in me all my chosen sees all good and all
ryghtwysnesse ; and so doth wykked spirites also, þough it be not
non lyght bot in her conscience. As yf a man that had lernede
lettruer wer putt in prison, þough he wer in derkenes and
25 myght nott see, yett he cowde the thynges he lorned to-for ;
ryght so feendes, þough they see nott in ryghtwysnesse in lyght
of my clernesse, yett they know as they see in her conscyence.
I am also as a thyng that partyth a thyng in too, for so do I to
ych as he desyrith.

30 After this our lord seyde to saynt Peter : thow art founder
of fayth and of my church ; sey þu in the heryng of all my
hevenly courte what ryghtwysnes wyl that be doo of these v
men.

Seynte Peter aunswerd, | and seyde : praysyng and wyrshuppe fol. 4 b
35 be to the, lorde, for thy cherite that thow doste with thin erth.
Blessedde be thu of all thy heuenly cowrte, for thu makys vs see
& know in the all thynges that ar doo and shal be do. For in
the we see and knowe all thynges. Thys is verray ryghtwosnesse, that the fyrst man that syttes in thy sete and hath

werk*es* of Lucifer leese w*ith* repreve þat sete wher-in he p*re*-sumyth to sette, & be made p*er*tener in peyne w*ith* Lucifer. Of the ij, ryghtwyssenesse ys that, for he hath gone from thy [1] fayth, he descende to helle w*ith* hys hed downwarde and hys fete upwarde ; for he hath despysede the that shulde be his 5 hede, and loved him-selfe. Of the iij, ryghtwysnes is that he see nott thy face, bot that he be punysshed aft*er* hys malice & couetyse ; for they that ar in mysbyleue des*er*ue not to see thy syght. Of the iiij, rych[t]wysnes [2] is that, as madde man, he be closed and putt in derke plase. Of the v, ryghtwysnes ys that 10 helpe be sente to hym.

Thes thynges herde, our lorde aunswerde and seyde : I swer by God the fader, whose voyce Iohn Baptyste herde in Iordan, I swere by the body þat Iohn Baptyst see & towched in Iordan, I swer by that spirite that in Iordan apperid in lykenesse of a 15 colu*er*, that I shal do ryghtwosnes vppon these v men.

Aft*er* this our lorde seyde to the fyrst man of the v, that is, to the clergye : the swerde of my cruelte shal enter in-to thy body. And it shal be-gyn to enter at the ou*er*-p*ar*te of thyn hede, and so myghtyly it shal be smytten in that it shal nev*er* 20 be drawe out. Thi seete shal be throwe dovn as a ston most heuy that abydyth nott tyl it come to the loweste depnes of hell. Thyn fyngurs, that is to sey thyn assissours, shal brinne in fyr and brymston that neuer shall be whenched. Thyn armes, þat ys to say, thy vycares, whych owe to be strechede 25 out to þe p*ro*fette of sowles and now ar streched oute to the p*ro*fyte & wyrship of the world, shal be dampnede w*ith* the payne that Dauid spekyth of, sayinge : 'Fiant filij eius orphani' & ' vx*or* ei*us* vidua & alieni accipiant substanci*am* ei*us* ': that fol. 5 a is, ' hys | chyldren mote be faderlesse and hys wyf a wydow, & 30 alyenes motte take hys wyrshyp and goodes '. What is his wyfe bot hys sowle, whych shall be for-sake from the blysse of heuyn and made wydow from God. Hys sonnes, that is to say, hys vertues that he semede to haue and my simple peple that was vnder hem, shall be departed frome hem. And her 35 worthynes and goodes shall passe to other & þey for her worthy-nesse shall enherett endeles confuc*ion*. And then shall the

---

[1] Y *written over original* a.   [2] MS. ryghwynes.

aray of her hedes be drownede in the fylth of hell, from whense
they shall nev*er* a-ryse. Bot as they ascendede above other
here by wyrshyp and pride, so shall the[y]¹ be drowned by-
neth other in hell so depe þat it shall be inpossible to hem
5 eu*er* to a-ryse. Her membres and soiett*es*, that is to sey her
followers and her clerk*es* and fawtoures, shall be kytt of and
descended from hem as a wall that is dystroyde, wher no stone
is lefte vppon other, ne wher morter clevyth to the stones. For
m*er*cy shall no[t]² come apon hem, for my cherite shall nott
10 make hem hote. Ne they shall nott be beld in endeless beldyng,
dwellyng in heuyn, bott w*ith* her hedes shall be tourmented
w*ith*-oute ende, departed from all goode.

To the ij man, that is, to the lay peple, I sey: for thow wyll
nott hold the fayth that thu haste by-hote me ne haue cherite
15 to me, I shall sende to þe a beste þat shal come oute of a sharpe
rennyng flode, and swalow the ine; & as a rennyng flode goth
away downwarde, so shall that best lede the dovn in-to the
iner p*ar*tyes of hell. And as þu may nott goo vpp ayeine a
myghty & hasty rennyng flode, so shal þu neuer mowe rysse
20 from þe pytte of hell.

To the iij man, that is, the Iewe, I sey: for thow, Iew, wyll
nott now by-leve þat I am comen, þ*er*-for when I com*me* to þe
ij doome, þu shall nott see in my blysse, bot in thy conscienc*e*,
and p*re*ve that all þat I seyde was trewe. And than shall thu
25 haue peyne, as þu hast deserued.

To the iiij man, þat is, the paynem, I sey: for thu takest no
kepe to byleve ne wyll nott know the ryght feyth, þ*er*-for thy
derkenes shall shyne vn-to þe, and thy herte shal be lyghtned,
that þu shall know that my domes ar trew; & yett shall þu
30 nott come to endelesse lyght.

To the v man, þat is, Godd*es* s*er*uaunt*es*, I sey: iij thyng*es*
shall I do vn-to the. Fyrst, I shall³ | fyll the w*ith*-inne wyth fol. 5 b
myne hete. Secund, I shall make thi mouth herder and
stabler than any stone, so þat stones cast the shall turne agayn.
35 Thryd, I shall arme the w*ith* myn armour, þat noo sperr shall
noye the, bot all thyng shall melte to-fore the as wex ayeneste
the fyr. Therfor be comforted and stonde manfully. For as

---

¹ MS. the; *Latin* hi.   ² MS. non; *Latin* neque.
³ MS. shall/shall.

a knyght that in a battell he hopeth to hafe help of hys lorde
fyghtyth as longe as only lycour ys in hym, soo stounde þu
sourely and fyght. For thy lorde God shall yeve þe helpe,
whom noon may with-stounde ; and for þu haste bott a lytell
and a small noumbre, I shall wyrshyp þe & encrese the.   5

Loo, my frendes, these þinges ye see and know in me, &
thus stondes þe worlde to-for me. These wordes that I haue
now seyde shall be fullfylled, and they shall neuer enter my
kyngdom as longe as I am kynge bot yf they amende hem, for
heuyn shall be yeuyn to noon bote to hem that meke hem-selfe 10
and do pennans.

Then aunswerde all the courte of heuyn : praysyng be to the
lorde God that art with-owte begynnyng & wyth-owten ende.
Amen.

Revela-
tions,
Book IV,
Chap. 37. **Owr lorde Ihesu Cryste tellyth saynte Birgitt of herde** 15
sentence of ryghtwesnesse that he wyll doo ayainste all
mankynde botte yf they amende hem.

The sonne of God askyth of saynte Birgitte and sayth:
doughter, how stondeth the worlde now ?

She vnswerde : it stondes as an open sake to whom all 20
rynne, and as a man reynyng nott rekkyng whatt folow after.

Then seyde our lorde : ther-for ryghtwosnes is þat I go with
my plowgh apon all the erth and worlde, both heethen and
crysten. I shall neuer spar olde nor yong, poor ne rych. Bott
ych shall be demed after ryghtwysnesse and ych shall dye 25
in hys synne ; and her howse shall be lefte wythout dwellers ;
and yet shall I nott make an ende of the worlde.

Seynt Birgitte sayde : o lorde, be dyspleased [not]¹ þough I
speke. Send some of thy frendes to warne hem and monysh
hem to-for of her perell.   30

Our lorde aunswerde : it is writen that the rych man in
fol. 6 a hell, despayring of his own helth, asked | that on myght be
sente to warne his brethern that they peryshed nott on þe
same wyse. And it was aunswerde to him, 'that shall nott
be, for they haue Moysen and the prophettes, of whom they 35
may be tawght'. So sey I to the. They haue the gospell &
saynges of profettes ; ` they haue ensamples and wordes of

---

¹ *Latin* ne (inquit) indigneris.

doctors ; they have reson and vnderstondyng. Vse they these
and they shall be sauyd. For yf I sende the, thow may nott
crye so lowde to be herde ; and yf I sende my frendes, they ar
bott few ; and yf they crye, vnneth they shall be herde.
5 Neuer-the-lesse I shall sende my frendes to sych as me lykyth,
and they shall make redy a way to God.

Owr lorde Ihesu Cryste techyth seynte Birgitt the Revela-
dyfference be-twyx good deth and euyll deth, and how tions,
Book IV,
goddes seruantes owe nott to be hevy þowht they be[1] in Chap. 40.
10 this lyf.

The sonne of God spekyth to seynte Birgitte thus : dowghter,
drede the nott ; thys woman that is seke shall nott dye, for
hyr werke plese me. And whan the same woman was dede,
the sonne of God seyde ayayne to seynte Birgitte : loo,
15 dowghter, it is trewe that I seyde, thys woman is not dede,
for hyr blysse is grete. For the departyng of body and sowle
of ryghtfull men is bott a slepe, for they awake in endelesse
lyfe. Bot that is veraly to be called deth when þe sowle,
departede from the body, lyuyth in deth euerlastyng. Þer is
20 mony that takyth noo kepe of thynges to come desyris to dye
in cristen deth. Bot what is cristen deth, bot for to dye as I
dyed, innocentely, wyllfully, and pacyentely ? Am I therfor
to be dispicede, for my deth was dyspisable and herde ? Or ar
my chosen therfor foules, for they sufferede dyspysable tor-
25 mentez ? Or come it of fortune, or was it wrought be the
course of planettes & of sterris ? Nay, bot þer-for I and my
chosen sufferede herde passyon to showe in worde and in
exsample that the way to heuyn is herd, and that it shulde
besyly be hadde in mynde how mych nede the wyked haue to
30 be clensede seth the innocentes & chosen sufferede so sharpe
thynges. Therfore wete þu well | that he dyth dispysabley and fol. 6 b
evyll that lyuyng dissolutly dyeth in wyll to synne, and while
he that forth goyng in the worlde desyrith to lyffe longer and
can not thanke God ; bot he that lovyth God with all hys herte
35 and is trowbled innocentely with dyspysable deth or grevede
with longer sekeness, he lyves and dyeth blessedly. For a

---

[1] *Space for another word follows in* MS.

sharpe deth lassyth synne and payne for syn, & morith the
rewarde in blysse.

    Loo, I brynge too men to thy mynde that after mannes dome
dyede in bytter & dyspisable deth, whych, bott they had gott
such deth of my grete mercy, shuld neuer haue bene sauede. 5
Bott for God punysheth nott twyse hem þat ar contrite in
herte, þer-for they come to the crovne of endeles rewarde.
Ther-for the frendys of God owe nott to be hevy, þough they
haue her temperall tribulacion or þough they dye by bitter
deth. For it is moste blessede to sorowe her for a tyme and to 10
be trowblede in the world, that he come not to more grevouse
purga[to]rie [1] wher is no fleyng ne tyme of laboring.

Revela-
tions,
Book II,
Chap. 24. **Of the tribulacion and sorow that our lady sufferede &
of the fruyte of [2] owr lordys wordys. And of iij howses
þat Cryst and mannys sowle owe to haue to-geder.** 15

    Oure blessede lady spekyth to seynte Birgitt and seyth :
lyke as ther wer a grete hoste of men, & one þat hadde a grete
and a heuy byrthn one hys bak and on hys armys and his eyne
full of teres wente forth by hem, and lokede yf eny of hem
wolde haue pitee on hym and help hym of hys byrthen, ryght 20
so was I ; for frome the byrth of my sonne vn-to hys deth I
was full of tribulacion. I bare a ryght grete byrthen on my
bakke, for I entendede contynually to the labour of Goddes
seruice, and I suffered pacyently all that euer come vn-to me.
In my armes I bar most heuy byrthene, for I sufferde tribula- 25
cion & soro of herte mor than euer dyde any creatur. I hadde
myn eyne full of teres when I byheld in the members of my
sonne þe place of nayles, & hys passyon þat wa[s] [3] to come,
and when I see fullfylled in him all that I had herde to-fore
fol. 7 a profyciede of profettes. But now I loke vn-to all þat | ar in the 30
worlde, [l]este [4] y myght fynde any þat hadde pyte & compassyon on me and wolde thynke on my sorow. And y fonde
bot fewe that thenke on my sorowe and tribulacion. Þerfore,
thu my dowghter, of I be foryette and lytell sett by, yett for-
yette þu nott me, bot see my sorow and folow yt as mych as 35
þu may. Be-holde my sorow and teres and be sory ; for the

---

[1] MS. purgarie ; *Latin* purgatorium.   [2] MS. of of.
[3] MS. wat ; *Latin* passionem eius futuram.   [4] MS. beste ; *Latin* si forte.

frendys of God ar bot fewe. And now stonde stabley, for, loo, my sonne comyth vn-to the.

Then come our lorde Ihesu Cryst and sayde : I that speke with the am thy God and thy lorde. My wordes ar as flowres
5 of a goode tre ; for lyke as all flowres, þough þei come oute of on rote of oo tre yett þei come not all to effecte of fruyte, so my wordes are as flowres comyng oute of the rote of godly cheryte, whych, þought þei be receyuede of mony, yett they bryng not forth fruyte in all ne wax nott ripe in all. For some take hem
10 and kape hem for a tyme, and after caste hem owte, for they ar vnkynde to my [1] spiritte. Bot some take hem and holde hem, for they ar full of cheryte and in hem þey wyrke fruyte of devocion.

Therfor, þu my spouse, for thow art mine of godely ryght, it
15 byhoueth [2] vs to haue iij howses. In the fyrste awe to be sych necessares as enteryth in-to þe body, as mete or drynke. In the ij awe to be clothes to helen the body with-oute. And in the iij, necessarie Instrumentez that longeth to þe profette of howsholde.

20 In the firste howse awe to be iij thynges : brede, drynk, and sowlle. In þe ij, other iij thinges ; that is, lynen cloth, wollen cloth, and cloth of sylke that is made of the worke of wormes. In þe iij, oþer iij thynges ; first, Instrumentes and vessells þat shall be fylled wyth lycour ; secunde, quyk Instrumentes as
25 horse, assys, and oþer ; the iij, Instrumentez artyficiall, be whych quyke thynges ar mevyde.

Merke how in the fyrst howse awe to be brede of god wyll, drinke of godly premeditacion, and sowlle of goddely wysdom.
Revelations, Book II, Chap. 25.

30 I that speke with the am maker of all thynges and made of none. To-fore me no thynge was, ne after me eny thing may be ; for y was and am all way. I am also þat lorde whos power none may wythstonde, and of me is all power & | lorde- fol. 7 b shyp. I speke to the as a man spekyth to hys wyfe. My
35 wyfe, vs moste haue iij howses. In one moste be brede and

[1] MS. my *inserted above line before* to.
[2] *Marg. gloss.* : Nota de tribus domibus.

drynk and sowle. Bot thu may aske what meneth thys brede,
whether y mene the brede that is in the auter. For-soth þat
is brede to-for tho wordes ; 'Hoc est enim corpus meum '.
Bot tho wordes seyde of the preste, 'It is nott brede bot my
blessede body that I toke of the virgyn and was crucifiede on 5
the crosse ', thys brede mene nott I here ; bot the brede þat vs
muste gader into one howse is a good and a clene wyll.
Bodely brede, yf it be clene and pure, it profetyth to ij thynges.
Fyrst, it comforteth and yifes strenght to all the vaynes and
senowes of the body. Secounde, it gadereth to it all inwarde 10
fylth, and þer-with it goth owte fro man, and so man is
clensede. Ryȝt so a clene wyll. Fyrst, it comforteth ; for
yf a man wyll nothyng but that god wyll, ne laboryth no
thynge bot to the wyrshyp of God, and desyryth wyth all his
herte to be owte of the worlde and to be wyth God, this wyll 15
comforthyth a man in God and encresyth the wyrshyp of God
and makes the worlde vyle and fowle. It strenght pacyence
and makyth stronge the hope of gettyng of blysse, so myche
that he takyth & sufferyth gladly all that fallyth to hym.
Seconde, a good wyll drawyth oute all fylth that noyse the 20
sowle, as pryde, covetyse, and lecherye. Bot when the fylth
of pryde or of any oþer synne comyth into the mynde, than it
goth away yf a man thynke thus : pryde is veyne, for it is not
semly hym to be praysed þat takes yiftes ; bot þe yeuer is to be
praysed.   Couetyse ys vayne, for all erthely thynge shall be 25
lefte, and lechery ys bot stynke. Þer-for I wyll nott ther-of ; bot
I wyll folowe the wyll of my God, whos rewarde shall neuer
haue ende, nor hys goodes waxe not olde.

   The drynke that vs muste haue in our howses ys godly
thynkyng to-for in all thys that ar to be doo. Bodely drynke 30
is veyleable in ij wise. Fyrst, it maketh goode dygestyon.
For who euer purpose to do any goode dedes, yf he byholde
fol. 8 a in him-selfe & bysely caste in hys | mynde, or he do owght,
what wyrshyp shall come to God þer-of, what avayle to
hys neghtburr, and what profette to hys sowle, and that he 35
wyll nott doo bot he perseyve some godely profett in hys werke,
than the werke shall haue good processe & goode ende as a
good dygestyon. Than, yf any vndiscrecion happen to come in
doynge of that werke, it shall sone be perceyved, and then, yf

owgh⌊t⌋ [1] be wronge, it may lyghtly be amendede, and hys
werke shall be ryght & resonable edyficacion in the syght of
man. For he that hath not [2] godely thynkynge to-fore in hys
worke neþer sekyth profette of sowle ne the wyrshippe of God.
5 Then of his werke hafe processe for a tyme, yette in the ende
it shall turne to noght, bot yf the entente be corrected and
amendett. Secunde, drynke quenchyth thyrste. What is
wers thirste þan synne of wykede desyr and of yr? Bot and
a man thynk to-fore what profette comyth thereof, how
10 wrechidly it is endede, and what reward if it be with-stounde,
anon be the grace of God thilke wyked thyrste is quenched,
and the hetee of godely charite and of good desyr comyth to
the sowle, and gladnes ryseth in him that he dyde notte þe
thinges that come in hys mynde. And he sekyth occasion how
15 he may from thensforth flee thoo thynges that he shuld haue
be deceyuyde with, hadde nott thynkyng to-for haue holpe.
And he shall be the more besy after to be-war of sych thynges.
Thys, my spowse, is the drynke that we awe to gader into owr
celar.
20   Thirde ; ther muste be sowle þat doth twoo thynges. Fyrst,
it makyth better sauer in the mouþe, and it is more con-
ueniente to the body than yf brede wer alon. Secunnde, it
makyth the body more delycate and the blode better than brede
and drynke onely. Ryght so doth gostely sowlle. What is
25 this sowlle bot godely wysdom? For who that euer haue a
gode wyll, and wyll ryght noght botte tho thynges that longe to
God, yf he haue also goddely thynkyng to- | fore, doynge no fol. 8 b
thynge but yf he knowe fyrst that it is to the wyrshyp of God,
to hym wysdom sauoreth ryght well. But now myght thu
30 aske what is this godely wisdame, for ther ar mony so sympell
that can nott her pater noster and vneth that ryght. Other
ar of grete letruer and depe connyng. Is that godely wysdome?
Naye. For godely wysdom is nott onely in letturis, bot in
herte and in goode lyvyng. Who euer he be that thenkyth
35 bysely the way vn-to deth and the qualite of the selfe, deth and
the dome after deth, he is wyse. And who caste from hym
þe vanyte of the worlde and all superflew thynges, and is contente wyth hys onely necessaries, and trauelyth in the love of

---

[1] MS. owgh.   [2] MS. not *inserted above line.*

God as mych as he may, he hath sowle of wysdome, by whych the brede of gode wyll and drynke of godely forthynkyng sauouryth mych the bett*er*. For when a man thynk*es* on hys deth, and how naked he shall be frome all thyng*es* in hys deth, and when he p*er*ceyuyth the dredefull dome of God, wher 5 no thyng ys hydde, no thynge left vnpunished, and whe*n* he thenkyth also the unstablenesse and vanyte of the worlde, Ioythe he not than, and sauo*ur*[i]th [1] it nott swetely in hys herte that he hath loste hys wyll to Gode, and ab- stenede hym frome synne? Is not than hys body com- 10 fortede and hys blode bettered? That is to say, all sekeness of sowle as slewth and dissoluc*i*on of maners is dryve away, and the blode of goodely cherite is fresh. For he sees it is mor resonable to loue thoo thynges that ar eu*er*lastynge than thoo thynges that ar faylynge. Ther-fore goodely wysdome is not 15 onely in lettrur, bot in goode werke. For ther ar mony ryght- wysse aft*er* the worlde and to here own desyris, bot they ar all vnwyse to the commaundement*es* of God & to hys wyll and to refreynynge of her flesh. And they ar not wyse, bot vnwyse and blynde; for they know and co*n*ne tho thyngis that shall 20

fol. 9 a vayle and ar profytable; bot ryght | a lytell whyle and they dyspyce eu*er*lastynge thynges. Other þ*er*be tha[t] [2] ar vnwyse to the delytes of the worlde and to the wyrshyp ther-of. And they ar wyse to be-holde thoo thynges that longyth to God and ar feruente in his s*er*uice; and thes ar verely wyse, for the 25 byddyng of God and hys wyll is sauo*ur*ye vn-to hem. Thes ar verely lyghtned & hath her eyne open, for they loke alwaye how they myght come to verrye lyfe and lyght. Bot the other goth in derkenes; and it semeth to hem more delectable to be in derkenes then to seke the way by whych they may come to 30 lyght.

Ther-fore, my spowse, gadre we in-too owre howses these thre; that is to say, goode wyll, goodely forthynkynge, and goodely wysdome. For these thynges be wher-wi*th* vs muste make merye. Bot þofe I speke onely to the, yette I mene by 35 [the] [3] all my chosen in the world; for the sowle of a ryghtwosse man is my spowse, and I am hys maker and hys ayayne-byer.

---

[1] MS. sauo*ur*rth. [2] MS. thar; *Latin* alij sunt insipientes.
[3] *Latin* in te.

Merke how seynte Laurence folowed the pacyence and Revela-
passyon of our lorde Ihesu Cryst in lyfe & deth. And how tions,
Book II,
in the secunde howse muste be lynnen cloth of pece and Chap. 26.
pacyence, and wollen cloth of dedes of mercy, and sylken
5 of abstenance from euyll.

Owre lady saynte Marie spekyth to seynte Byrgitte and seyth :
festne to þe roch of the passyon of my sonne as seynte Laurance
festned it to hym.   For he thought thus in hys mynde : my God
is my lorde, and I am his seruante to the same.   Lorde Ihesu
10 was nakede and scorned ; how myght it þer-fore be semely that
I that am his seruante be with-owte sorow and tribulacion ? And
ther-for, when he was streynede oute apon the coles, and when
his grese molte and ranne in-to the fyre, and fyre enflawmede
all the membres of his body, he loked upp to heuyn with his
15 eyn and seyde: ' Blessede be þu, my god and my maker, Ihesu
Criste.   I know that I haue not well lyved in my days, and þat
I haue do lytell to thy wyrshyp.   Ther-for thy mercye ys moste, | fol. 9 b
I pray the do with me after thy mercy.'   And wyth thys worde,
the sowle departed from the body.   Loo, my doughter, he that
20 loved my sonne so mych and suffered such paynes for hys
wyrshyp, ȝett he lett [1] him-selfe vnworthy to gett hevyn.   How
then ar they worthy that lyven after her own wyll ?   Ther-for
by-holde the passyon of my sonne and hys sayntes ; for they sufferede nott so grete thynges wyth-owte cause, but for to yif oþer
25 ensample of lyvynge, & for to showe how streyte a rekenyng my
sonne shall aske of synne, that wyll notte that the leste synne
be with-owte amendement.

Then spake the son of God to hys spowse, seynte Birgitte,
and seyde: I told the to-for what muste be in our howsys.
30 And a-monge other I seyde that ther muste be iij maner of
clothyng: fyrst, lynen cloth that growyth of the erth ; seconde,
cloth of woll, or of lether that is made of bestes ; and þe iij,
cloth of sylke that is made of wormes.

Lynen cloth hath ij goodes : fyrst, it is softe and esy to the
35 bare bodye ; secunde, it lesyth nott hys coloure, bot the ofter it
is wesh, the clenner it is.   Wollen also hath ij goodes : fyrst,
it heleth fro nakednes ; secunde, it makyth hote aȝaynes

---

[1] *Latin* dixit.

C

colde.　Syulke also hath ij godes : fyrst, it semyth ryght feyr
and delycate ; secunde, it is ryght der to bye.

The lynnen that is able to the naked body betokenes peese
and a-corde.　That awe a deuoute sowle to haue to God that he
haue peese with hys lorde, wyllyng ryght noght nor in other 5
wyse þan he wyll, nott offendyng him by synne.　For be-twix
God and the sowle is no pese, bot if synne be sesed, and wordely
and fleschly desyre refrened.　He oweth also to haue peese with
hys neghtborr, doyng hym no herme, bot helpyng[1] hym yf he
haue wher-of, and suffrynge hym yf he trespas aȝaynes him. 1
fol. 10 a For what distrow- |[2] bleth the sowle more wrechedly than all
way to desyr synne and neuer to be full þer-of, all way to
couett and neuer reste?　And what prykketh the sowle mor
bitterly than to be wroth ayanste hys neghtbor and to haue
envye at his goodes and welth?　Ther-fore the sowle must 1
haue peese vn-to God and to hys neghtborr ; for ther may no
thyng be more restefull than to seese fro syn and nott to be
besy abowte the worlde.　Ther is also no thynge so lyght þan
to Ioy of the good of his neghtbor and to wyll to him as himselfe.
Thys lynnen cloth aweth to be to the naked body ; for to the 2
herte wher in God wyll reste peese from synne muste cleue
moste nyghe and moste principally amongest all other vertues.
For thys is the vertue that bryngyth God in-to the herte and
holdeth hym when he ys browght ine.　This peese springyth
owt of the erth as lynnen ; for verry peese and pacyence 2
spryngyth of beholdynge of a mannes own frelte.　For if a man
that comyth of the erth beholde hys owne feblenesse, how sone
he is wrothe and hevye yf he be offendede, hurte, or dyssesed,
yf he thenke thus, he awe nott to do to a-nother that he may
nott ber hymselfe, thenkyng in him-selfe thus : as I am frele, 3
so is my neghtborr ; and yf I wyll nott suffer such thynges, no
mor may he.　For then peese lesyth nott hys colowr, that is to
sey, hys stablenesse.　But it is the mor stable and sadde ; for
the beholdynge in hym-selfe of his neghtborrs freelte maketh a
man gladely to suffer all disese that cometh.　And yf it happe 3
that peese be fowled in any wyse be vnpacyence, than the
ofter and the sonner it be wesshed be pennance, the whitter it
fol. 10 b is anenste God ; and the more it is trowbled and | ofter weshed,

---

[1] MS. helpyng helpyng.　　　　　[2] bleth the *catch word.*

the gladder and redyer it is to ber and suffer. For it Ioys in
hope of rewarde that itt hopeth is to come to it for peese ; and
ther-for it is the besyly war that it fall nott by vnpacyence.

The secunde cloth that is of wolle or of lethur betokeneth
5 the werk*es* of m*er*cy. This clothyng is made of skynnys of
dede best*es*, which ar my seyntes þ*at* ar symple as best*es*.
W*ith* her skynnes oweth the sowle to be clothede ; that is, it
oweth to folow & to[1] do the werk*es* of her m*er*cye. These
werk*es* doth ij thyng*es*. Fyrst, they hylle the nakednes &
10 shame fastefullnesse of the synffull sowle, and clense it that it
apper nott fowle in my syght. Seco*n*nde, they defende the
sowle aȝaynes cold, which coldenesse is bott hardenes of the
sowle vn-to my love. Ayaynste this colde, the werk*es* of
m*er*cye ar veyleable that cloth the sowle so that it is not
15 disessed w*ith* cold. For by thes werk*es* God vysetyth the sowle,
that it nygh alway ner & ner vn-to God.

The thrid clothyng, that is, of sylke, that is made of wormes
and semeth ryght dere to buye, betokeneth pur abstynence.
For þ*at* is fayr both in syght of God and angell*es* and men.
20 Thys is der to bye, for it semyth herde to man to refreyne hys
mowth from mych spech and vayne, and to refreyne the desyre
of hys flesh from sup*er*fluite and his delices. It semyth eke
harde to go & doo ayanste his will ; bott þof it is herde, ȝit it
is p*ro*phetable in all wyse and feyr. Ther-for, thow my spowse,
25 by whom I vnderstonde all trew cristen men, gadre we in-to
owr secunde howse peese to God & to owr neghtborr, werk*es* of
m*er*cye be compassyon and helpyng of wreches, & abstinenc*e*
frome euyll desyris and lust*es*. For this cloth of abstynenc*e*,
as it is derrer than other, so it is fayrer than other ; so much,
30 that w*ith*-owte that, non other vertue semeth feyr. And this
abstinenc*e* muste be drawe frome wormes ; þ*at* is to sey, oft-
thynkyng of hys trespasse aȝeneste | his God, and of my meke- fol. 11 a
nes and abstinenc*e*, that was made lyke a worme for the loffe
of man. For yf man bethinke him in hys herte how mych and
35 often he hath synned aȝenste me, and what amendes he hath
made, he shall fynde ine him-selfe that he is nott sufficiente to
make amendes w*ith* none abstinenc*e* nor labor of þ*at* he hath
offended me. If he take kepe eke of my payne and of my

[1] MS. to *inserted above line*.

c 2

sayntes, why and in what wyse we sufferede, he shall verely
vnderstonde that seth I asked so grete streteness of my-selfe
and of my sayntes that obeyed vn-to me, how mych nor strayte
vengeance shall I aske of heme that obey me nott. Ther-for
a good sowlle muste gladly take abstynence apon hym, and to 5
haue mynde on his synnes, how evell they be þat as wormes
gnowe þe sowle ; and so of fowle wormes he shall geder preciose
sylke, that is pur abstynence in all hys membres. Wher-of
God shall Ioy, and all the company of heuyn ; and he that
gaderith it shall deserue þer-fore endelesse blysse, whych, 1o
hadde þat not holpe, shuld haue hadde euerlastyng woo and
weylynge.

Revela-
tions,
Book II,
Chap. 27. **Of the Instrumentes of the thirde howse, that ar good
thoughtes, verteus, maneres, & verry confession. And of
the sperrynge of all thre howses.** 1s

The sonne of God spekyth to hys spowse and sayth : I told
the to-for, that in our thride howse muste be iij maner of
instrumentes. Fyrst, sych as liquour is kepte in. Secunde,
instrumentes that londe is tylled wyth, as ploghe & haroo and
axes and such other, wher-with þinges ar made ayeine when they 2o
ar broke. Thride, quyke Instrumentes, as assys and horses and
other lyke, by whome both whykke thynges and dede ar
caryede.

In the fyrst howse that licour ar jne muste be ij maner of
Instrumentes : oon, wher-in ar kepe thyne lycowres, & swete, 25
fol. 11 b as oyle, water, & wyne, | and such other ; anoþer, to kepe in
bitter and thykke liquores, as mustarde, meele, and such other.
For-soth, these lycoures betoken thoughtes of the sowle, goode
and euyll. For a good thought is as swete oyle and dilectable
wyne, and an evyll thought is a bytter mustarde, for it maketh 3o
the sowle bytter and troblesse. And as a man nedeth other
whyle thyke lycoures, for þof they profett nott mych to þe sus-
tenance of the body, yett they profette to purgynge and helynge
of the body and brayne, right so ar euyll thoughtes ; for þof they
hele nott nor make not the sowle fatt as oyle of goode 35
thoughtes, yett they profett to purgynge of the sowle, as
mustarde doth to purgynge of the brayne. For bot yf evyll
thowghtes come other whyle amonge, els man shulde be an

angell, and no man ; and he shulde wene to haue all of him-
selfe. Ther-fore, that man vnderstonde the freltee that he hath
of him-selfe, and the strenghth that he hath of me, it is nedefull
that he be other while, be suffrance of my grete me*r*cye,
5 temptede w*ith* evyll thought*es* ; to which thought*es*, if man
consente nott, they ar purgac*io*n of hys sowle and kepynge of
hys verte*us*. And þof they be as mustarde, bitter to bere, ȝett
they hele the sowle full mych, and gyde it vn-to endelesse
lyffe and helth, which may not be had w*ith*-owte bytt*er*nes.
10 Ther-fore the vessells of the sowle, wher goode thought*es* shall
be putt, muste besily be made redy, and contynually clene.
For it is p*r*ofitable that euyll thowght*es* come other whyle for
prefe and more merette ; and ther-fore the sowle must besyly
labor that it consent nott to hem, ne delyte notte in hem. For
15 elles the swettenes and encrese of the sowle shal be powred
owte, and the bytt*er*nes only shall abyde.

Ine [1] the secunde howse muste be also ij man*er* of Instrument*es* ; fyrst, owtwarde Instrument*es* wher-w*ith* the londe
is made redy to be sowe, & thornes and wedes turned
20 upp by the rote, as [2] | plow and harow ; secunde, p*r*ofitable fol. 12 a
Instrume*n*tes to þat that is necessarie both wyth-in and with-
owte, as axes and such other. The Instrumentez that londe is
tylled w*ith* betokenen the wyttys of man, which ar ordend to
the p*r*ofette of hys neghtbor, as a plowe for the londe. For
25 vykked men ar as londe or erth, for they thenke alway apon
erthely thyng*es*. They ar baron and drye fro compu*n*ccion
and soroe for her synnes, for they sette her synne at noght.
They ar elke colde from the lofe of God, for they seke ryght
noght bot þer own wyll. They ar elke hevy to do goode dedes,
30 for they ar swyfte and redy to the wyrship of the worlde. Þer-
for a goode man oweth to tyll hem by owtworde wytt*es*, as a
goode man tyllyth his londe w*ith* þe plowgh. Fyrst, he oweth
to tyll hem w*ith* his mowth, spekyng to hem sych þynges as is
p*r*ofytable to the sowle, & enformynge hem to the way of lyfe ;
35 afft*er*-warde, in doyng þe goode that he may, that his neghtborr be enformed with wordes and stired wyth werk*es* to do
goode. And then-aft*er*, he tylleth hys neghtborr [3] to be fruyte-

---

[1] MS. Ine In.   [2] MS. as/as.
[3] MS. hys neghtborr hys neghtborr.

full wit*h* all hys oþer membres, þat is to sey, wyth symple eyn,
that he beholde nott vayn and vnchaste thynges, þat his varray
neghtborr may lerne to kepe sobreness in all his membres. He
muste also tylle wit*h* hys erres, that he here no vanton thynges,
and wit*h* hys feete and hondes, þat he be redy to all goode 5
werk*es*. To such erth thus tylled, I God shall ȝeue the rayne
of my grace be labor of the tyll man, and so he laboryth shall
Ioy of the fruyte of the londe that was drie, when it begynnyth
to borione. The Instrument*es* that ar necessarie to make
thin[g]es [1] wit*h*-in-forth, as axes and sych other, betokenen dis- 10
crete entente & goodely discussynge of his werke. For what
eue*r* a | man doo, he awe nott to do itt for wyrship and pr*a*ys-
yng of man, bot for the love of God to endeles rewarde. Þer-
for a man oweth to examyn hys deyly dedes bysely, for what
entente and for what rewarde he doth hem ; and if he fynde in 15
hys werke any pride, that he kitte it anon away wit*h* the axe
of descrecion. That as he tylleth hys neghtborr outwarde,
whych is as it war wit*h*-owte þe howse, that is to sey, oute of
the companye of my fryndes be evyll dedes, ryght so he fruyte
to himselfe inwarde be the lofe of God. For lyke as þe werke 20
of a tylle man that hath none Instrument*es* wher-wit*h* to
rep*er*ell hys tooles when thay ar blonte or broke is sone turnede
to noght, ryght so bot yf a man examyn hys werk*es* wit*h* wyse
dyscreci*o*n, how he shall eese hem yf they be trauelowse, and
how he may rep*er*ell hem yf they be broke, he shall not brynge 25
hem to p*er*fecci*o*n. Therefor a man aweth nott only to labor
effectualy outwarde, bott also bysely to loke onwarde, how and
for what entent he laboryth.

In the thirde howse must be quyke Instrument*es*, that
caryth both quyk and deth, as horse, asses, and other best*es*. 30
These Instrument*es* ar verray confession ; for it caryth and
moveth both quyke and deth. What betokeneth the quyke
bott the sowle that is made of my godhed and lyveth wit*h*-
owten ende ? For by verray confession it neghyth eu*er*y day
mor and more to God. For ryght as a beste, þe ofter and better 35
it is fedde & norysshede, is stronger to ber and farrer to see ;
ryȝt so confessyon, þe ofter and the more diligentely it is made,
as well of the leste as of the moste, so mych mor it fortheryth

fol. 12 b

[1] MS. thinkes.

þe sowle. · & so mych it plesyt God, þat it bryngyth þe sowle
evyn to the herte of God.   And what betokeneth the dede þat
confession caryeth and meveth, bot goode werkes that ar slayn
be dedely synne. | For the selfe goode dedes that a man hath fol. 13 a
5 doo dyeth when he doth dedely synne, and ar dede anenste
God.   For no goode dede may please God, bot if synne be fyrst
correctede and amendett other in perfyte wyll or dede.   For
stynkynge thynges and swete thynges may not wele acorde to
gadre in one vessell.   Bot yf any man slee hys goode dedes by
10 dedely synnes and after-warde make verray and trew confessyon of the synnes that he hath doo, with wyll to amende
and to be-whar frome thens forth, than anon be that confession
and vertue of mekenes, hys goode dedes takyth lyfe ayayne
that war slayne a-fore, and profettes hym to endeles helth.
15 Bot and he dye wyth-oute confessyon, than hys goode dedes,
that neþer may in all wyse be dede and torne to noght, neþer
for that dedely synne deserue euerlastyng lyffe, shall profett
him to suffre mor esy payne, or elles to helth of other, so that
he dyde the goode dedes with goode entente and too Goddys
20 wyrship.   For and he dyde hem for wordely wyrshyp and for hys
own wordely profette, then they dye with him þat dyde hem ;
for he hath receyved hys mede of the worlde þat he labored for.
    Ther-for, my spowse, by whom I vnderstonde all my frendes,
gader we in-to our howses thoo thynges wher-with goode wyll
25 gostely be delytede wyth an holy sowle.
    Fyrst, into our fyrst howse brede of clene wyll, wyllyng no
thyng bot that God wyll.   Secunde, drynke of goodely thynkyng to-for,[1] doyng nothyng bot it be thought to the wyrship of
God.   Thirde, sowle of goodely wysdome, thinkyng all way
30 what is to come, and how thynges ar to be gouerned that ar
nowe.
    Gadre we in-to our secunde howse peese from synne vn-to
God and | peese from stryfe to our neghtborr.   Secunde, werkes fol. 13 b
of mercye with which we be profitable to our neghtborr in dede.
35 Thirde, perfyte abstynence, refrenynge thoo thynges that myght
trowble peese.
    And gadre we in-to our [2] howse goode & resonable thoughtes
to array our howse with-ine.   Secunde, well rewled and tem-

---

[1] *Latin* praemeditationis.   [2] *Latin* tertia *omitted.*

*per*atte wyttes to shyne to our frendis wyth-owte. Thride,
trew confessyon, wher-by, þof we be seke, we may lyf ayayne.

Bot þof we haue howses, we may nott kepe þ*at* is gadered in
hem bott yf they haue doores ; ne the doores may nott honge
wyth-owte hynges, ne be shytte w*ith*-oute lokk*es*. Þer-for, that 5
our thynges gadered may be safe, þer moste be sette a door on
our house ; þat is to say, syker hope that it be broke w*ith*
none adu*er*site. And this hope must haue too hyngges, that
man noþer dyspeyr to gette blysse, ne p*re*sumpte to skape
payne ; bot in all dysese he truste all way ine the m*er*cy of 10
God, hopynge in bett*er* amendement. The loke of the door
must be godely charite, wher-w*ith* þe dor moste be sperrede,
that the enmye come nott ine. For what avaylyth it to haue a
dor w*ith*-owte a lokke, & what hope is it to haue hope w*ith*-owte
cheryte ? For if a man hope to haue endeles blysse, and hope 15
also in þe m*er*cye of God, & yett dredyth nott God nor loue
him, he hath a door w*ith*-owte loke, by which hys dedely enmy
may come ine and slee when he wyll. Bot right hope is þat
he that hopyth do þe goode that he may, wyth-oute which he
may nott gete heuyn, if he cowth and myght do good and 20
wolde nott. Bot if eny vnderstonde þat he hath do amysse &
not doo the goode þat he myght, yett yf he haue a good wyll
to doo the goode that he maye, and also that he may nott, latt
hym hope sycurly that he may negh vn-to God by that goode
wyll and goodely cherite ; that as a loke hath mony wardes 25
wyth-in that þe enmye open it notte, ryght so in the lofe of
God and of goodely charite | muste be a man*er* besynes, that
God be nott offendede ; a love-drede[1] that God goo not from
hym ; a brennyng feruo*ur*, how God may be loved ; a dili-
gence, how to folow him ; a sorow, that he may nott do as 30
mych as he wolde and as he vnderstondeth that he is bonde ;
and a mekenes, by whych he holdeth notte all that he doth ine
regarde of hys synne. W*ith* thes wardes the lokke muste be
strenghthed, that the fende oppen nott the lokke of cheryte
and sende in hys love. Þe keye to open and sparr oweth to be 35
only desyr of God acordyng wyth gudely cherite and wyth
godely werke, so that man wyll ryght nott haue bot God, þough
he myght ; & that for hys moste grete cheryte, thys desyre

fol. 14 a

---

[1] *Latin* sit charitiuus timor.

speryth God in the sowle and the sowle in God, for þer is bot
o wyll of hem both. . Thys key owe no man to haue bote the
husbonde and the wyfe alone ; þat ys, God and the sowle :
that as often as God wyll enter and delyte hym in goodes and
5 verteus of the sowle, he hafe fre entre be the kay of stable
desyre ; and as often as the sowle wyll entre to the herte of
God, it may frely, for it desiryth ryght nogh bot God. Thys
kay is kepte be wakernesse of the sowle and be mekenes, wher-by
it arecheth all the gode that it hath vn-to God. This key is
10 kepte eke be the power of God, and cherite, that þe sowle be
notte deceved of the fende. Loo, my spouse, what cherite and
love of God is to mannes sowle. Stonde þer-for seurely, and
do my wyll.[1]

Our lorde Ihesu Crist techyth seynt Birgitt howe actyfe
15 **lyf and contemplatyf owe to be kepte be ensample of**
Marie and Martha ; & fyrst, of contemplatyf lyff.

Revela-
tions,
Book VI,
first part
of Chap.
65.

The sonne of God seyth : Birgitt, ther ar ij lyffes þat ar
lykened to Marye and Martha ; which lyfes, what man or
woman will folow | he muste fyrst make clene confessyon of
20 all hys synnes, takyng to him verray contricion for hem,
hauyng wyll neuer to synne mor. The fyrst lyfe, as the lorde
beryth wyttenes, Marie chese ; and it ledeth to contemplacion
of heuenly thinges ; and this is þe best parte and days
Iournay to euerlastyng helth. Þerfor euery man and woman
25 that desyrith to take and holde þe lyff of Marie, it is I-now
to him to haue ij thinges that ar necessarie to the body : þat
is, clothing with-owte vanyte or shewyng of pryde, and mete
and drinke in scarsenes and not ine superfluyte. He muste
eke haue cherite with-oute any evell delectacion, and resonable
30 fastyng after the ordynaunce of holy chyrch. And in his fastyng he muste take kepe þat he be nott seeke of vnresonable
abstynence, leste be sych sekenes hys prayers or prechyng or
other goode dedes þer-by be lessede, by whych he myght profett both to his neghtbor and to him-selfe. He muste also
35 besily examyn him-selfe, that be his fastynge he be neþer made
dull or hasty to the rygour of ryghtwisnes or slow to the
werkes of pytee, for to punyshe hem that ar rebell, and to make
vnfeythfull men soiett vn-to the yoke of fayth. It is nede as

fol. 14 b

---

[1] MS. & e ; *Latin ends with* fac voluntatem meam.

well to haue bodely str[e]ngth [1] as gostely.   Ther-for eny that
is seke or feble, that wolde rather to my wyrshyp faste than
etee, he shall haue as grete rewarde for his goode wyll as he
that fasteth resonabley of cherite.   And on the same wyse he
that etyth for holy obydience, wyllyng rather faste than ete, 5
shall haue þe same medee as he þat fasteth.

Secunde, Marie oweth nott to Ioye of the wyrship of the
werlde ne of the prosperyte þer-of ; ne he owght noght to sorowe
of the aduersyte þer-of, bott in that he oweth to Ioy þat wyked
men ar made deuoute and at lovers of the worlde ar made 10
louers of God, and that godemen profett in godenesse and, by
fol. 15 a laboring in the seruice of God, ar made more deuote.   Of this ¦
also oweth he þat is Marie to sorow : that synneres fall into
wers, and that God is nott lovede of hys creator, & that Goddis
commaundementes ar dispised and nott kepe.   15

Thirde, Marie oweth not to be idelle no mor then Martha ;
bot after he hath take his nedefull slepe, he aweth to aryse, and
with inworde attendaunce of herte thanke God that of hys
cherite and love made all thinges of noght ; and of that ylke
cherite, takyng a body of man-kynde, he made all thynges 20
aȝayne ; shewyng by his passyon and deth his love vn-to man,
more þan þe which myght noon bee.   Marie muste eke thanke
God for all tho þat ar sauede ; and for all tho that ar in purgatorie, and for hem that ar in the worlde, prayinge God mekely
that he suffeur hem nott to be temptede ouer her strenghthes. 25
Marie muste also be discrete in prayer, & ordinate in the
praysynge of God ; for yf he haue the necessaries of his lyvyng
with-oute bysenes, he oweth to make þe longer prayeres.   And
if he wax tediouse in praying, and temptaciones grow apon
him, then he may labor with his hondes some honeste and 30
profitable werke, oþer to his owne profette if he have nede, or
ells to the profette of other.   And yf he be werye and tediouse
both in prayer and in labor, than he may haue some honeste
occupacion, or here wordes of other edificacion with all
saddenes, and with-oute dissolucion and vanyte, till the body 35
and sowle be made mor able and quyke to the seruyce of God.
If he that is Marie be sych that he haue nott bodely sustynaunce
bott of hys own labour, then he muste make his prayer the

---

[1] MS. strongth.

shorter for sych nedefull werk ; and that same labour shall be
profetyng and encresyng of prayer. If Marie kan nott wyrke,
or may nott, then be he nott ashamed nor hevy to begge, bot
rather Ioyfull ; for then he foloweth me, the sonne | of God ; fol. 15 b
5 for I made my-selfe poor that man shulde be made rych. And
yf he that is Marie be soiett to obedyence, lyf he after the
obedyence of hys prelate, and the crowne of rewarde shall be
dowble the mor þan he war in hys own lyberte.

Forte, Marie aweth nott to be couetouse, no mor than was
10 Martha. Bott he oweth to be ryght large ; for Martha ȝeuyth
temperall goodes for God, so oweth Marie to yiffe spirituell
goodes. And ther-for, yf Marie haue lovede God enterly in
hys herte, be he[1] warr of that worde that mony haue in her
mowth, saynge : ' It is I-noght to me, if I may helpe myn
15 own sowle. What is it to me the werkes of my neghthborrs ?'
Or thus : ' I be goode ; what longeth it to me how other men
lyff ? ' O dowghter, they that say and thinke such wordes, if
they see her frende trowblett or vnhonestely tretede, they
shulde renne vn-to the deth to delyuer her frende frome tribu-
20 lacion. So muste Marie do ; he oweth to sorow that hys God
is offendede, and that hys brother, hys neghtborr, is hurte ; or
if eny fall in-to synne, Marie oweth to laborr as mych as he
maye þat he be delyuered,—neuer-the-leesse, with discrecion.
And yf for that Marie be pursewed, he muste seke a-nother
25 place mor sewr. For I my-selfe that am God bad so sayng :
' Si vos persecuti fuerint in vna civitate fugite in aliam ' ; that
is, yf they persewe yow in one cite, fleth into oþer. And so
dide Pawle, for he was necessarie anoþer tyme ; and ther-for he
was latte dovn by the wall in a lepe.

30 Ther-fore, that Marie be large and pytefull, fyve thinges ar
nedefull to hir : first, an howse þat gestes shall slepe ine ;
secunde, clothes to cloth þe | naked ; thirde, mete to fede the fol. 16 a
hungery ; forte, fyr to make the colde hote and warme ; fyfft,
medecyn for the seke.

35 The howse of Marie is his herte, whos wyked gestes ar all
the thinges that come to him and troble his herte : as wrethe,
hevenes, s[l]awth,[2] couetyse, pride, and mony other, whych
enter ine by the v wyttes. Ther-for all þese vyces, when they

---

[1] MS. he *inserted above line.*   [2] MS. shawth.

come, they owe to lye as gest*es* þat slepe in reste. For lyke as
an hosteler receyvyth gest*es* both good & badde w*ith* pacyence,
so oweth Marye to suffer all thinges for God by the vertue of
pacyenc*e*, and nott consente to synne nor delyte in hit, bot
remeve hit fro his herte as mych as he may by litell and litell 5
by the helpe of grace of God ; and yf he may nott remeve hem
and putt hem a-way, suffer he hem pacyentely aȝeynst his wyll,
as gest*es* knowyng certenly that they shall p*r*ophett him to
more rewarde, and in no wyse to dampnaci*o*n.

Secu*n*de, Marie oweth to haue clothes too cloth hys gestes : 1c
that is, mekenes, inwarde and owtwarde, and compassion of
herte in diseese of eyn cristen.   And if Marie be dispisede of
men, re*n*ne he then anon to hys mynde, thinkyng how I, God,
was dispisede, repreved, & suffered it pacyentely ; how I was
demed, and spak nott ; how I was scourgett and crownede 15
w*ith* thornes, and gurched nott.   Marie muste also take hede
that he shew no tokennes of wreth or vnpacyenc*e* to hem þat
repreve him or dispise him ; bott he oweth to blesse hem that
p*er*sewe him, that they þat se it may blesse God, whom Marie
foloweth ; and God him-selfe shall yif blessyng for cursynge. 20
Marie eke muste be-war that he nother bakbyte nor repreve
hem that hevy him or troble him.   For it is dampnable to
fol. 16 b bakkebyte and to here a bakbyter and to repreve his neghtbour |
wyth impacyence ; and therfor, that Marye may haue p*er*fytely
the gyfte of mekenes, he muste study to monysh and to warne 25
hem of hur p*er*elles þat bakbite other, exhortynge hem w*ith*
cheryte in worde and exsample to verrey mekenes.   Also the
cloth of Marye oweth to be compassyon ; for if he see his eyn
cristen syn, he ogh to haue compassion of hem, & to prey to
God to haue m*er*cy apon hem.   And yf he sees hys neghtborr 30
suffer wronge or harmes or repreves, he owght to be sorye þer-
of, and to helpe him w*ith* hys p*r*ayeres and oþer helpe and
besinesse.   Yee, anenste þe grete men off the worde ; for
verrey compassion sekyth nott that longyth to him-selfe, bott
to evyn cristen.   Bot yf Marie be sych þat is nott herde 35
anenste princesse & grete men and at the goynge oute of his
cell p*r*ofyteth nott, than p*r*ay he to God besily for hem þat ar
disesede ; and God, be-holder of the herte, shall for the cherite
of him þat p*r*ayeth turne the hertes of men to peese of him

that is disesed. And other he shall be delyuered of his tribulacion, or ells God shall gyf him pacyence, so that his rewarde in
heuyn shall be dowbled. Þer-for such a cloth of mekenes or of
compassyon oweth to be in Maries herte ; for þer is noo thynge
5 that drawes God so in-too a sowle as mekenes and compassyon
of his euyn cristen.

Thirde, Marie muste [haue] [1] mete and drinke for gestes.
For grevouse gestes ar logett in the herte of Marie, whan the
herte is rauyshed oute of it-self and hath appetite to see delec-
10 table thinges in erth & to haue temperall thinges ; when the ere
disiryth to her his own wyrship ; when the flesh sekyth to
delite in fleshely thinges ; when the spirite pretendeth excusa-
cion of frelte and lyghting of synne ; when | þer comyth fol. 17 a
tedyousnes to do gode and for-yettynge of thinges that ar to
15 come ; when goode dedes ar counted money and evyll few and
for-yett. Aȝayne such gestes Marie hath nede of consell, that
he dissimule nott ne begynne nott to slepe. Ther-for Marie,
herted with feyth, must arise strongely and vnswer thus vn-to
these gestes : ‘ I wyll hafe no thyng of temperall thinges, save
20 onely necessarie sustinaunce of my body. I wyll not spende
the beste howr or tyme, bot to Goddes wyrship. Ne I wyll
take hede of feyre or fowle, ne what is profettable or vnprofetable to the flesh, ne what is sauorye or vnsauorye to the taste,
saue onely the plesaunce of God and profett of the sowlle ; for
25 me lyst not lyff on howr, bot to the wyrship of God.’ Sych
a wyll is mete [2] to gestes that comen, and such vnswer
qwenchyth inordinate delytes.

Ferte, Marie muste haue fyr 'to make her gestes hote &
warme, and yif hem lyght. This fyr is the hete of the holy
30 goste ; for it is impossible any man to forsake his own wyll or
carnall affeccion of his frendes or love of rich, bot be þe worching inspiracion and hete of the holy goste. Nor ne Marie
himselfe, be he neuer so perfyte, may nott begynne ne contynue
ony good lyfe with-out swetenes and informacion of the same
35 holy goste. Ther-fore that Marie shine and lyghten to the
gestes that comen first, he must thenke thus : God made me
for that skyll that I shulde wyrship him, love him, and drede
him above all thinges ; and he was boor of a virgyn to tech the

---

[1] *Latin* habeat.   [2] MS. mete meete.

way to heuyn, which I shulde folowe with mekenes. And after, with his deth, he opened heuyn, þat be desyring and comyng I shulde haste me theder. Marie muste eke examyn all his werkes and thoughtes & desires, & how he hath offended God, and how pa|cyentely God suffered man, and how in mony wyse 5 God callyth man to him. For such thowghtes and other lyke ar the gestes of Marie, which ar all in derkenes; bot yf they be lyȝtenede with the fyr of the holy goste, whych fyr comyth to the herte when Marie thenkyth it is resonable to serue God, and when he wolde rather[1] suffre all payne than wyttyngly 10 provoke God vn-to wreth, be whose goodenes his sowle is made and bowght aȝayne with hys blessed blode. The herte eke hath lyght of this goode fir, when reson thenkyth and discern-eth by what entent ych geste, þat is ych thowghte, comyth, when the herte examyneth yf the thowght goo vn-to euerlast- 15 ynge Ioy or to transitorie Ioy; yf it lefe no thowght vndis-cussed, none vnpunyshed, none with-owten drede. Þer-for, that this fyr may be gote, and kepte when it is I-gote, it nedeth that Marie beer to-geder drye wode, by whych this fir may be noryshed: that is, that he take kepe bisely of the styrringes of 20 the flesh, that the flesh begynne not to wax wanton; and that he putt to all diligence, that the werkes of pitee and deuoute prayer be morede and encresede, in which the holy goste delyteth. Bot soffraynly it is to wytt & see þat wher fire is kyndelede in a close vessell and hat no vsshe, the fyr is sone 25 quenchede and the vessell waxeth colde. And ryght so it is with Marie; for if Marie desyr to lyf for not elles bot to do Goddes wyrship, then it is nedefull to him that his mouth be opened and the flaume of hys cherite go[2] owte. Than is þe mouth openede, when by spekyng in feruent cherite he geteth 30 spirituall | sonnes vn-to God.

But Marie muste take hede besily that he open the mowth of hys prechinge when they that be goode may be made more feruente, and they that be wykked may be amendede, wher rych[t]wosnes[3] may be morede and evell costome do away. 35 For my apostell Paule wolde some tyme haue spoke; bot he was forbede by my spirite, and þer-fore in acceptable tyme he

fol. 17 b

fol. 18 a

---

[1] MS. rather *inserted above line.*   [2] MS. go goo.
[3] MS. rychwosnes.

was stylle, and in tyme conuenient he spake ; and some tyme
he vsede softe wordes, and some tyme sharpe ; and all hys
wordes and dedes was to the worship of God and to comforth of
the feyth. But if Marie may nott prech, and hath wyll &
5 kunnyng to prech, that he muste do as a fox that goyng abowte
seketh mony places with his feete ; and where he fyndyth
places beste and moste able, þer he makyth a denne to reste jne.
So Marie muste with wordes, exsamples, and prayers assay the
hertes of mony ; and when he fyndeth hertes more able to
10 receyve the worde of God, ther muste he terye and abyde,
monyshing and styrringe what he may. Marye must also
labour that a conuenient yshew be yeve vn-to his flame of fyr ;
for the mor that the flawme is, þe mor [1] ar lyghtned and en-
flawmed þer-of. The flawme hath than a conuenient yshew,
15 wher Marie noþer dredeth reprefe or shame, ne sekyth his own
praysyng, when he dredeth neþer contrariose thinges, nor
delytes in welth and prosperyte. And than it is mor acceptable
to God þat Marie do his gode dedis in open than in prevey, to
that extent þat they þat se hem may prayce and wyrship God.
20   Also Marie owe to yif owte ij flawmes, on in prevey, anoþer
in open : that is, to haue dowble mekenes ; þe fyrst in þe herte,
inwarde, the oþer, owtwarde. The fyrst is that Marye | thenke fol. 18 b
him-selfe vnworthy and vnprofetable to all godenes, and that
he prefer notte ne exalte him-selfe in his owen conceyte to-fore
25 ony creatur ; and that he desyr nott to be see nor praysed, bot
that he flee all pride and hyghnes, desiringe God above all
thinges and folowyng his wordes. Yf Marye sende owte such
a flame in his dedes, then shall his herte be lyghtened with
cherite, & all contrariose thinges þat come to him shall be ouer-
30 come and esely sufferde. The secunde flame muste be in opyn ;
for yf verrey mekenes be in the herte, it oweth to aper in
clothyng and to be herde of the mowth and to be fullfylled in
dede. Verray mekenes is in clothing when Marie chesyth
rather cloth of lesse price, of which he may haue hete and
35 profette, than cloth of more valeve, wher-of he myght haue
pride and owtwarde shewyng. For cloth þat is litele worth and
is calledde of men vile and abiecte is verely feyr anenste God,
for it prouoketh mekenes. Bot that cloth that is bowght with

[1] *Latin* plures.

grete price & is called fayr is fowle anenste God; for it beryth
a-way þe fayrenes of angells, þat is, mekenes. Neuer-þe-lesse if
Marie be compelled be any resonable cause to have better clothinge than he wolde, be nott trowbled ther-for; for by that
[his] [1] mede shall be morede.   5

Also Marie oweth to haue mekenes in mowth, spekyng meke
wordes [2]; fleyng vayne wordes and such as sterris to lawghing;
beynge war of mych spech; nott vsyng sotell nor gay wordes;
nor prefessyng hys own wyll or wordes to-fore the wytte and
felynges of hem that ar better. And if Marie be praysed for ony 10
good dede, be he nott lyft vp þer-by in pride, bot aunswer he
thus: 'laus sit deo qui dedit omnia'; that is, praysing be to
God that yove all goodenes. For what am I bot powder be-for
the face of wynde; or what goode comyth of me, erth [3] with-out
water? & if he be repreuede, be nott he hevy bott vnswer he 15
thus: 'It is worthi; for I haue so often offended in the syght
of God and not done pennaunce for which I am worthie |
gretter tormentes. Þer-fore praye for me that by suffraunce of
temperall repreues, I may escape euer-lastyng.' If Marie be
prouoked to wreth to ony mysgouernance of his evyn cristen, 20
he muste be wysely war of vndiscrete aunswer; for pride is
ofte-tyme associate to wreth, and þer-for it is an holsom consell,
that when wreth and pride come, þat he holde to-geder hys
lippus so longe tyme tyll þe wyll may eske halpe of God of
suffraunce and pacience; and tyl he may be avysed what & how 25
it is to a [4] vnswer; or til he may over-come him-selfe. For
then wrath is quenched in the herte, and man may aunswer
wysely to hem that ar vnwyse.

Know þu also þat the devell hath grete envye at Marie; and
þer-fore if he may nott lett him be brekyng of Goddes com- 30
maundementes, þan he sterith him to be lyghtly meved with
grete wreth, or els to dissolucion of vayne myrth, or els to
dissolute and gamefull wordes. Þer-fore Marie muste aske helpe
of God þat all his spekyng and wyrkynge be gouernede of God
and dressed vn-to Gode. Also Marie muste haue mekenes in his 35
dede, þat he doo ryght noght by-cawse of erthely praysyng; þat
he attempte nothinge of nowe; þat he be ryght noght ashamed

fol. 19 a

---

[1] MS. he; *Latin* eius.   [2] MS. wordes wordes.
[3] *Preceded in Latin by* qui sum.   [4] a *inserted above line before* vnswer.

of mekenes; that he flee synglarte in his werk*es*; that he
wyrship all; and þat in all thing*es* [he] holde [1] him-selfe vnworthy.   Also Marie oweth rather to sytte w*ith* the poor þan
w*ith* þe rich ; rather to obey than to be abeyde ; rather to kepe
5 silence than to speke ; rather to be alon solytarie þen be c*on*n-
staunte amonge the grete of the world or amonge his wordely
frindes.   Marie must hate his own wyll and eu*er* haue mynde
on his deth ; Marie oweth nott to be idle, ne no gurcher, ne
foryettfull of þe rightwyssnes of God and of his own affecc*io*nes.
10 Marie must be feruent to c*on*fession, besy in his temptac*io*nes,
desiri*ng* | to lyffe for ryght nott ells bott for þat the worshipe of   fol. 19 b
God and helth of sowles be encresede and morede.

þer-for if Marie þat is thus disposede as I haue now seyde be
chose by Martha, and obeying for the love of God takyth the
15 gou*er*nance of mony sowles, ther shal be yeve to him dowble
crown of rewarde, as I shew the be a lykenes.   Ther was
a c*er*teyn lorde of grete power that hadde a shippe chargede
w*ith* p*re*co*u*se marchaundyse, and seyde vn-to hys s*er*uantes:
' Goth to sych ane havyn, and ther shall be grete wynnyng to
20 me, and gloriose fruyte.   Yf the wynde arise ayaynste yow,
travelleth manfully and be nott werry ; for yo*ur* rewarde shall
be grete.'   Then the s*er*uantes sayled forth.   And the [wind] [2]
wex myghty, and tempestes arosse, and the shipp wasse grevously bete.   Wherfor the gou*er*nor of the shippe waxe wery,
25 and all they dispeyrede of her lyfe.   And then they acordede
to-geder to come to sych ane hauyn as [3] þe wynde wold blow
hem to, & nott to þat hauyn [3] that þe lord assygned hem.   When
one of the seruant*es* that wasse mor trew than oþ*er* herde this,
he weylede & of feruente love and [z]ele [4] þat he had to his
30 lorde, he toke violently þe gou*er*nall of þe shippe, & w*ith* grete
strengthes he browght þe shippe vn-to the hauen desired of
the lorde.   Ther-fore thys man þat thus manfully browght the
shipe to þe hauen is to be rewarded w*ith* mor singler rewarde
then oþ*er*.

35   In lyke wyse is it of a goode p*re*late þat for love of God and

---

[1] MS. be holde ; *Latin* reputet se.
[2] *Latin* ventus.
[3] MS. as . . . hauyn *inserted in margin.*
[4] MS. yele ; *Latin* zelo.   *Due to a scribe copying* zele *as* yele.

helth of sowles takyth charge of gouernaunce, nott rekkyng of
worshipe, for he shall haue dowble rewarde : fyrst, for he shall
be partener of all the goode dedes of hem þat he hath browght
to þe hauyn ; secunde, for his Ioy & blisse shall be morede
with-outen ende.   And so shall it be ayayne warde of hem that 5
fol. 20 a desir worshippes & prelacies ;[1] | for they that shall be partener
of all peynes and synnes of hem that they haue take to gouerne.
Secunde, for þer confucion shall be with-owten ende.   For the
prelates þat desyr wyrshippes ar mor lyke to strompettes than to
prelates.   For they disseyve sowles with her evell wordes and 10
exsamples ; and thay ar vnworthy to be calde oþer Marie or
Martha, bot they amende hem with pennaunce.   Fyft, Marie
oweth to yeve his gestes medecyn : þat is, glad and comforth
hem with Goddis wordis.   For to all thynges that euer be-fall
hym, wheder they be Ioyfull or hevy, he oweth to say : ' thus 15
I wyll ; what euer God wyll, I do ; and to hys wyll I am redy
to obey, þough I shulde goo to hell '.   For such a wyll is
medecyn ayenste euyll thynges that fall to þe herte, and þis
wyll is delite in tribulacion and a good temperer in prosperyte.
Bot for Marie hath mony enmys, þer-for he muste make con- 20
tynually confession.   For as longe as he bydeth in synne &
myght be shryfe and is necligent and takyth no kepe þer-of,
than is he rather to be called apostata a-for God þan Marie.

Revela-
tions,
Book VI,
Chap. 65,
com-
pleted.
**Of the dedes of actyf lyfe þat is vnderstonde be Martha.
Cap. xj.** 25

Know þu also þat þough the parte of Marie be beste, ȝett þe
parte of Martha is not euyll, bot prayseable and well plesinge
to God.   Þer-for I shall tell the how Martha oweth to be
gouerned.   For he oweth to have v goode thinges as well as
Marie.   Fyrst, the ryght fayth of Goddys church.   Secunde, to 30
know the commaundementes of the godhed & the conseles of
the trowth of the gospell ; and thes oweth he perfitely to kepe
in herte and werke.   Thirde, he oweth to kepe his tonge from
evyll wordes þat is aȝayn God and his neghtbor, and his honde
from all vnhoneste and vnlefull wyrkyng, and hys herte fro 35
ouer-mych couetyse & delyte.   He oweth also to be contente of
goodes þat God hath yeve him, and not to desyr superflew

---

[1] for they þat, *catchword half cut off.*

thing*es*. Foourth, he oweth to fullfyll þe dedes of mercye
resonably and mekely, þat | for truste of thoo dedes he offende fol. 20 b
in no thing. Fyfte, he oweth to love God above all thinge and
mor than himselfe.   So dyde Martha, for he yafe Ioyfully him-
5 selfe, folowyng my wordes and werk*es*; and aft*er* she yave all
hyr godd*es* for my love.   And therfor she lothed temp*er*all
thyng*es*, and sowght heuynly thing*es*, and suffered heuenly
thing*es* pacyentely, and toke kepe and cur of other as of hyr-
selfe.   And therfor she thought all way on my cherite and
10 passyon; and she was gladde in tribulac*io*nes and loved all as
a moder.   The same Martha also folowed me euery daye,
desyryng nothyng bot to her word*es* of lyffe.   She had compassyon on hem þat wer in sorow; she comforted the seke; she
neþ*er* cursed nor sayd evyll to ony.   Bot she dissimiled the
15 frowardnesse of hyr neghtborr, and prayed[1] for all.   Þ*er*-for
euery man þat desyrith cherite in actyf lyffe oweth to folow
Martha in love of hys neghtbor, to brynge him to heuyn, bot
nott in favoryng and norishyng his vyces and synnes.   He
oweth also to fle hys own p*ra*ysyng, pryde, and dowblenesse.
20 Eke wreth or envye oweth he nott to kepe.

   But marke well that Martha, praying for hyr brother Lazar
when he was dede, come fyrst to me.   Bott hyr brother was not
raysed anon, tyll Marie come aft*er*, whe*n* she was called.   And
then for both systeres her brother was arered fro deth to lyfe.
25 So in sp*iritu*ell lyf he þat p*er*fytely desyrith to be Marie muste
fyrst be Martha, laboryng bodely to my wyrship.   And he
oweth fyrst to conne wi*th*-stonde[2] þe desyris of the flesh and
the temptac*io*n of the fende and aft*er*-warde he may wyth
dilib*era*c*io*n ascende up to the degre of Marie.   For he that is
30 nott p*re*ued and tempted, and he that hath not ou*er*comen þe
styrryng*es* of hys flesh, how may he contynually entende and
cleve to heuynly thing*es*?   Who is þe dede brother of Marie
and Martha, bott an vnp*er*fyte werk? | For ofte sythes a good fol. 21 a
werke is doo wyth an vndyscrete entente and wyth an vnavysed
35 herte, and þ*er*-fore it goth dolly and slawly forth.   Bot þat the
wyrkyng of gode dedes be acceptable to me, it muste be arered
and quykened by Martha and Marie; that is, when the neghtbor
is clerely loved for God & to God, and God allon is desyrid

[1] MS. p[ra *abbre.*]rayed.   [2] *Latin* scire debet prius resistere.

above all thing*es*. And than eu*er*y good werke of man is
plesing vn-to God. Þ*er*-fore I seyde in the gospell that Marie
chese the beste p*ar*te ; for than is the p*ar*te of Martha good,
when he soroweth for the synnes of his evyn crysten ; & then
is þe p*ar*te of Martha bett*er*, when he laboryth that men abyde 5
in goode lyvyng wysely and honestely, and that only for the
love of God.

Bot the p*ar*te of Marie is beste when he beholdeth onely
heuenly thing*es* and the lucre of sowles. And the lorde enter-
eth in-to the howse of Martha and Marie when þe herte is 10
fullfylled w*ith* gode affecc*i*ones ; and pesed from the noyse of
wordely thing*es* ; and thenkyth [God][1] as all way p*re*sente ;
and nott onely hath mynde and meditac*i*on in his love, bot
laboreth þ*er*-ine day and nyght.

Our lorde Ih*es*u Criste telleth seynt Birgitt of his blessed 15
incarnac*i*on ; & how man offendeth God & brekyth þat he
behyght in hys baptem ; & mercy to hem þat amendeth
hem ; and of herde dome to heme þat amende not ; & how
swetely he callys douowte sowles to hys blysse. Cap. xij.

I am maker of heuyn and erth, one in godhed w*ith* the fader 20
and the holy goste. I am he þat spake to p*ro*fett*es* & patriark*es*,
& whom they abode ; for whos desyr and aft*er* myn awn by-
heste I toke a body w*ith*-oute synne or luste, entering þe
madenes wombe as the sonne shynyng thorow a cler ston.
For as the sonne enteryng the glasse hurtyth it not, so þe 25
madened of the virgine bode incorrupte and vnsowled in
fol. 21 b takynge of my man-hod. For so [2] | toke I a body þat I lest nott
the godhed ; nor I was not the lasse in godhed wyth the Fadre
and the holy goste, all thyng*es* gou*er*nyng and fullfyllyng,
thowgh I wer in my manhode in the virgyns wombe. For as 30
bryghtnes is neu*er* dep*ar*ted from fyr, so my godhede was neu*er*
dep*ar*ted from my manhode ; not in deth, forþ*er*-mor. I wold
suffer my body that was moste clene frome synne to be crucified
for þe synnes of all mankynde, and to be all-to rente fro þe
soole of þe foote vn-to the toppe of the hedde. This same body 35
is also now eu*er*y day offered on the awt*er*, that man shuld love
me so mych the mor, as he had my benefett*es* often in mynde.

[1] *Latin* Deum.   [2] c ij.

Bot now I am all for-ȝett, dispised, and sett att noght.   And
as a kynge caste owte of his own kyngdom, ine whose place
a wykked thefe is chose and wyrshiped, I wold my kyngdome
hulde be in man.   & of him I awght of ryght to be kynge and
5 lorde, for I made and bowght him ; bot now he hath broke and
defowled the feyth þat he behyght me in baptym ; he hath
broke and dispised my lawes that I yaue him ; he louyth his
own wyll, and liste not to here me ; & mor-ouer he enhanseth
the wyked thefe, the fende, above me & to him hath yove hys
10 feyth which is verely a thefe.   For he robbyth to him the
sowle of man þat I bought with my blode be suggestyon off
wyll and fals byhestes ; ȝett he robbyth nott as he wer myghteer
than I, while I am so myghty þat I may do all thinges with on
worde, and so ryghtfull þat I shuld nott do þe leste thinges
15 ayanste ryghtwosnes, þof all saynte prayed me.   Bot man that
is yove to fredome, wylfully leuying my commaundementez,
consenteth to the fende ; and þer-for it is ryghtfull that man
have experyence of hys tyrauntrie. | For the fende of me was fol. 22 a
made goode, bot throw hys own evyll wyll he fell and is as my
20 seruante to the vengeance of the wyked.   Bot þough I be now
thus dispised, yett I am so mercyfull that who euer aske my
mercy and worthely meke him-selfe, I foryeve them that they
haue trespaced, & I shall delyuer hem fro the wyked thefe.
And they þat abyde in my offence and dispite, I shall vysett
25 apon them my ryghtwosnesse.   So that all that her it shall
tremell and wake for fere.   And they þat fele it shall say :
allas ! þat euer we war borne and conceyved. Allas ! þat euer we
prouoked the lorde of maieste to wreth.

Bot þo[u][1], my dowghter, whom I haue chose, and wyth
30 whom I speke with my spirite, love þu me with all thyne
herte, nought as thy sonne, thy dowghter, thy fader, thy
moder, or other frendes, bot mor than any-thing in the werld.
For I that made the spared none of my membres to putt hem
to torment for the ; and yett I love thy sowle cheritably, that
35 rather than I shuld fayle itt, I shuld be crucyfyed aȝayne, yf
it wer possible.   Folow thu my mekenes ; for I, kyng of blysse
and angells, was clad in pour and vyle clothes, and I stode
naked at a pyller and herde with myn eres all repreves &

[1] MS. of ; *Latin* Tu autem filia mea.

scorn*es*. I putt also my wyll to-for thy will, for my modor,
thy lady, wold neu*er* other thing than I wold fro the begynnyng of hur lyf vn-to the ende.   If þu do thus, than shall thy
herte be wyth my herte, and it shall be enflaumed wyth my
love, as a drie stykke is lyghtly enflaumede w*ith* fyr.   So thy 5
sowle shall be fullfylled of me, & I shall be in the ; so that all
temp*er*all thing*es* shall be bitter vn-to the, and all fleshely luste
as venum.   Thu shall reste in the armes of my godhed, wher
is no luste of the flesh bot Ioy and dilectac[*i*]on [1] of sprite, w*ith*
fol. 22 b which a sowle delyted is full of joy w*ith*-|in and w*ith*-owte. 10
And itt desyryth or thinkyth no-thinge bott the Ioy that it
hath.   Love me þ*er*-fore onlye, and thu shalt haue all thing*es*
that þu wylt plentevously.   Is itt nott wryte that the oyle of
the videw fayled nott tyll Good yaue rayne apon the erthe,
aft*er* the worde of the pr*o*phete ?   I am a trew and a verray 15
pr*o*fette.   Yf þu yif fayth to my wordes and full-fyll hem,
Oyle, Ioy, and gladenes shall neu*er* fayle the wyth-outen ende.

Oure lorde Ih*e*su Cryst telleth seynte Birgitt of the
synne & of vnclennes of cristen peple ; and how they may
haue m*er*cye yf thay wyll amende ; and elles how herde 20
they shall be punyshede.   Cap. xiij.

The sonne of God spekyth vn-to hys spowse and sayth :
Crysten men do now vn-to me as some tyme dyde the Iewes.
The Iewes keste me owte of the tempull and hadd fulle wyll
to slee me.   Bot for my tyme was [not] [2] yett I-comme, 25
I wente owte of her hondes.   So do now cristen men w*ith* me.
They caste me owte of her temple of her sowles, which aught
to be my temple, and gladely thay wold slee me yf they myght.
I am in her mouth as roten as stynkyng flesh, and I seme to
hem as a man spekyng lesyng*es*, and they reke ryght not of me. 30
They turne hur bak to me, & I shall turne my bakke to hem.
For in her mouth is no thyng bott couetyse, and in þ*er* flesh
no thinge bot luste and lecherye.   In ther heryng onely pride
pleseth hem, and in her syght þe dilectable thing*es* of the
worlde.   My passion and my cherite is to hem abhominable, and 35
my lyf is grevouse to hem.   Ther-for I shall do as doth that

---

[1] MS. dilectacon.   [2] *Latin* non dum.

beste that hath mony dennys, when he is persewed of hunteres
in one denne, he fleth to a noþer, so shall I do; for crysten
men persewe me with her evyll dedes, and caste me owte of the
denne of her hertes. Þer-for I wyll enter in-to þe hethen, in
5 whos mowth I am now bytter & saffren; & I shall be in her | fol. 23 a
mowth swetter than hony. Neuerlesse I am yett so mercyfull
þat who euer aske foryevenesse and say, 'lorde, I knowlege that
I haue grevously synned and fayne wold mende me by thy
grace; haue mercy apon me for thy bitter passyon'; I shall
10 gladely receyve hym to mercye. Bot thay þat abyde in her
evyll, I shall come vn-to hem as a gyaunte that hath three
thinges: dredefullnesse, strenghth, and sharpenes. So shall
I come to cristen men so dredefull þat they shall nott der sterr
ayaynste me her leste fynger. I shall come so stronge þat
15 thay shall be as a g[n]att[1] to-for me and I shall come to hem
so sharpe that they shall feele woo here in thys lyffe and woo
with-outen ende. Amen.

Owr lorde[2] tellyth seynte Birgitt by exsample that noo
thing plesyth God so mych as he be loved above al thinges.

Revela-
tions,
Book VI,
Chap. 50.

20 The moder of God spekyth to the spowse of Cryste seynte
Birgitt and seyth: no-thing plesyth God so mych as þat man
love him above all oþer thynges. Loo, I shall telle the by ensample of a hethen woman that knewe ryght not of cristen
fayth; bot she[3] thus by hyr-selfe: 'I knew', she sayth, 'of
25 what mater I am, and wher-of I come in-to the wombe of my
moder. I byleve also that it is impossible me to haue body,
Ioyntes, and bowelles and wyttes, bot if some had yeve it me.
And þer-for ther is some creator and maker that made me so
fayr a person of mankynde, and wolde nott make me fowle as
30 wormes and serpentes. Ther-for it semeth to me that þough
I had mony husbondes, if they all cleped me, I shulde rather
go att one callyng of my maker than at the callyng of hem all.
I haue also mony sonnes and dowghteres, yett if I see hem
haue mete in her hondes and I know þat my maker hungred,
35 for-soth I wolde take a-way the mete fro my childrens hondes

[1] MS. gatt; *Latin* culex.
[2] *The chapter heading is incorrect, since only* 'the moder of God spekyth
to the spowse'.
[3] *Latin* cogitauit *omitted.*

fol. 23 b and gladely yeve it to my maker.   I haue also mony pos-[1]|ses-
sions which I dispose at myn owen wyll.   Yett if I knew the
wyll of my maker, I wolde full fayne leve myn own wyll and
dispose hem to hys wyrship.'

But see, dowght*er*, what God dide w*ith* this hethen woman. 5
For-soth, he sende to hyr hys frende, that enformede hir in the
holy fayth.   And God him-selfe visett hir herte, as þu mayst
well vnderstonde be þe womans word*es*, for when þat man of
God pr*e*ched to hir þat þ*er* was one God w*ith*-out*en* begynnyng
& ende which is maker of all thing*es*, she aunswerde : 'It is 10
well to be beleved, þat he þat made me and all thing*es* hath no
maker above him.   And it is well lyke to be trew þat his lyffe
is eu*er*-lastyng þat myght yif me lyf.'

When this woman herde that the same maker toke man-
kyn[d]e [2] of a virgyne and pr*e*ched w*ith* hys own mowth, she 15
aunswerde : 'It is well to be-leve of God all v*er*tues werk*es*.
Bot thu, frende of God, tell me what be tho wordes that come
of my maker ?   For I wyll leve my own wyll and obey till
him aft*er* all the wordes of hys.'

Then, the frende of God pr*e*chinge to hir of the passion, 20
crosse, and resurrecc*i*on of him, she aunswerde wyth wepynge
eyn and seyde : 'Blessed be that God that so pacyently shewed
hys cherite in erth that he had vn-to vs in heuen.   Þer-for if
I haue loved him 'fyrste, for he made me, now I am mych mor
bounde to love him, for he shewed me the ryght way and 25
bought me w*ith* hys holy blode.   I am also bounde to s*er*ue
him w*ith* all my myght*es* and all my membres, for he bowght
me w*ith* all hys membres.   And forther-mor, I am bounde to
put fro me all myn own will ̓& desyr þat I had to-for to my
godes, possession, children, kynne, & frendes, and only to 30
desyr my maker in his blysse & in that lyf that neu*er* hath
ende.'

Then sayde the moder of God : loo, dought*er*, thys woman
gate mony-folde rewarde for hyr love, & so is eu*er*y day yeve
rewarde to ychon aft*er* that god whyle he lyveth in this 35
world.

[1] c iiij.   [2] MS. mankynge.

**How our lady & seynte Petre kept a woman fro fallyng
to | synne, by whose [consell]¹ she changed hir lyf; & of
special gr*a*ce she fell in sekenes, & so was purgett and
went to heuen.   Cap. xv.**

₅ The spouse of Cryste seynte Birgitte see in sprite a woman
sitty*n*g in a rope, whos oo fote a fayr man bar upp, and a virgyn of me*r*velouse fayrenes bar vp the other fote.

Than our lady apperede and sayde : This lady that þu
knoweste is wounde in mony bysenes of the flesh and the
₀ worlde, and mervelously she hath be kepte that she fell nott.
For she hath hadde often wyll to haue synned, bot neu*er* place
nor tyme.   And that made þe p*r*ayer of Petre the apostle ² of
my sonne, whom this woman loved. Some tyme she had tyme
& space, bot thoo not wyll ; & þat made the lofe of me þat am
₅ the moder of God. And þer-for now for hir tyme neghith nye,
seynte Petre concellyth hir to take apon hir some sharpenes in
clothinge and werynge, puttynge a-way softe clothing. For he
was soue*r*ayne apostle ; and yette he suffered nakednes, pris*on*,
and hunger, all-though he war mighty in heuyn and erth. I also,
₀ moder of God, þat passed neu*er* howr in erth wi*th*-owte tribulac*i*on and dysese of herte, consell hir that she be nott ishamed
to be meke and to obey the frendes of God.

Af*ter* this anone saynte Peter the apostle appered and seyde
to seynte Birgitte : Thu now, spowse of our lorde God, goo aske
₅ of thys woman whom I haue loved and kepte, if she wyll all
holy be my dought*er*.

When seynte Birgitte had asked, & she, consentynge, sayde,
' I wyll, wi*th* all myne herte,' seynte Petre aunswerede : I shall
purvey for hyr as for my dought*er* Peronell, and take hir to
₀ my kepyng.

Than anon as this lady herde thys, she changed hir lyf.
And nott longe aft*er*, she fell seke that endured all the tyme of
hir lyfe, tyll she was purged and wyth ryg[ht] ³ grete deuocyon
yaue vp the spritte. For when she come to the ende of hir
₅ lyfe, she see seynte Pet*er* arayde lyke a byshop, and seynte
Petir þe martyr in habite of freer p*r*echou*r*s, for he was of that
ordre ; ⁴ | whych both she loved enterly in hyr lyfe.

---

¹ *Word omitted ; Latin* quorum consilio.   ² *Latin* & Filii mei.
³ MS. rygth.   ⁴ c iij (*foliation should be* c v).

And than she sayde openly: what ar these [m]y[1] lordes? When þe ladyes and wymmen that stode abowte hyr asked her what she see, she aunswerede: I see, she seyth, mervelowse thing*es*. For I see my lordes Petre the apostle arayed pontifically and Petre the martir in habyte of p*r*echowres, [5] whom I haue eu*er* loved and eu*er* hoped in her helpe. And anon, crying: blessed be God. Loo, I come, she paste to owr lorde.

Revela-
tions,
Book I.
Chap. 3. **Owr lorde Ih*esu* Cryst steryth his spouse to love him, & telleth hir how lyttell love mony hath to him, & how mych** [1] **to the werlde.   Cap. xvi.**

I am thy lorde God, whom þu wyrshyppest. I am he þat by my power bere vp heuen and erth; and it is bor vpp w*ith* non oþ*er* arch nor pyllers. I am he þ*at* ych day am offered on the auter verray God and man. I am the same that hath [1] chose the. Worship my father. Love me. Obey to my sprite. Do reu*er*ence to my moder, as to thy lady. Wyrship all my sayntes. Kepe the ryght feyth, which he shall tech the that hath felde in himselfe þe stryfe of ij spirit*es* of falsehod and trewth; and be myn helpe he ou*er*-comyn.[2] Kepe thow verray [2] mekenes; that is, a man to shew him-selfe sych as he is, and to yeve p*r*aysinge to God for hys yifte.

Bot now þ*er* is mony that hateth me. My wordes and dedes they holde bot sory and vanyte; and the auovterer, þe fende, they halse and love. What-eu*er* they do for me, it is w*ith* [2] gurching and bytt*er*ness. Ne they wold not knowleghe my name, if thei shuld nott be confunded of me. The werlde they love so clerly that they ar nott wery to labor ther-abowte nyght and day; and alway they ar feruent in love þ*er*-of, ther ser*u*ice is so plesynge to me as yf a man yave his enmy mony to slee [3] hys own sonne. So doth they þat ʒeveth me a lytell almosse. And they worship me w*ith* ther lippes to thentente þ*at* thei may encrese in wordely p*r*osperyte, and abyde in wyrship and fol. 25 a in synne; wher-for her good wyll | is slayne from p*r*ofetyng in God. [3]

Bot if thu wyll love me w*ith* all thyne herte and desyre no

---

[1] MS. any.
[2] MS. ouer comercomyn; *Latin* deuicit.

thyng bot me, I shall draw the vn-to me by cherite, as the
adamaunte draweth to him irn. & I shall sett the in myne
arme, that is so stronge þat non may draw it owte, and so
myghty that when it is stretched owte, none may bowe it. It
is also so swete þat it passeth all swettenes ; and it haueth no
comparison with dilectaciones of the werlde.

How saynte Birgitte see in gostely vision the dome of
a sowle whome the fende accused, and at the laste was
holpe by our lady ; & how she see all hell and purgatorie
& monye oþer mervelles ; & how nedefull it is to helpe hem
þat be in purgatorie. Cap. xvij.

Revela-
tions,
Book IV.
Chap. 7.

It semed to a person wakynge in prayer and not slepynge, as
þough she had see in spirituell vision a palasse of vnspectable
gretenes, wher-in wer folke innowmerable, cladde in white and
shynyng clothes. And ech of hem semed to haue a propur sete
to him-self. In this palyse stode principally a seete of dome,
wher-in was as it had byn a sonne ; and the bryghtnes that wente
fro thet [1] sonne was mor þan may oþer be tolde or vnderstonde,
in lenght, depnes, and brede. Þer stode also a virgyn nygh þat
sete, hauyng a precyouse crown on hir hede. And all þat þer
wer seruede the sonne syttyng in þe seete, praysyng him with
ympnes and songes.

Then appered þer an Ethiope, ferefull in syght and beryng,
as þof he had byn full of envy and gretely an aungered. He
cried & sayd : O þu ryghtfull Iuge, deme to me this sowle, &
her his werkes ; for now hys lyf is nygh at the end. Suffer
me þer-fore to punysh the body with the sowle, till they be
departede in sunder.

When this was seyde, it semed to me that one stoode afor
þe sete as it had be a knyght armed clenly, and wyse in wordes,
& sobre in heryng, þat sayde : | Thu Juge, loo, her ar his goode fol. 25 b
werkes that he hath do vn-to þis howr.

And anon ther was herde a voyce oute of the sonne syttynge
in the seete : her is vices, he sayth, moo then vertues. And it
is nott ryghtwosness þat vyce be Ioned to hym þat is souerayn
verteu.

---

[1] *Final t inserted above line.*

Then aunswerde the Ethiope: þer-for it is ryghtfull that þis sowle be Ioned to me; for if it haue any vyce in it, so in me is all wykkednes.

The knyght aunswerde: the mercy of God foloweth euery person vn-to[1] the laste poynte of hys lyffe, and then-after is the dome. And in this man that we speke of ar yett both sewle & body Ioned togeder, and dyscrecion abydeth in him.

The Ethiope aunswerde: the scriptur sayth, that may nott [li]e:[2] þu shalt love God above all thynges, and thy neghtbor as thy-self. See þu therfor, þat all the werkes of thys man be do of dred, and nott of love & cherite as they aught. And all the synnes þat he is shryve of, þu shalt fynde hem shrive with lytell contricion. And þer-for he hath deserued hell; for he hath forfett the kyngedome of heuyn. And þer-for hys synnes ar her open to-for the ryghtwosnes of God. For he gatt yett neuer contricion of goodely cherite for þe synnes that he hath doo.[3]

The knyght aunswerde; for-soth, he hoped and byleved to gete verray contricion to-fore his deth.

Thu, he sayde, hast gedered all the dedes þat euer he dyd well, and þu knowes all hys wordes and his thoughtes to the helth of his sowle. And all thes, what-euer þay be, may nott be lykened to þat grace had be contricion of the love of God with holy fayth and hope, and mych lasse they may nott do a-way all his synnes. For ryghtwyssnes is in God from with-owte begynnyng, that no synner shall enter heuyn þat | hath no perfite contricion. And þer-for it is vnpossible þat God shuld deme ayanste þe disposicion ordened from with-oute begynnyng. Therfore the sowle is to be demed to hell & to be Ionede wyth me in euerlastyng payne.

When thes war sayde, the knyght helde his pees and aunswerde nott to his wordes. After thes appered fendes innowmerable, lyke vn-to sparkles rynnyng abowte oute of an hote fyr. And all they criede with one vyce sayinge to him þat satt in þe seete as a sonne: we, þay say, knowe that þu arte oo God in iij persones, with-oute begynnyng & ende, and ther is non oþer God but þu. Thu arte þat cherite to which is Ioned mercy and rightwysnes. Þu was in thy-selfe from with-oute

fol. 26 a

---

[1] MS. vn to & vn to.   [2] MS. be. *See Notes.*   [3] s *cancelled.*

begynnynge, hauynge ryght nott lassede ne to lytell in the ne
changeble, as it semyth God with-owte þe is right nott, and no
thyng hath Ioy with-oute þe. Þer-for thy cherite made angelles
of non oþer mater bot of the power of thy godhede. And þu
dedyste as mercy sterrede the. Bot after that we ware brente
wyth-in with pryde, envye, and couetyse, thy cherite, louynge
ryghtwosnes, keste vs oute of heuen with the fyr of our malyce
in-to dyrke and vnspectable depnes that is now called hell. So
dyde þi cherite, than, which shall nott yette be departed from
þe dome of thy rightwysnes, wheder it be after mercye or after
equite. And yett we say mor, if that thinge that thu loveste
to-fore all thinges, the virgyn þat bare the, þat neuer synned,
hadde synned dedely & diede with-oute godly contricion, þu
loveste so ryghtwysnes þat hir sowle shuld neuer haue gotte
heven, bot it shuld haue be with vs in hell. Ther-for, þu Jugge,
why demeste þu nott this sowll to vs, that we may punysh it
after his werkes?

After thes was herde as it had be þe sown of a trumpe, & | all fol. 26 b
that herde it wer styll. And anon was herde a voyce seynge:
be styll and lysteneth ye, all angelles, sowles, and fendes, what
the moder of God spekyth.

And than anon, the same virgyne apperinge to-fore the seete
of dome and havynge vnder hyr mantell as it had be some
grete pryve thinges, sayde: O O ye enmyse, ye pursue mercy
and wyth-owte cherite ye love ryghtwysnes, þof here apper
defaute in goode werkes for which this sowle oweth not to gett
hevyn, yett seeth what I haue vnder my mantell.

And when the virgyn hade opnede both the lappys of hyr
mantell, vnder þe one appered one as it had be a lytell church,
wher-in semede to be some men of relygion; and vnder the
oþer apperede women and men, frendes of god, religiose and
other. And all thay cried with oo voyce saynge: haue mercy,
mercyfull lorde.

Than after was kepte silence and the virgyne spake and
seyde: the scriptur seyth, he þat hath parfyte fayth may þer-by
translate mountanes in the worlde. What than may and owe
the voyces of thes do, that had fayth and also serued God wyth
cherite? And what shall thoo frendes of God do, whom this
man prayed to pray for him, that he myght be departede from

hell and gette heuen? And he sowght no noder rewarde for
his goode werkes bot heuynly thyng*es*, wher all ther teres and
prayers may nott or be nott of power to take him and lyfte
him vpp so þat he gete godely contric*ion* w*ith* cherite to-for his
deth, and forther-mor I shall adde to my p*r*ayers wyth þe
p*r*ayer of all sayntes that ar in heuyn, whom thys man specyally
wyrshipped. Yett than forþermor sayde the virgyn: o o ȝe
fendes, I commaunde yow by þe power of the Iuge to take kepe
fol. 27 a to thes thyng*es* that ye se now | in ryghtwysnes.

Then they all aunswerde as it had been w*ith* one mowth: we
see, thay seyde, that in the worlde a lytell water and a grete
ayer peese the ire of God. And so be thy prayer is God pesede
vn-to mercye wyth cherite.

Aft*er* thys was herde a voyce from the sonne, saying: for the
p*r*ayers of my frendes shall now this man gete goodely contri-
c*ion* to-fore his deth, in so mych þat he shall [not]¹ come ine
hell; bott he shall be purgett w*ith* him that sufferith moste
grevouse payn in purgatorie. And when the sowle is purgede,
he shall haue rewarde in heuen w*ith* hem þat had fayth & hope
in erth w*ith* ryght litell cheryte. ·

When thes was sayde, the fendes fledde her way. Then-
aft*er*, it semed vn-to the spowse as if þer had openede a ferefull
place and a dyrke wher-in appered a fornace all brennyng
w*ith*-in; and that fyr had not elles to brenne bot fendes and
quyke sowlys. And a-bove þat fornace aperede þat sowle whos
dome was ryght now to-fore. The feete of the sowle wer
festened to the fornace, and the sowle stode vp lyke a p*er*son.
It stode nott in the hyeste place nor in the loweste, bot as it
wer on the syde of the fornace. The shap of the sowle was
fereful and m*er*velowse. The fyre of the fornace semede to
come vp by-twyx the feete of the sowle, as when wat*er* ascendyth
vp be pyp*es*. And that fyre ascended vp-on hys hede, and
vyolentely thryste him to-geder; so mych that the pores stode
as vaynes rennynge w*ith* brennyng fyr. Hys eres semede lyke
smythes belowes that mevede all his brayne w*ith* contynuall
blowyng. Hys eyn semede turnede vp so downe and sounke
ine as they had be festenede to the bake p*ar*tye of the hede.
fol. 27 b Hys | mowth was open and his tonge drawe owte by his noose

¹ *Latin* non.

th[r]illes [1] and hynge doun to his lypp*es*. Hys teth wer as irn
nayl*es* fastenede be his palate. His arm*es* wer so longe that
they streched down to his feete. Both his hond*es* semede to
haue & to presse to-geder a man*er* of fatnes w*ith* brennyng
5 pykke. The skynne þat semede apon the sowle semede lyke the
skynne apon a body, and it was as a lynnen cloth al byshede
wyth fylth ; whych cloþe was so colde that yche on that see itt
tremeld and shoke. And þ*er* come þ*er*-fro as whiter of a soor
w*ith* corupte blode, and so wykked a stynk þat it myght nott be
10 lykenede to the werste stynke in the werlde. When his tribulac*i*on was see, ther was herde a voyce of the sowle þat sayde v
tymes, ' wo, wo, allas, allas,' cryinge. w*ith* teres and all his
mygthis.

Fyrst he sayde : alas and woo to me, þat I loved God so litell
5 for his ryght grete verteus and grace yove vn-to me. The
secunde : allas and woo to me, þ*at* I haue nott drede the ryghtwysnes of God as I aught. The thirde : allas and wo to me,
þat I lovede the body and the luste of my synfull flesh. The
ferte : allas and wo to me, for my wordely ryches & pride.
10 The v[te] : allas and woo to me, that eu*er* I see yow, Ludowyke
and Iohane.

Then sayde the angell to me : I wyll expowne to the this
vysion. This paleys þat þu haste seen is the lykenes of heuen.
The multitude of hem that þat wer in the seet*es*, cladde in white
5 and shynynge clothes, ar angles and sowl*es* of seyntes. The
sonne betokenes Criste in his godhede. The woman betokeneth
the virgyn that bar God. The Ethiope betokeneth the fende
that accuseth the sowle. The knyght betokenyth the angell
that telleth the goode werk*es* of the sowle. The fornace be-
10 tokenyth hell, þat is so bren- | nyng w*ith*-ine, that yf all the fol. 28 a
werld brynte w*ith* all thing*es* that be þ*er*-in, it wer nott lyke
the gretenes of that fornace. In this fornace a[r] [2] herde
dyu*er*se voyces, all spekynge ayanste God, and all begynnyng
her voyces w*ith* ' woo and allas ', and endyng in lyke wyse. The
15 sowles appered as p*er*son*es* whos membres ar streched owte
w*ith*-oute comforth and hath neu*er* reste. Know þu also þe
fyre that semed to the in the fornesse brynnyth in eu*er*-
lastynge derkenes, & the sowles that brynne þ*er*-ine haue nott

---

[1] MS. thilles.   [2] MS. as ; *Latin* audiuntur.

all one lyke payne. The derkenes that appered abowte the
fornace ar called limb*us*, & it comyth of the derkenes that ar
ine the fornes and yett they ar both one place and one hell.
Who þat eu*er* come ther shall neu*er* haue dwellyng w*ith* God.
Above this derkenes is the gretteste payne of purgatorie that
sowl*es* may suffer.   And by-yonde this place is a-noþ*er* place
wher is lesse peyne, that is none oþ*er* bott lake of myghtes ine
strenght, fayrnes, and such oder : as I telle the by a lykenes,
as yf ther wer a seke man ; and when the sekenes and the
payne wer sesede, he wer lefte so feble þ*at* he had no
strenghtes, tyll he recou*er*ede by litell and litell.   The
thirde place is a-bove, wher is non oþ*er* payne bot desyre of
comyng to God. And that þu shuldeste the bett*er* vnderstonde
in thy conscience, I telle the by a lykenes, as yf oþ*er* metall wer
medled w*ith* gold and brynte in moste hote fyr & shuld so longe
be purgett, tyll the other metallys wer wasted away ; and the
gold abode pur and clene the more that þe oþ*er* metall were
stronge and thikke, so mych it shuld nede the hott*er*e fyr, tyll
the golde wer as rennyng wat*er*, and all brynnyng.   Then the
master of the werke putteth þe golde in an oþ*er* place, wher it
shall take his trew forme and shappe ine syght and touchyng.
And after that, he puttyth itt in-to the iij place, wher it is
fol. 28 b kepte tyll | it be *pre*sentede to the ower.

So it is gostely.   In the fyrst place above the dyrkenes is the
greteste payne of purgatorie, wher þu see þe sayde sowle be
purged.   Þ*er* is towchyng of fendes. Ther is appere by lykenes
venemouse wormes & lykenes of wode best*es*.   Þ*er* is hete and
cold.   Þ*er* is derkenes and confuc*i*on þat come of the payn þat
is in hell.   Þ*er* have some sowles lasse payne & some mor, aft*er*
that her synnes wer amended or noght, while tyme the sowle
abode w*ith* the body.   Then the mayst*er*, that is, the ryghtwysnes of God, putteth the gold, that is, the sowles,[1] in oþ*er*
places, wher is not bot defaute of myght*es*, ine whych sowles
shall abyde tyll thay haue refreshing of her frendes or of con-
tynuell suffrage of holy church.   For a sowle, the more helpe
it haue of fryndes, the rather shall it wax stronge & be delyu*er*ed from þat place.   After thes, the sowle is bore to the iij
place, wher is no payne bot desyre of comyng to the *pre*sence

[1] MS. þ*at* is.

of God & to his blessed syght. In this place abyde mony, and
ouer-long, with-oute hem þat had perfyte desyr whyle they
lyved in þe werld to come to þe presence and syght of God.
Know þu also that mony dye in the worlde so ryghtfull and
5 innocentely, that anon they come to þe syg[ht] [1] and presence of
God. & some haue so amended her synnes with good werkes,
þat her sowles shall fele no payn. Bot few þer be þat come
nott in the place wher is desyr of comynge to Godde. Þer-for
all sowles abydynge in thes iij places hath parte of the prayers
10 & goode werkes of holy church þat ar do in þe werlde : namle,
of thoo þat thay dyd while thay lived, & of þoo that ar do of
her frendes after her deth. Know þu also þat as synnes ar
monye and dyuerse, so ar peynes mony and dyuerse. Þer-fore as
the hungorie Ioyeth of mete when it comyth | to his mouth, fol. 29 a
15 and the thiristy of drynke, and as [2] he þat is hevy is glad of
Ioy, and the nakede of clothinge, and the seke of commynge to
his bedde, so sowles Ioy and be perteneres of the goode dedes
at ar do for hem in the werlde.

Then sayde the angell forþermor : blessede be he þat in the
20 werld helpeth sowles with prayers, goode werkes, and labor of
hys body. For the ryghtwosnes of God may nott lye þat sayth
þat sowles oþer muste be purgede after her deth with peyne of
purgatorie, or ells rather be lowsed be goode werkes of her
frendes.

25 After thys was herde mony voyces oute of purgatorie, saynge :
O lord Ihesu Cryste, ryghtfull Iugge, sende thy cherite to hem
that gostely haue power in þe werlde ; for then shall we mowe
haue more parte than we haue nowe, of her songe, redyng, and
offrynge.

30 Above thys space fro when this crie was herde, semede as it
had bene a howse in which wer herde mony voyces, sayng :
rewarde be vn-to hem of God þat sende vs helpe in owre
defautes.

In the same howse semede to go forth as it had bene þe
35 springe of a day, and vnder þat day springe apperede a clowde
þat had ryght not of the lyght of the mornetyde. Oute of
which come a grete voyce, saying : O lorde God, yife of thyne
vnspekable power to ych of hem in þe werld an hundreth fold

---

[1] MS. sygth.   [2] MS. as *inserted above line.*

E

rewarde, that with her good dedes lyfte vs vppe in-to the lyght
of thy godhede, and in-to þe syght of thy face.

Revela-
tions,
Book IV,
Chap. 8
and
part of
Chap. 9.

Then-after tellyth the angell the paynes of the sayde
sowle, and seyth:

That sowle whos dispocion þu haste see, & herde his dome, 5
is in the moste grevouse peynes of purgatorie. And that is
þer-for, for it vnder-stondyth nott wheder it shall come to
reste after purgacion, or ells be dampned; and this is the

fol. 29 b

ryghtwysnes of God, for he had | conscience [1] and grete discre-
cion, which he vsede bodely to the worlde and not gostely to 10
hys sowle. For he was to necligent and for-yette God to mych,
as longe as he lyved. Þer-for his sowle suffreth now brennyng
of fyre, and it tremeleth for cold. It is also blynde of darke-
nes and dredefull of the horrible syght of fendes. It is deffe
of the fendes crie, hungrie & thiresty with-in-forth, and all 15
wrapped in confusion with-owte-forth. Neuer-the-lasse, God
ʒaffe it oo grace after deth; þat is, þat it shulde nott come to
the touchinge of fendes. For he spared and for-ʒaffe grevouse
defautes to his cheffe enmyse, only for the wyrship of God;
and he made frenship and a-corde with his cheffe enmye. 20
Know þu also þat what euer he dyd of good and what euer he
by-hyght & ʒaff of well goten riches, & moste the prayers of the
frendes of God, lassen and refreshen his payne, after it is deter-
mynede in the ryghtwysnes of God. Bott oþer goodes þat he
yave, þat wer not well I-gotte, profyte þat to-for had hem ryght- 25
fuly in possession gostely or bodely, if they be worthy after
the dispocion of God.

After this þe angell calde, forþer-more, of the dome of the
sayde sowle, & sayde: þu haste herde to-for that for þe prayers
of the frendes of God, this man gatt goddely contricion of 30
cherite for his synnes, a litle to-for hys deth; which contricion
departed him fro hell. Þer-fore after his deth, the rightwysnes
of Gode demede þat he shulde brenne in purgatorie þe sexe ages
þat he had, from that howr þat he dide fyrst wyttyngly dedely
syn, vn-to the tyme þat he repentede fruytefully of godely 35
cherite, bot he gatt helpe from Gode, of the world, or from þe
frendes of God. The fyrst age was þat he loved nott God for

[1] MS. cons | conscience.

the deth of his noble body, & for his monye folde tribulaciones,
þat he sufferede for non oþer cause bot for the helth of sowles.
The secunde age was þat he loved nott his own sowle as a
cristen mann [1] | aught ; nor he thonked not God for his fol. 30 a
5 baptem, for that he was neþer Iewe neþer hethenman. The iij
age was þat he knew well tho thinges that God commaunded,
and he had full litell wyll to fullfylle hem. The ferte age was
þat he knew well tho thinges þat God for-bade hem þat wyll
go to heuen ; and bodely he dyde ayaynste hem, nott folowyng
10 þe prikkynge of his concience, bot his own carnall affeccion.
The fyfte age was þat he vsede nott grace and confession as
longed to hym, while he had so longe tyme. The vi age was
þat he rowght lytell of the bodye of Criste, nott wyllynge ofte
receyve it, for he wold nott kepe him-selfe fro synne ; neþer
15 he had no cherite to receyve the body of Cryst tyll in the ende
of hys lyfe.

After this appered one as it wer a man right sobre in Revela-
syght, whos clothes wer white & shynyng as a prestes tions,
albe ; he was gyrde with a lynnen gyrdele & a rede stole Book IV,
20 abowte his necke & vnder hys armes ; & he began his concluded.
wordes on this wyse :

Thu þat sees thes thinges, take kepe, merke, and commende
to thi mynde tho thinges that þu seest and þat be sayde vn-to
the. For ye þat be lyvyng in þe werld may not vnderstonde
25 the power of God and the euerlastyng settyng þer-of, in the
same wyse as we that ar wyth hym. For the thynges that ar
anenste God do in a poynte of tyme, may not be vnderstonde
ane[n]st [2] yow, bot with wordes and lykenes after the disposi-
cion of the world. I am on of hem whom this man that is demede
30 to purgatorie wyrshiped wyth his ʒiftes in hys lyfe. Þer-fore
God hath granted me of hys grace þat yf ony man wolde do
thes thynges þat I tell the, then his sowle myght be translate
to an hier place, wher it shuld gett his trew | shappe, and fele fol. 30 b
non oþer payne bot as he shulde suffer that had a grete soore,
35 and all the sorowes ware agoo, and he lay as a man with-oute
strenght ; and yett he shulde Ioye, for as mych as he shulde
knowe certenly þat he shulde come to lyve.

---

[1] aught, *catchword*.   [2] MS. anest.

Þer-fore, as þu herde þe sowle of this man hath criede v tymes woo and allas, so say I now to hym v thing*es* of comforth.   The first wo was þat he loved God to lytell.   Þer-fore, þat he may be delyu*er*ed from this, be þ*er* ȝeve for his sowle xxx chalesse, wher-in the blode of God be offered, and God 5 him-selfe more wyrshipped.   The secunde woo was þat he drede nott God.   Þer-for, for to do away this, be þ*er* chose xxx prest*es* þat aft*er* the dome of the man be deuote, & ych of hem sey xxx masses, when they may: ix of marteres, ix of confessors, ix of all sayntes, þe xxviij mass of angell*es*, þe xxix 10 of oure lady, and the xxx of the holy trinite.   And all they muste pr*a*ye ententevously for his sowle, þat the ire of God be swaged, and his ryghtwysnes bowed vn-to m*er*cye.   The thirde wo was for his pride and couetyse.   Þer-fore, to do away thys, be þ*er* receyved xxx poor men, whos feete be wesshede w*ith* 15 mekenes, and mete and drynke and mony & clothes be yeve vn-to hem, wher-wyth they be comforted ; and ych of hem, both he þat wasshed, & thay þat ar wash, pr*a*ye God mekely, þat for his mekenes and bytt*er* passion he foryeve this sowle þe covetyse and pr*i*de þat he hath doo.   The ferte woo, for the 20 lecherye of hys flesh.   Þer-fore, who eu*er* yife a mayden in-to a monaster & a wydewe eke, & a mayde in-to trewe wedlok, ȝevyng w*ith* hem so mych goode as they myght be sufficiently founde in mete drynke & cloth ; þane shuld God for-ȝeve the synne of this sowle that he dyde in his flesh.   For thes ar iij 25 fol. 31 a lyves þat God | hath co*m*maunded and chose to stonde in thys world.   The v woo was for he hath doo monye synnes in tribulac*i*on of mony other.   Þat is to say, for he did all hys power þat tho tweyn named to-fore shuld come to-geder in wedloke, which wer no less nye of kynne to-geder than yf they 30 hade be both of the nexte kynred ; and this mariage he pr*o*cured more for himself than for the realme, and w*ith*-owte requeste of the pope, ayeynste þe pr*a*yseable [1] dispoc*i*on of holy church.   And for his dede, mony wer made m*a*rtres, þat such thing*es* shuld nott be suffered ayanste God and holy church 35 and cristen man*er*s.

If any man þat wold do a-way þis synne went to þe pope, and seyde : ' a c*er*ten man dyde sych a synne ' (not expr*e*ssyng

------

[1] MS. prayse able.

the person), 'neuer-the-lasse in his ende he repented [1] & gatt
absolucion, the synne nott amended. Puttyth to me þer-fore
what pennance ȝe wyll, that I may ber; for I am redy to
amende þat syn for him.' For-soth, if þer wer putt to him no
5 mor bot oo pater noster, it shulde be vayleable to þat sowle to
the lessynge of his payn in purgatorie.

   **Wordes of praysyng bytwix our lady & hir son & what
grace our lady getteth to hem that ar in purgatorie and in
the werld. Cap. xviij.**

Revela-
tions,
Book 1,
Chap. 50.

10   Marie spak vn-to hir sonne and sayde: [blessede] [2] be thy
name with-outen ende with thi godhed, which is with-oute
begynnyng and with-owten ende. In thi godhed ar iij mervelowse thinges: þat is to say, power, wysdom, & vertue. Thy
power is as fyre brynnyng moste hote, to-fore whos face all
15 that is seur and st[r]onge [3] is as it were a drie strawe in the
fyre. Thy wysdom is as it war the see that for gretenes may
nott be drawe owte; which, when it encresyth and ouer-
flowyth, it hilleth [4] | mountaynes and vales. So thy wysdom fol. 31 b
may nott be comprehended ne full know. How wysely þu
20 haste made man and sett him above all thi creatures in erth!
How wysely þu haste disposed birdes in þe ayr and bestes on
the erth and fishes in the see, & to ych of hem þu haste ȝyve
his tyme and ordre! How mervelously þu ȝeveste and takest
away lyf to and fro all thinges! How wysely þu ȝeveste wys-
25 dom to the vnwyse and takeste it away from þe prowde! Thi
vertue is grete as it wer þe lyght of the sonne þat shyneth in
heuenes and fylleth all erth with hys light. So thy vertue
fyllyth hie and low thynges, & all thynges. Þer-fore blessede
be þu, my sonne, þat arte my God and lorde.

30   The sonne aunswerde: my moste der moder, thy wordes ar
swete to me, for they come owte of thy sowle. Thu arte as
the morentyde procedyng with clerenes. Þu haste yeve owte
þi bemes above all heuenes, and thy lyght and clerenes passeth
all angelles. Thu haste draw vn-to þe with thi clerenes þat
35 verray sonne þat is my godhed, so mych þat the sonne of my
godhed, commyng in-to the, hath festened it-selfe in the. Of

[1] MS. repetented.   [2] *Latin* Benedictum.
[3] MS. stonge; *Latin* forte.   [4] d ij.

whose hete þu arte warmed with my cherite above all ; of whos
bryghtnes þu arte lyghtned above all oþer wyth my wysdom ;
and the derkenes of erth ar drive awaye, and all hevenes ar
lyghtened be the. I sey in my trowth þat thi purenes, which
plesed me above all angelles, drowgh my godhed in-to the, that 5
thu shuldeste be enflamed with the hete of the holy goste,
wherby þu closdeste in thy wombe verray god and man ; wher
throwe man is lyghtned, and angelles gladed. Þer-fore blessed
be þu of thy blessed son. And þer shall no peticion be þat þu
fol. 32 a askes of me, bot þat it | shall be herde. And all that aske 10
mercye with wyll to amende be the, they shall haue grace ; for
as hete procedyth fro the sonne, ryght so be the all mercye
shall be yove. For þu arte as a well moste plenteous, oute of
which mercy floweth vn-to wreches.

The moder aunswerde to her son : all verteu and glorie be 15
to the, my sonne þat arte my God ; & my mercye and all
godenesse þat I haue is of the. Þu arte as a sede þat was
nott sawe, and ȝit it ȝave of it-self a hondreth fold and a thou-
sande fold fruite. For of the procedyth all mercye, which, for
it is vnnowmerable and vnspekable, it may well be lykened in 20
the noumbre of an hondreth, in whych is notted perfeccion ;
for of the is all p[er]feccion [1] and profett.

The sonne aunswerd to his moder : verely, moder, þu
lykenest me well to a sede þat was nott sawe and yett it grewe,
for I come in-to the wyth my godhed, and my manhode was 25
nott sowe be eny medelyng of man. And ȝett it grew in the ;
wher-of mercye floweth vn-to all. Þer-fore þu saydeste well.
And now, þer-for, for as mych as þu draweste mercye of me be
the moste swete wordes of thy mowth, aske what þu wylte,
and it shall be yove vn-to þe.   30

The moder aunswerd : my sonne, for I haue gote mercy of
the, þer-for I aske mercye and helpe to wreches. For þer ar
iiij places. Þe fyrst is hevyn, wher ar angelles and holy
sowles ; and they nede no thynge bot the, whom they hafe,
and in the they have all goodenes. The secunde place is hell ; 35
and they þat dwell þer ar fyllede with malyce and excluded
from all mercy ; and þer-fore þer may be ryght nott of gode,
noþer enter vn-to hem. The iij place is purgatorie ; and they

[1] MS. profeccion.

þat ar þer hath nede of iij folde mercye, fur they ar tormented
in iij wyses. They ar trowbled in her heryng, for they here
nott bot sorowes & paynes &[1] | wrechednes. Thei ar tor- fol. 32 b
mented in her syght, for they see ryg[ht][2] noght bot her
5 wrechednes. They ar tormented in her towchyng, [for they][3]
fele flaumes of fyre vnsuffereble and of grevouse payne. My
lorde and my son, ȝeve hem thy mercye, for my prayers.

The sonne aunswerde : full gladely, moder, for þe I shall yeve
hem iij folde mercy. First, her herynge shall be relesed ; her
10 syght shall be esed ; and þe payne of felynge shal be more soft
& esy ; and mor-ouer, from this tyme furth who euer be in þe
gretteste payn of purgatorie shall come to the medell payn.
And þay þat ar in þe medle payn shall come to the leste. And
tho thatt ar in the leste payn shall passe in-to blysse.

15 The moder aunswerde : praysyng & worship be to the, my
lorde. And then she sayde forþer : the ferte place is the world ;
and the dwellers þer-in haue nede of iij thinges. Fyrst, contricion for her synnes ; secunde, satisfaccion ; thirde, strenght
to do goode dedes.

20 The sonne aunswerde : who þat euer call apon thy name &
hath hope in the, with purpose to amend that he hath do amysse,
thes iij thinges shall be yove him & the kyngdom of heuyn
þer-to. For þer is so mych swetenes to me in thy wordes þat
I may not denye þat þu askes. For þu wyll no thing bot þat
25 þat I wyll. For þu arte as a flawme bryght brynnyng, wherby
candels quenched ar lyghtned. And þ[o][4] þat ar not well
brynnyng ar amended. Ryght so of þi charite, þat ascended
in-to myn herte and drowgh me vn-to the, they þat ar dede in
synne shall be arered to lyfe and tho þat ar leuke warme, as is
30 blak smok, shall be made stronge in my cherite.

**How our lorde lykneth our lady to a flour þat sprong in
a vale and grew vppe above mountaynes. Cap. xix.**

Revela-
tions,
Book I,
Chap. 51.
fol. 33 a

The moder of God spake vn-to hyr sonne : blessed | be thy
name, my sonne Ihesu Criste. Wyrship be to thy manhode
35 above all thynges made. Glorifie be to thi godhod a-bove all
thinges, whych is with thy manhod oo God.

[1] d iij.
[2] MS. rygth.
[3] *Latin* quia sentiunt.
[4] MS. þu ; *Latin* & inaccensa conualescunt.

The sonne aunswerd: my moder, þu arte lyke to a flowr þat grew in a vale, a-bowte which vale wer v high mountaynes. And þat flour grew oute of iij rootes, with a ryght shafte þat had no knottes. This flowre had v leves full of all swettenes. And this vale grew vp with this flour above thes v moun- 5 tayns, and the leves of the flour sprede hem abrode above all the hyghnes of heuyn and above all the quores of angels. My loved moder, þu arte þat vale, for thy mekenes þe which þu haddeste a-fore all oþer. This vale passed v mountaynes. The fyrst mountayne was Moyses, that is called a mountayne for 10 power. For he hadde so grete power in the lawe apon peple, as if he had hade hem closed in his fyste. Bott thu closed in thy wombe the lorde of all lawes; þer-for þu arte hyer than that mountayne. The ij mountayne was Hely, which was so holy, þat wyth body and sowle he was take vp in-to an holy place. 15 Bot thu, my moste der moder, thy sowle was take vppe above all queres of angeles, vn-to the trone of God; and þer is thy moste clene bodye with thy sowle. Þer-fore þu art hier þan Hely. The iij mountayn was the high strength of Sampson, þat he had above all men. ȝett þe fende dyceyved him thro 20 his slyght. Bot þu ouer-come the fende with thy strenght; þer-fore þu arte stronger than Sampson. The iiij mountayn was Dauid, þat was a man after myn[1] | herte and wyll; and ȝett he fell in-to synne. Bot thu, my moder, foloweste all my wyll and synneste neuer. The v mountayn was Salamon, that 25 was full of wysdom; and ȝett he was fonned. Bot þu, my moder, was full of all wysdom and þu wer neuer no foole ne deceyved; þer-for þu art hier than Salamon. The flowr all-so spronge owte of iij rotes. For þu had iij thinges fro thy ȝonge age: that is, obedyence, cherite, and godely vnderstondyng. 30 Out of iij rotes grew a shafte moste ryght with-oute any knott: that is to say, thy wyll þat neuer was bowed bot after my wyll. This flour had also v leves that grew above all quers of angelles. For-soth, my moder, þu arte þe flour of these v leves. The fyrst leve is thin honeste, in so mych þat myn angelles þat ar 35 honeste to-for me, beholdyng thy honeste, see it be above hem and mor excellent than her honeste and holynes. Therfor þu arte hyer than angeles. The secunde lefe is thy mercye, þat

fol. 33 b

[1] d iiij.

was so mych that when þu see þe wrechidnes of all sowles, thu
had compassion apon hem. In my deth þu sufferest most
payn. Angelles ar full of mercye, ȝett they suffre neuer sorow ;
bot þu, moste pitefull moder, had mercy on wreches when thu
felst all sorow of my deth. And for mercy þu woldest rather
suffer sorowe than be exempt þer-from. Þer-fore thi mercy
passeth the mercy of all angelles. The iij leve is thy myldenes.
Angelles ar myld and wyll gode to all. Bot þu, my moder
dere, to-fore thy deth had in thi body and sowle a wyll as a
angell, and dyd good vn-to all ; and yett þu· denyeste non þat
askyth resonably to his profett. And þer-for thy myldenes is
more excellent than angelles. The iiij^te leve is thy fayrenes.
For angelles beholdes ych oþers | fayrenes and they mervell þe fol. 34 a
fayrenes of sowles and bodies ; bot they see the fayrenes of thy
sowle above all thinges made, and the honeste of thy body passe
all men or wymmen þat euer wer. And so thy fayrenes passed
all angelles and all thinges made. The v leve was thy goodly
delectacion, be which no thinge delyted the bot God. Þer is no
thing þat delyteth angelles bot God, and ych on of hem feleth
his delyte in him-selfe. Bot when they see in the thy delyte
vn-to God, it semed to hem in her conscience þat her own
delyte brente in hem, as it had be a lyght in goddely cherite.
Bot thei see thi delyte in God, as it had bene a fyr most hot,
brynnyng with most fervente flaume, and so hie þat it neyght
vn-to my godhed. And ther-fore, moste swete moder, thy
goodely delectacion brynte hote above all queres of angelles.
This flour þat had thes v leves, þat is to sey, honeste,
mercye, myldenes, fayrenes, and souerayn delyte, was full of
all swettnes. For who þat wyll taste swettnes, he moste negh
vn-to swettnes & receyve it in-to him-selfe. And so did þu,
my good moder. For þu were so swete to my fader þat he
receyved þe all in-to his spirite, and thy swettnes plesed him
above all. A flowr also beryth a seede of he[t]e ¹ and verteu
of the sonne, wher-of groweth fruyte. Bot blessede be þat
sonne þat is my godhed, that toke manhode of thy madynly
bowelles. For lik as sede, wher-euer it is sowe, bryngeth furth
sych flowres as the seede is, ryght so my membres wer lyk
vn-to thy membres in forme & in face. ȝett I was a man, & þu

¹ MS. hede ; *Latin* ex calore.

a virgyn woman.   This vale was heved above all mountayn*es*
w*ith* his flowr, when thi bodye was heved above all queres of
angell*es* w*ith* thy [1] | moste holy sowle.

Our lady p*r*ayeth þat thes revelac*i*ones mote be roten in
me*n*nys hert*es* and spred o-brode in the werld; and how
our lorde prayseth owr lady and graunteth hir askyng, and
byddyth þat thes be [2] bore to the pope & to oþer p*r*elat*es*.
Cap. xx.

The blessed virgyn Marie spake vn-to hir sonne and seyde:
blessed be þu, my sonne and my God, & lorde of angels and
kynge of blys.   I p*r*aye þe þat þe word*es* þat þu hast spoke be
roted in the hert*es* of thy frendis ; and so sykyrly that they
mote cleve in her mynd*es* as the glewe whyt the which the
shippe of Noe was glued, which neu*er* tempestes nor wynd*es*
myght lowse a-sonder.   Thy word*es* mot also be spred in the
world as branches and flowres moste swete, whos swete smell
spredeth far o-brode.   They mott also be fruytefull and swete
as the date, whos swetenes delyteth mych mann*es* lyffe.

The sonne awnswerd : blessed be þu, my moste dere mod*er*.
Gabriell myn angell sayde vn-to the, ' Blessed be þu, Marie,
to-fore all women,' and I bere the wyttnes þat thu art blessed
and moste holy above all queres of angell*es*.   Thu arte as a
flowr in a garthen wher, þought mony swete flowres stonde
abowte, ȝett it passyth all in swetenes, feyrenes, and verteu.
Thes flowres are all þe chosen from Adam to the ende of the
world, which wer planted in the garden of the werld and haue
shyned and flowred with dyu*er*se verteus.   Bot amongeste all
þat eu*er* war or shall be, þu wer moste excellente in swete smell
of gode lyvynge and mekenes, and yn fayrenes of moste accept-
able virgynyte, & in verteu | of abstynence.   For I ber the
wyttenes þat þu wer in my passyon more than martyr.   In
thyn abstynence þu arte more than any confessore.   In m*er*cye
and goodenes þu arte more than a angell.   Þer-fore, for the my
word*es* shal be roted as in moste stronge [glewe] [3] in the hert*es*
of my frend*es*; they shall sprede o-brode as flowres smellyng
most swete ; and they shall sauor as a date alther swettyste.

Then sayde our lorde to his spouse, seynt Birgitt : sey to my

---

[1] d v.   [2] *Poorly written* bor *erased*.   [3] *Latin* bitumen fortissimum.

frende, thy fader, hos herte is after myn herte, þat he expoune
dylygently thes wordes þat ar wryte; and that he take hem to
the archebysshop and afterwarde to an oþer bysshoppe, and
when they ar wysely enformed, then þat he sende hem to the
5 thirde bysshoppe.　Say also to him on my be-halffe : I am þi
maker and the raunsoner of sowl*es*.　I am he whom thu loveste
to-fore all oþer thinges.　Be-hold and see þat the sowles which
I bowght w*ith* my blode ar as it wer þe sowles of hem þat
knew nott God.　And they ar take prison*er*es of the fende so
10 horribly þat he punyshet hem in all membres, as it were in a
streyte press.　Þer-fore if my wound*es* sauour þe in thyn herte,
if þu sett ought be my scorgyng and by my sorowes, shew in
thyn werk*es* how mych þu loveste me ; and make my word*es*
that I haue spoke w*ith* myn own movth to come in open, and
15 bere hem thy-self vn-to þe hede of the church.　For I shall
ȝeve the my sprite þat wher-eu*er* is eny debate by-twix tweyn,
thu shalt mow make hem acorded in my name by þe v*er*teu
þat is ȝeve the, yf they ȝiffe fayth and credence to my word*es*.
And for the more obydence of my word*es*, þu shalt ber to the
20 byshopes the wyttnes of hem | to whom my wordes sauo*ur* and ┆ fol. 35 b
delyte.　For my wordes ar as it war fatt grece or talowe þat
melteth so mych þe sonner as a man hath w*ith* ine him more
kyndely hete ; for wher is no kyndely hete a man casteth oute
sych fattnes and receyveth it nott in-to his stomak.　So ar my
25 wordes.　For þe mor feruent a man in his cherite that eteth
and choweth hem, þe more fatt he waxeth in swetenes of
heuenly Ioy and inwarde love, and the more he brennyth in
my love.　Bot they to whom my wordes plese nott, haue as it
wer fattnes in her mouth which they taste, and anon they
30 caste it owt & trede it vnder her fote.　So my wordes are dispised of some, for the swettnes of sp*irit*uall thing*es* sauo*ur* hem
nott.　The p*r*ince of the londe whom I haue chose in-to my
membre and made verely myn shall helpe the manfully ; and he
shall ȝeve the thin necessaries for the way of well gote goodes.

35 　An angell tellyth seynt Birgitt a difference by-twyx þe
good spirite and the evell; and how a man shall do þat is
combered w*ith* þe evyll spirite.　Ca. xxj.

Revela-
tions,
Book I,
Chap. 54.

　An angell spake vn-to the spouse of Cryst seynt Birgitt and

seyd : þer ar ij spirit*es*, on vnmade and a-noþer made.[1]   The spirite vnmade hath iij thing*es* : Fyrst, he is hote, secunde, he is swete ; thirde, he is clene.   He is hote, for he makyth hoote not w*ith* eny thyng made, bot of him-self ; for he is, w*ith* the fader and the sonne, maker of all thinges and all myghty ; and than maketh he hoote when the sowll brennyth all to the love of God.   He is swete, when ryght noght is swete ne plesyth þe sowle bott God allon and the

fol. 36 a mynde on hys werk*es*.   He is clene, so þat | [noo][2] synne may be founde in hym nor nothinge fowle, corrupt, nor changeable. He makyth hoote, nott as ma*t*eriall fyre, nore as the visible sonne, þat melteth thing*es* ; bot his hete is the inwarde born-yng love of the sowle and a desyre fullfyllynge and swelowynge the sowle in-to God.   He is also swete to the sowle nott as desiderable welth, luste, or any sych wordely thinge ; bot that swettnes of the sprete is vnlykely to all temp*er*all swettnes and the vnthinkable to all hem that neu*er* sau*er*ed it.   Third, þat spirite is so clene as the bem*es* of the sonne, wher-in may be founde no spott.

The secunde spirett, þat is, a spirite made, hath also iij thing*es* : for he is brennyng, he is bytt*er*, and he is vnclene. Fyrst, he is brynnyng and wastyng as fyr.   For þe sowle þat he hath in possessyon, he brennyth all wyth the fyre of lecherye and of wyked desyr ; so that þe sowle may ryght noȝt think ne desyr bot the fullfylly[ng][3] þer-of ; so mych, þat some tyme tem-perall lyfe and all worshipp and comfort is loste þer-by.   Secund, he is bitter as the gall ; for he enflaumeth the sowle w*ith* his delectac*i*on, þat þe Ioyes þat ar to come seme to hem right nought, and endeles good*es* seme to him folye ; and all thyng*es* þat ar of God and that he oweth to do to God ar bitt*er* to him and abhorable, as if it wer a vomyte or gall.   Thirde, he is vnclene ; for he maketh the sowle so vile & redy to syn þat he is ashamed of no synne, ne he shulde leve noo synne, bot if he dred mor shame of man then of God.   And this spirite is brynnyng as fyre ; for he is brynnyng in him-selfe vn-to wykednes & so

fol. 36 b brynneth oþer w*ith* him.   And he is bytt*er* ; for all goode is bitt*er* to him, and he makyth oþer bytt*er* w*ith* him.   And he |

---

[1] MS. vn [made] *cancelled.*   [2] *Latin* nullum.

[3] MS. fully filly.   *See Notes.*

is unclene ; for he delyte[t]h ¹ him in vnclenes, and he sekyth
to haue oþer lyke to him.

Bot now þu myght aske & say to me : art nott þu a spirite
made as he is ? Why arte þu þer-for [nott] ² sych on as he is ?
I vnswer : for-soth, I am made of the same God þat he is ; for
þer is bot on God, fader and sonne and holy goste, and they ar
not iij Goddes bott on God. And we both wer well made and
to a good ende, for God made neuer ryght noght bot goode.
Bot I am as a sterr, for I stode in the goodenes and cherite of
God, where-in I was made ; and he is as a ded coole, for he
wente from the cherite of God. Þer-fore as a sterr is not with-
outen bryghtnes and shynnyng, and a coole is nott with-oute
blakenes ; so a good angell, þat is, a sterr, is neuer with-oute
lyghtnes, þat is to say, the holy goste. For all þat he hath he
has of God, þat is, fader and sonne & holy goste, by hos love
he is hote and by hos shynyng he is bryght. And to him he
cleveth besyly and conformeth him to his wyll, and for he
wyll neuer ony thinges bot as God wyll ; & þer-for he is hote and
clene. Bot the devell is so fowle blak coole and mor fowll then
all creatures. For as [he] was mor fayr þan oþer, so muste
he be fowler þen oþer ; for he was contrarie to his maker.
And as the angell of God shyneth with-oute sesyng by the lyght
of God & brynnyth in the lyght of his cherite, ryght so þe fend
brynneth and is aungwesshed in hys malyce. & as his malice
may neuer be fylled, so þe goodenes of þe spirite of God and
the grace of God ar vn-spekable ; for þer is non so rotted with
the fende bott that the goode spirite some tyme vysetes and
stirreth his | herte. So is þer also non so goode in erth bot þat fol. 37 a
þe fende is besy gladely to toch him with temptacion. For þer
ar mony good and ryghtfull þat ar tempted of the fende be þe
suffrance of God. Bot þat is not for her harme, bot to þe more
glorie. For þe sonne of Godd, þat is on in godhed with the
fader and the holy goste, was tempted in his manhod. How
mych rather his chosen muste be tempted to her more reward.
Þer ar also mony goode folke þat some tyme fall in-to synne ;
and her conscience is derked be falsehed of the fende ; bot by
verteu of the holy goste, they rise mor myghtly and stonde
more strongely. Neuer-the-lesse, þer is non bott he vnder-

---

¹ MS. delyteh.   ² *Latin* non.

stondeth in his conscience wheþer the suggestyon of the fende
leede to the fylth of synne or to goode, if he wyll besyly thinke
and examyn it. Þer-fore, þu spowse of my lorde, haste nott for
to dowte of the spirite of thy thoughtes, wheþer it be good or
evyll ; for thy conscience telleth the which thynges ar to be
lefte and which to be do. Bot what shall he do with whom the
fende is full ? For þe goode spirite may nott enter in him, for
he is full of the evyll spirite. iij thinges aweth he to do. Fyrst,
that he haue pure and hole confessyon of hys synnes which,
þof it may not be a-non in a contrite [1] herte for herdenes of
herte, ȝett for that confessyon þe fende yeveth stede to the
good spirite and a maner of sesyng and skyppyng away.
Secunde, he muste haue mekenes, þat he purpose to amende
the synnes which he hath don. Thrid, to thentent þat he gett
ayayn þe good | sprite, he oweth to praye God with meke prayer
and to be contrite for his synnes þat he hath do with verrey
cherite. For cherite to God fleeth the devell ; for he had leuer
die an hundreth tymes þan a man shuld yeve the leste goode of
cherite to his God, so envyous and malycyus he is.

After this spake þe blessed virgyn our lady to the spowse of
Cryste seynte Birgitt and seyd : thu new spowse of my sonne,
cloth þe in his clothes and sett thin owch on thy breste ; þat
is, þe passion of my sonne.

Seynt Birgitte aunswerd : my lady, sett thu þat owch on my
breste.

Our lady seyde : þat wyll I doo. For-soth, I wyll telle the
how my sonne was disposed and why he was so fervently
desyred of holy faders. For he stode as a man be-twyx two
cytes ; þat is, heuen & hell. Oute of the fyrst cite cried a
woyse to him & sayde : 'Þu man þat stondeste in myde way
between the cites, þu art a wyse man and can be-war of perelles
þat fall. Þu arte stronge to suffer herde thinges þat þe betyde ;
and þu art myghty herted, for þu didest right noght.[2] We
haue desyred the and abydes the. Þer-fore open our ȝate, for
oure enmyse besege it þat it be nott opened.' Oute of the
secunde cite was herde a voyce, saying : 'Thu man moste man-
full and stronge, here our querell and weylyng. We sytt in

fol. 37 b

____
[1] MS. an vncontrite ; *Latin* contrito corde.
[2] *Latin adds* quia nihil times.

derkenes and we suffer hungur and thruste vnsufferable. Þer-
fore be-hold our wrechednes and our wreched pouerte.   For
we ar smyte as gresse þat is smyte with a syth ; and we ar
dried from all goode, and all our strenght fayleth.   Come to vs
5 and save vs ; for the onely we haue abyde, and the we hope to
be our delyverer.   Come and louse our pouerte and turne our
weyling in- | to Ioy.   Be þu our helpe and our helth.   O moste fol. 38 a
worthi and blessed body þat was bore of a pure virgyn, come.'
Those ij voyces herde my sonne oute of ij cites, heuen and hell ;
10 and þer-fore he was moved with mercy ; and by his moste
bitter passyon and ȝevyng oute of his blod, he opned the yate
of hell.   Thes thinges, my dowghter, thinke þu ; and haue hem
all way to-fore thyn eyn.

   After owr lady hade sende mony reuelaciones to a kyng,   Revela-
15 at laste she sente hym on and seyde þat it shuld be þe last tions,
letter that shuld be sente him.   Bott in this reuelacion BookVIII,
folowyng, our lady spekyth aȝayne to þe same kyng and Chap. 48.
declareth her fyrst sayng, & enformeth seynt Birgitt why
þe wordes of God ar spok so derkely þat they may haue
20 dyuerse vnderstondynges.   Here is also shewed þe blessed
trinite vnder lykenes of a pulpit; & of iij bemes of iij
dyuers colores ; & of þe dome of iij kynges, of which on
was olyve, ane oþer was in hell, & þe thirde in purgatorie.
Cap. xxij.

25   The moder of God speketh to þe[1] spowse and seth : doughter, I told the to-for þat that shuld be my laste letter þat
shulde be sente to the kynge, my frend ; that is to be vnderstonde of tho thinges that towches his syngler person and myn.
For if a man herde a profetable thinge song þat longed to his
30 frende, & he sat &[2] herde itt for to tell it to him, wheþer it
wer a songe of myrth or a letter of holsome blamyng, both he
þat endited it & he þat sounge it were worthy rewarde.   Ryght
so þe ryghtwysnes of God, demyng in evennesse and Iustyfyyng
in mercye, wyll synge ryghtwysnes and mercy.   And þer-fore
35 who euer wyll heer, heer he.   For | it is no letter of blamyng, fol. 38 b
bot a song of ryghtwosnes & cherite.   Some tyme when a letter
was sent one, it contened warnyng and blamyng ; for it blamed

---

   [1] MS. e *inserted above line.*   [2] MS. sat & *inserted above line.*

vnkyndenes of benefetez and warnde and stirred to conuersion
and amendynge of maneres. Bot now þe ryghtwysnes of God
syngeth a feyre songe, þat longeth vn-to all ho euer here it,
beleve it, & receyve it in werkyng, he shall fynde fruyte of
helth and fruyte of endeles lyffe.

   Bot þu myght aske why þe wordes of God ar sayde so derkely
þat they may be dyuersely vnderstounde & some tyme thay ar
oþer-wyse vnderstounde of God and oþer while of men. I
aunswer : God is like to a man þat makyth brynnyng wyne.
For this man hath mony pypes, some goynge vpp and some
don, by which the wyne rynneth now vp & now down be
wyrkyng of the hete of the fyre tyll it be made perfyte. Ryght
so doth God in his wordes, for some tyme he goth vppe be
rightwysnes, and some tyme he comyth down be mercye ; as it
is shewed in kynge Ysache, to whom, I say, þe profett seyde of 1
ryghtwysnes þat he shuld dye, and yet afterwarde mercye
addyd to him mony ʒeres to lyve. Some tyme also God comyth
dovn be simple shewynge of wordes be bodely expressynge, bot
he goth vp ayayn be spirituall vnderstondyng ; as it was in
Dauid, to whom mony thynges wer seyde vnder the name of 2
Salamon which wer vnderstonde & fullfylled in þe sonne of
God.   Some tyme also God spekes of thinges to come as it wer
of thinges paste, and towcheth both thinges presente and thinges
to com ; for all thynges, both present, paste, and to come, ar
in God as oo poynt. And þu owe not to mervell þof God speke 2
in dyuerse wyse, for it is do for iiij causes. Fyrst, þat God
shuld shew his grete mercye, þat no man herynge þe rightwysnes of God shulde dispeyr of his mercye. For when a man
chongeth þe wyll of synne, þen Gode chaunges þe strettenes of
hys sentence.   The secunde cause is þat they þat yeve fayth to 30
the ryghtwysnes and to the behestes of God shulde be crowned
& rewardede þe more largely for fayth and abydyng. The third
cause is for if the counsell of God wer know in certen tyme,
some shuld be gretely trobled be-fore, knowyng of contrarie
cases, and oþer for werynes shuld sesse of her feruour and 35
desyre. And þer-for when I write any wordes to ony, it is nott
expressed to the in þe conclusion wheþer tho wordes shall be
receyved & be beleved with effecte of him or noo.   Ne it is
declared to the wheþer he shall beleve and fullfyl the wordes

fol. 39 a

ine dede or no, for it is nott lefull to the to know it. The iij
cause is þat non shulde presume bodely to discusse þe wordes
of God, for he makyth him lowe þat is hyght, and of ane
one he makyth a secunde. The fourte cause is þat he þat
5 sekyth occasion to departe from God may fynde itt, and thay
that be fowle be mor fowle, and tho goode be made mor
know.

After this, þe sonne of God spake to saynte Birgitt and
seyde : yf a man spake be a pype þat hade iij howles, and seyde
10 to the herrer, þu shall neuer her my voyce be thys hole, he war
not to blame þof he spake afterwarde be the ij other hooles. So
it is now in our spech ; for þough the virgyn my moder sayde
þat shuld be þe laste letter to be sent to þe kynge, þat is to be
vnderstond | of his person. Bot now I God, þat am in the fol. 39 b
15 moder and moder in me, sende my messynger to the kynge, als
well for hem þat ar now present olyve as for hem þat ar nott
yett borne. For ryghtwysnes and mercye ar in God endelesse,
for eternally this rightwysnes was in God, þat whill God was
to-fore Lucyfer full of wysdom of gudenes and of power. He
20 wold þat mony shuld be pertyneres of his godenes. And þer-
fore he made angelles ; of which some, beholdyng here feyrenes,
desyred to be above God. & þer-for they fell and ar made vnder
þe feete of God wykked fendes. And yett in hem God in
a maner hath mercy ; for when the fende by the ryghtwysnes
25 and suffraunce of God fullfylleth the evell þat he desyrith, he
is as it wer in a maner comforted of the prosperyte of his malice.
Nott at the payne of the fende is lessned þer-bye ; bot as a
seeke man that hath an enmye moste stronge is comforted be
þe herynge of his deth, þof the peyne of his sekenes be nott
30 lessned be that heryng, ryght so the fende of Envye, wher-in
he is hote brynnyng, Ioyeth and is glad when God doth ryghtwysnes ayenst men ; for the thruste of his malyce is in maner
refresshed and esed. Bot after þe precypitacion of the fendes
God, seyng lake ine his oost, made man, þat he shuld obey to
35 his preceptes and brynge forth fruyte, tyll as many men and
women were ascended in-to heuen as angelles fell owte of
heuen. Þer-for man was made perfyte ; which, when he had
take þe comaundement of lyf, he toke no hede to Gode ne to his
worship. Bot consentyng to the suggestyon of the fende, he

F

fol. 40 a trespased, sayng, ' Ete we of the tree of lyffe, and we shall[1] | know
all thyng*es* goode and evell '.   Th[u]s [2] Adam and Eue wold nott
herme to God, as the fende ; noþ*er* they wold be above God, bot
they wold be wyse as God.   And the[y] [3] fell, bot not as the fende ;
for the feende hadd envye to God, and hys wrechednes shall neu*er* 5
have ende.   Bot man wold oþ*er* than God wolde he shuld wyll,
and þ*er*-fore he des*er*ued and suffered rightwysnes w*ith* m*er*cye.
Than felt they ryghtwosnesse when [4] they had nakednes for
clothyng of glorie and hung*er* for plente, styrryng of the flessh
for virginite, drede for seekernesse, and labor for reste.   Bot 10
anon they gate m*er*cye : þat is to say, clothynge aȝanste nakednes, mete ayanste hunger, sykernes of co*m*myng to-geder for
enc*re*syng [5] of man-kynde.   For-soth, Adam was of moste
honeste lyffe, in that he had neuer wyf bot Eue, ne oþ*er* woman
bot hyr allon.   Allso God hath shewed rightwysnes and mercy 15
i*n* bestes, for God hath made iij worthy thing*es* : fyrst, angell*es*
þat hath sprete bot no bodye ; secunde, manne þat hath sowle
and body ; thirde, best*es* þat hath body bot noo sowl*es* as man
hath.   Þ*er*-fore angell, because he is a spirit, he cleveth con-
tynualy to God and nedeth no man*n*es helpe.   Bot man, for 20
he is flesh, may not cleve contynually to God, tyll þe dedely
bodye be dep*ar*ted from the sowle.   And þ*er*-for, þat man may
lyfe, God hath made to his helpe vnresenable best*es* to obeye
and s*er*ue to his bett*er*.   And in thes vnresenable best*es* God
hath grete m*er*cye, for they haue no shame of her membres, 25
nor sorow of deth tyll it come.   And they ar content wyth
simple lyvelod.   Also aft*er* the flode of Noe was paste, God
dyd ryghtwosnes w*ith* m*er*cye.   For God myght haue browght
well ye peple of Isr*a*ell in-to the lond of beheste in shorte
fol. 40 b tyme.   Bot it | was ryght that the vesselles þat myght hold 30
beste drynk shuld fyrst be p*re*ued and purged and aft*er*-ward
halowed.   To whom allso God dyd grete m*er*cy, for by þe
prayer of one man*n*e, þat was Moyses, her synne was done
away & þe grace of God ȝeff.   On the same wyse, aft*er* myne
Incarnac*io*n, ryghtwysnes is neu*er* vsed w*ith*-owt m*er*cy ne 35
m*er*cy w*ith*-oute ryghtwysnes.

[1] know all *catchword*.   [2] MS. thes ; *Latin* scilicet.
[3] MS. ther ; *Latin* ceciderunt.   [4] MS. when when.
[5] MS. enc*re* syng.

Then sewed þer a voyce on hie, sayng : O moder of mercy,
moder of endeles kyng, purchase þu mercye ; for to the ar
comen thoo prayers and teres of thy seruant, the kynge.   We
know well þat right is þat his synnes be punyshed, bot gett þu
5 mercy þat he be conuerted & do pennaunce and wyrship to God.

Then aunswerd oure lorde Ihesu Cryst and sayde : þer is iiij
fold rightwysnes in God.   The fyrst is þat he þat is made and
is endelesse be worshiped above all thinges ; for of him and in
him ar all thinges lyve, and haue her beynge.   The secunde
10 rightwysnes is þat to him þat euer was and is and was temper-
ally bore, in tyme afore ordened, be do seruice of all ; & for þat
he be loved in all clannesse.   The thirde rightwysnes is that
he þat of himselfe may not suffer bot of hys manhode was
made able to suffer ; and in the dedelynesse þat he toke hath
15 deserued to man vndedlenesse, be desyred to man above all
thinges þat may be desyred or ar to be desyred.   The fourte
rightwysnes is þat they þat ar vnstable do seeke verrey stable-
nes, and they thar in de[r]kenes[1] desir lyght, þat is, the holy
goste, askyng his helpe with contricion and verrey mekenes.
20 Bot of this kyng, þe seruante of my moder, for whom mercye is
now asked, rightwysnes seyth þat his tyme is nott | sufficiante fol. 41 a
to purge worthely, as rightwysnes askyth, the synnes that
he hath doo ayenste þe mercye of God, ne his body myght
nott suffer the payn þat he hath deserued for his synnes.
25 Neuerthelesse þe mercye of the moder of God hath deserued
and gatt mercye for the same, hir seruant, þat he shall her what
he hath doo and how he may amende him, yf he wyll in
happes be compuncte and conuerted.

Then anon, sayth seynte Birgitt, I see in heven a howse of
30 mervelouse fayrenes and grettenes.   And in þat howse was
a pulpite, and in the pulpite a booke.   And I see ij stondynge
to-for the pulpite ; þat is to say, an angell and the feende.

Of which þe on, þat is, the feende, spake and seyde : my
name, he sayth, is Waylleway.[2]   For this angell & I folow oo
35 thing þat is desiderable to vs ; for we see þe lorde moste
myghty purposeth to byld a grete thing.   And þer-for we
labour ; the angell to perfeccion of the thinge, and I to destruc-
cion of þe same.   Bot it happith þat when þat desiderable

---

[1] MS. dekenes ; *Latin* tenebris.   [2] *Latin* heu.

thing comyth some tyme in-to my hond*es*, it is so fervent and hote þat I may nott hold it; and when it comyth in-to þe hond*es* of the angell, it is so cold and sliper þat anon it slydeth oute of his hond*es*.

And when I, sayth seynt Birgitt, beheld*e* besyly wyth all consideraci*on* of my mynd vn-to the same pulpite, myne vnderstondyng suffyced nott to conceyve it as it was, ne my sowle myght nott compr*e*hende þe fayrenes þ*er*-of, ne my tonge expr*e*sse itt. For the apering of the pulpite was as it had be the sonnebeme, hauyng a red colour and a white colo*ur* and a shynyng colo*ur*[1] | of gold. The golden colo*ur* was as the bryght sonne. The white colour was as snow, most whyte. And the rede colour was as a roose. And yche colowr was see in oþ*er*. For when I beheld the gold colowr, I see þ*er*-wyth the white and the redde colowr. And when I see the white colowr, I see þ*er*-in þe oþ*er* two colowres. And when I byheld the rede colo*ur*, I see þ*er*-in the white and the golden colo*ur*. So that ych colo*ur* was see in oþ*er*, and ȝett ych was distincte from oþ*er* and by it-self; and no colo*ur* was to-fore oþ*er*, ne after oþ*er*, none lasse þan oþ*er*, nor mor than oþ*er*; bot ou*er* all and in all thing*es* they semed even. And when I loked vpwarde, I myght not compr*e*hende þe lenghth and the brede of the pulpyte; and lokyng downwarde, I myȝt nott see ne compr*e*hende þe grettenes ne þe depnes of it, for all was incompr*e*[hen]sible[2] to be consydered. After this I see a bok in the same pulpite, shynyng as gold moste bryght, þat had the shap of a boke. Which boke, and the scriptur þer-of, was not write w*ith* ynke, bot ych worde in the boke was qwhik and spak it-self, as yf a man shuld say, doo thys or that, and anone it wer do w*ith* spekyng of the word. No man redde the scriptur of that boke, bot what euer that scriptur contened, all was see in the pulpyte and in the iij colo*urs*. To-fore þis pulpite I see a kynge þat was o-lyve in the werld; and on the lyft syde of the pulpite I se a noþer kyng þat was dede and in hell; and on þe right syde of the pulpyte I se the iij kynge that was in purgatorie. The sayde kynge þat was o-lyf satt crowned as it had be in a vessell of | glasse close abowte. Above that glasse hange an horrible swerde w*ith* iij egges, neyghyng contynually

fol. 41 b

fol. 42 a

---

[1] e ij.　　　　　　　[2] *Latin* incomprehensibilia.

to þat glasse as a dyall in ane orelege neghith to his merke. On
the ryght syde of the same kynge stode an angell that had
a vessell of gold and his lapp open. And on his lefte syde
stoode a fende þat had a peyr of tounges and an hommer. And
boþe þe angell and þe feend stroffe wheþer of her hondes shuld
be mor ner the vessell of glasse when the iij egged swerde
shuld touch it and breke it.

Than herde I an horrible voyce of the fende, saynge : how
longe shall it be thus? For we both folow oo praye, and we
wot not who shall ouer-come.

Then anon þe ryghtwysnes of God spake to me and seyd :
thes thinges þat ar shewed to the ar not bodely bot gostely.
For neþer angell nor fende hath bodies ; bot they ar shewed to
the in sych wyse, for þu maiste not vnderstonde gostely thinges
bot by bodely lykenes. This lyving kynge aperyth to the as it
wer a vessel of glasse, for his liff is bot as it wer frele glasse
and sodenly to be ended, þe iij egged swerde is deth, for when
it comyth it doth iij thinges. It febleth the body, it chongeth
the conscience, & it fleeth all strengthes, departyng as a swerd
þe sowle from the body. That the angell and the fende seme
to stryve abowte the glasse betokeneth þat eyther of hem
desyrith to haue the kynges sowll, þat shall be demed to him
to whos consell he is more obedyent. That the angell hath
a vessell [1] | and a lapp betokeneth þat right as a child resteth fol. 42 b
in þe moder lappe, so laboreth þe angell þat the soule be presented to God as it wer in a vessell and reste in the lappe of
endeles comforte. Þat the fende hath tonges and a hammer
betokeneth that the fende draweth the sowle to him with the
tonges of wykked delyte & brekyth it asonder with þe hammer ;
þat is, with the consente and doyng of synne. That the vessell
of glas is some tyme [2] ouer hote and some tyme ouer cold and
slyper betokeneth þe inconstance and unstablenes of the kynge ;
for when he is in temptacion he thinkyth thus : þof I know
well þat I offende God, if I fullfyll now þe conceyte of my
herte, ȝett a[t] [3] this tyme I shall fullfille my conceyte in dede.
And so wyttyngly he synneth aȝanst his God, for he synneth
so wyttyngly he cometh in-to the hondes of the fende. After-

---

[1] e iij.   [2] MS. is some tyme is some tyme.
[3] MS. as ; *Latin* ista vici.

ward þe kynge takyth to him confession and contricion, & so
he ascapeth þe hondes of the fende and comyth in-to þe power
of the goode angell. And þer-for, bot if the kyng lefe his
inconstance, he stondeth full perlously, for he hath a feble
gronde.   5

After this I see on þe left syde of the pulpite þe dede kynge
þat was dampned in-to hell cledde in kyngely araye and
syttyng as it hadde be in a trone. Bot he was dede and pale
and ryght ferefull to loke on. To-fore his face was as it had
be a whele þat had iiij lynes in the ottmeste partye; and this   1
whele torned abowte att brething and blowyng of the kynge.
And ych of the iiij lynes ȝede vpwarde and donwarde as the
kynge wold, for þe mevyng of the whele was in the kynges |
power. The thre lynes wer wretyn bot in the fourte lyne was
writen right noght. On the right syde of this kynge I see an 1
angell as it had be a man most feyr, whos hondes wer voyde;
bot he serued to the pulpytt. On the lefte syde of the kynge
appered a fende whos hede was lyke to a dogg; his wombe
myght nott be fylled, his navyll was open and boyled out
venym, colowred with all maner of venemouse colours. And 2
in ych fote he hade iij clawes, grete, stronge, and sharpe.

Then was þer one þat shone mor bryght then the sonne,
that for bryghtnes was mervelouse to be-hold. And he seyde
vn-to me: This kynge whom þu seest is full of wrechednes,
whos conscience is now shewed to the as he was in his kyng- 2
dom, and whatt entent he was in when he dyed. Whatt hys
consciens was or he come to his kyngdome longeth nott to the
to know. Neuer-þe-lesse, know þu þat his sowle is nott to-for
thyne eyn, bot his conscience. And for the sowle & þe fende
ar nott bodely bot gostely, þer-fore þe fendes temptacions & 3
tormentes ar shewed to the [be]¹ bodely lykenes.

Tha[n]² onone þat dede kynge began to speke, not of his
mouth, bot as it had be of his brayne, and seyde thus: O ȝe my
conselleres, this is myn entent, that what euer is suggett to
the crown of my realme, I wyll hold it and kepe it. I wyll 3
also labor that the thinges þat I haue be encresed and nott
lessed. Bot in what wyse thoo thinges wer gote, þat I hold,

---

¹ *Latin* per similitudines corporales.
² MS. that; *Latin* et statim ille Rex.

what is it to me to aske? It is I-neught to me if I may
defende and encrese tho thing*es* þat I haue.

Then cried the fende and seyde: lo, it is thorowght. What
shall my hoke do?

5 Ryghtwysnes aunswerde oute of the boke that was in the
pulpite, saynge to the fende; [1] | pot*t* in thy hoke in the hoole fol. 43 b
& drawe to the.

And a-non as the worde of ryghtwysnes was spoke, þe hoke
was putt ine. Bot þer-wi*th* in the same moment come to-for
10 the kynge an hammer of m*er*cye w*ith* which the kyng myght
haue smyte away the hooke, if he wold have inquired the
trowght of all thing*es* and fruytefully haue chaunged his wyll.

Then spak the same kynge ayane and seyde: O my conselleres and my men, ye haue me to be yo*ur* lorde, & I haue take
15 yow to be my consellers. þer-fore I tell yow þat þer is a man
in my realme þat is a treyto*ur* of my wyrship and of my lyf,
þat lyeth in wayte to hinder my realme and to distrowble peese
and the comyn peple of the realme. In this, seyth the kynge,
þer yave credence to me both lerned and lewed, both lordes
20 and comyn peple, belevyng the wordes þat I seyde to hem, in
so mych þat þat man þat I defamed of treson toke grete herme
and shame, and sentence of exile was yeve ayanste him.
Neu*er*-the-lesse, my conscyenc*e* wyste well what þe trowth was
in all this dede, and I wyst well þat I seyde mony thinges
25 ayanste þat man for ambic*io*n of the kyngdom and for the
drede of lesyng þer-of, and that my wyrship shulde be spred
a-brode, & þat þe realme shuld cleve mor suerly to me and to
my successores. I thought also in myselfe þat þought I knew
þe trowth how this kyngdom is goten, and what wronge is don
30 vn-to him, yett if I receyve him aȝayn to my grace and | tell fol. 44 a
the trowth, then all þe rep*re*ve and herme shall fall apon my-
selfe. And þer-for I sett me suerly in myne herte þat I wold
rather die then tell the trowth or revoke myn vnryghtfull
wordes and dedes.

35 Then seyde the fende: O Juge, loo, how this kyng ȝeveth
me his tonge.

The rightwysnes of God aunswered: put þer-on thy snare.
And when the fende had don so, anone þer hounge to-fore the

[1] e iiij.

kynges mouth an irne most sharpe, wher-wi*th* he myght if he
had wolde haue kutt away the snare and all-to haue broke it.

Then spake þe same kynge and seyde : O my conselleres,
I haue concelled wi*th* clerk*es* and lettred men of þe state of the
realme, and they sey to me þ*at* yf I shuld resigne the realme 5
in-to oþ*er* menn*es* hond*es* I shuld do herme to mony, and be
a treyto*ur* of her lyves and godes and breker of the law of
ryghtwysnes ; and þ*er*-for þ*at* I myght kepe þe kyngdom &
defende it from enmys, vs be-hoves to thinke and ymagyn some
new thing*es*, for the old rent*es* of the escheker ar not suffy- 10
ciaunte to gou*er*nen and to defende þe realme.   And thus I by-
thought [1] me of new imposici*ones* of tributes and of gylefull
exacci*ones* to be putt in the realme, both to herme of hem
dwellyng þ*er*-in & of innocent peple þ*at* went by the way and
of marchauntes.   And in thes Inuenci*ones* I purposed to abyde 15
to my deth, al-though my conscience told me þ*at* they were
ayanst God, ayanest all ryghtwysnes, and ayanst comyn
honeste.

Then criede the fende and seyde : O Juge, loo, this kyng hath
fol. 44 b bowed both his hond*es* vn[der] [2] my | vessell of wat*er*.   What 20
shall I do ?

Ryghtwysnes aunswerd oute of the booke : putt thy venem
þ*er*-apon.   And anon as the venem of the fende was putt apon
his hondes, þ*er* come to-fore þe kyng a wessell of oyntement
wher-wi*th* the kynge myght well haue refreyned þ*at* venym.   25

Then the fende cried owte strongely and seyde : loo, I see
a mervelouse thinge þ*at* passeth my wytt to vnderstonde.   For
my hoke is putt to the herte of the kynge, and anon þ*er* is yeve
him an hammer in his bosn.   My snare is putt to his mowth,
and þ*er* is offred him an irne moste sharpe.   My venym is 30
powred apon his hond*es*, and þ*er* is yeve him a vessell of oyntement.

Ryghtwysnes aunswerde oute of the boke of the pulpite and
sayde : all thing*es* haue tyme ; and mercye and ryghtwysnes
shall met*e* to-geder.   35

Aft*er* this the moder of God spake to me and seyde : come,
doughte*r*, and heer & see what the good sprete styrreth to, and
whatt the evell ; for eu*er*y man hath infuci*ones* and visitaci*ones*,

---

[1] MS. by thought.   [2] MS. vn ; *Latin* sub.

some tyme of the good spirite and some tyme of the evell.
For þer is not bot þat he is visitted of [God]¹ longe as he
leveth.

And anon þer appered ayane þe same dede kynge, whos
5 sowle þe holy goste enspired while he lyved in this wyse: O
frende, þu owest to serue God with all thy strenghthes, for he
[y]aue² lyff, conscience and vnderstondyng, helth and wyrship ;
and yett he suffreth the in thy synnes.

The kynges conscience aunswerd, spekynge by a lykenes : it
10 is trew, he sayth, þat I am hold to serue God, be hos power I
am made and bowght, and hos mercy I lyfe and haue my
beyng.

Bot her ayaynste the wyked sprete styrred the kyng and
sayd : Broþer, I ȝeve þe good consell. Doth as he doth þat
15 paryth ane apple | for þe parynges, and the coor he casteth fol. 45 a
away, & þe pyght and the beste he kepeth to him-selfe. So do
þu. God is meke and mercyfull and pacyente and nedeth nothing. Þer-fore yeve him of thy goodes such as þu maste esely
forber, and oþer goodes þat ar mor profitable and desiderable
20 kepe to thy-self. Do also what þe lyste after thy flesh, for it
may lyghtly be amendett. And þat þat þe lyste nott to do,
þough þu be bounde to do it, lefe it ; and in-stede þer-of yeve
almes. For þer-by may mony be comforted.

The kynges conscience aunswerd : this, he sayth, is a pro-
25 fetable consell. For I may yeve some thinges þat I haue with-
oute any grete harme to me, and yett God settyth right mych
þer-by. And oþer thinges I shall kepe to myn own vse & for to
gete me þer-wyth frenshipe of mony oþer.

After this þat good angell þat was yeve to kepe the kynge
30 spake vn-to him by inspiraciones, sayng : O þu frende, thinke
þat þu, dedely, shall dye. Thinke also that this lyff is shorte
and God is a ryghtfull and pacyent Juge þat examineth all thy
thoughtes, wordes, and dedes from the begynnyng of thyn
vnderstondyng age un-to the ende, which also demeth all thy
35 wylles & ententes and leveth right noght vndyscussed. Þer-
for vse thy tyme and thy strenghthes resonably and gouerne
thy membres to the profett of thy sowle. Lyve sobrely, not

---

¹ *Latin* a Deo.   ² MS. haue ; *Latin* dedit tibi.

fullfyllynge the luste of thy flesh in desyres, for they þat lyven after the flesh and after her own wyll shall not come to the kyngdom of God.

Bot her ayayne anon þe fende wyth his suggestyones stired þe kynge and sayde: O þu broþer, | yf þu shalt yeve a reken-ynge to God of all thy tymes and momentes, whan shalt þu than Ioy? Bot here my consell. God is mercyfull and may esely be plesed, for he had nott bowght the if he wold haue lost the. Ther-for the scriptur of God sayth þat all synnes ar foryeve be contricion. Do þu þer-for as dyd he þat aught an-oþer xx pounde of gold. And when he had nott wher-of to pay, he come to his frende and asked him consell. And he conseled him to take xx pound of copur and gilt hit with oo pound of gold, and with þat gilte mony pay his creditour. & he dide after þe consell I-yeve him & payde his creditour xx pounde of coper ouer gylte ; & xix pounds of pure gold he kepte to him-self. So do þu. Spende xix howres to thy delyte, luste, and Ioy ; and on howr is suffyciante for the to be sory and compuncte for thy synnes. Þer-fore do þat delyteth the both a-fore [& after] ¹ confession ; for as coper þat is gylt semeth gold, so þe werkes of synne þat ar betokened in coper, when they ar ouer gylte with contricion, shall be do away, and all thi werkes shall shyne as golde.

Then aunswerd þe kynges conscyence : this consell semeth to me delectable and resonable. For if I do thus I shall mowe dispose all my tymes to myne own Ioy.

The good angell spake ayayn to the kyng be his enspira-ciones, saynge : O frende, thinke fyrst with what mastre God browght the oute of the streyte wombe of thy moder. Secunde, thenke with how grete pacyence God suffreth the to lyfe. Thirde, thinke with how grete bytternes God hath bowght the from endeles deth.

fol. 46 a   Bot ayane-ward | the fende styrrede the kynge, sayng : O brother, if God haue browght the oute of the streyte wombe of thy moder in-to the brede of the world, thenke also þat he shall lede þe ayayn oute of the world be herde deth. And yf God suffer the to lyff longe, thinke also þat þu hast in thy lyff

¹ *Latin* audacter ergo ante, & post confessionem. *Note that* audacter *is omitted in translation also.*

fol. 45 b

mony dyseses and tribulaciones ayanste thy wyll. Yf God
haue bought the with his herde deth, hoo compelled him?
Praydeste þu him?

Than the kynge aunswerd as it had be by spekyg with-in in
5 his conscyence: it is trew, he sayth, þat þu sayste. For I
sorowe more þat I shall die þan þat I was bore of my moderys
wombe. It is also more grevouse to me to bere the aduersites
of the world and tho thinges þat ar contrarie to my wyll þan
any oþer thing. For I wold, and I myght chese, rather to lyve
10 in the world with-oute tribulacion and to abyde in comforte
þer-of, than to be departed from the werld. And rather I wold
desyre to haue endelesse lyff in the werld with wordely felycite
þan þat Cryst had bowght me with hys blode. And I rowght
nott [þ]of¹ I come neuer in heuen, if I myght haue the werld
15 at my wyll in erth.

Then herde I a word oute of the pulpyte, sayng thus: take
now away from þe kynge þe vesell of oyntement. For he hath
synned in God the fader. For God the fader þat is endeles in
the sonne and in the holy goste ȝaffe a trew and a ryght law be
20 Moyses. Bot this kyng hath made an evell and a contrarie
lawe. Neuer-the-lesse, for this kyng hath done some goode² | fol. 46 b
dedes, all though he dyd hem nott with good entent, þer-fore he
shall be suffered to haue possession of the kyngdom whill he
lyveth, and so be rewarded in the world. Secunde tyme the
25 worde spake oute of the pulpite and sayde thus: bere a-way
the most sharpe Irne from this kynges eyn. For he hath
synned ayanste þe sonne. For he sayde³ in his new lawe that
doome shall be do wyth-oute mercy to him þat doth no mercye.
Bot this kynge wold not do mercy to him þat was vnryght-
30 wysly vexed ne amende his errour ne chaunge his evyll wyll.
Neuer-the-lesse, for some good dedes þat he hath doo, be it
yeve to him for reward þat he haue wordes of wysdom in his
mowth and þat he be hold wyse of mych peple. The thirde
tyme the worde of ryghtwysnes spake owte of the pulpite and
35 sayde: the hammer be take awey from the kynge, for he hath
synned in the holy goste. For the holy goste foryeveth synnes
to all repentaunte, bot this kynge purposeth to persuer in his

¹ MS. of.　　　　　² MS. some good | some good.
³ MS. for he sayde for he sayde.

synne vn-to the ende. Neuer-þe-lesse, for he hath do some
goode dedes, þer-for þat thing be yeve to him þat he desyreth
moste to the delyte of his body, þat is, þat woman which he
desyrith to be his wyfe, þe delyte of his eyn, and þat he haue
a fayr and desyderable ende after þat werld.   5

After this,[1] when þe ende of his lyff neghed, the fende cryed
and sayde : loo, the vessell of oyntement is bore a-way.   þer-
for shall I now make his hondes hevy, þat he shall do no fruyte-
fol. 47 a full goodes. And anon as the worde of the fende | was seyde,
þe kynge was prived of his strenghth & heleth. And then anon 10
the fende cryed and sayde : loo, the sharpe Irne is take away ;
þer-for I shall aggrege my snare apon him.

And anon the kynge was prived of hys spech. And in þe
poynte of hys priuacion, ryghtwysnes spake to the good angell
that was yove to the kyng to be his keper, and seyde : seeke in 15
the whele and see what lyne þer-of goth vpwarde, and rede the
scriptur þer-of.

The angell loked and the fowrte lyne yode vpwarde, wher-in
was ryght not wryte, bott all it had be rased. Then seyde
ryghtwysnes : for this sowle hath l[o]ved [2] þat is voyde, þer- 20
fore go he now to the delyte of his rewarde. And anon the
sowle of the kynge was departed from the bodye.

And anon as the sowle was gon owte, the fende cried and
sayde : now shall I brek and all-to rente þe herte of this kyng,
for I haue his sowle in possession.   25

And then I see how the kynge was all chaunged fro the
toppe of the hede vn-to the sowle of the foote, and he semed
horrible as a beste all flayn. His eyn wer oute and his flesh
all clobbed to-geder. Then his voyce was herde, saynge : wo
vn-to me, for I am made blynde as a whelpe þat is bor blynde, 30
sekynge the hynder partyes of the moder. For be myn vnkyndenes I se nott the moderes tetis. Woo vn-to me, for I see
fol. 47 b in my blyndenes þat I shall neuer see God, for my con- | scyence
vnderstondeth now fro whens I am fall, and what I awght to
haue do and dyd nott. Wo vn-to me, for by the providence of 35
God I was bore in-to the werld and bore ayane be baptem. And
yett I was neclygent and foryett God. And for I wold not
drynke of the mylke of the swettenes of God, þer-for I am now

mor lyke to a blynde dogge þan to a whyke and a seyng chyld.
Bot now ayanest my wyll, þowgh I wer a kynge, I am compelled to sey trowth.   For I was bound as it had be wit*h* thre
ropes for to s*er*ue God : þat is to say, for baptem, for wedloke,
5 and for the crown of kyngdom.   Bot the fyrst I dispised when
I turned myn affecc*io*n and wyll to the vanyte of the world.
To the secunde I toke non hede when I desyrede a-noþ*er*
mann*es* wyff.   The thrid I dispised when I was prowde of
erthely power and thought not of the power of heuen.   Þer-
10 fore, þough I be now blynde, I se in my conscience þat for the
contempte of my baptem I owe to be bounde to the hatefullnes
of the fende.   And for the inordinate sturryng of the flesh I
owe to suffer þe fendes luste.   And for my pride I owe to be
bounde to the fendes feet.
15   Then aunswerde the fende : O brother, now it is tyme þat I
speke and wit*h* my spekyng I shall wyrke.   Therfore come vn-
to me, nott wit*h* cherite bot wit*h* hate ; for I was fayrest of
angell*es*, and þu wer a dedely man.   & God most myghty [1] | fol. 48 a
yave me fre chose my wyll.   Bot for I meved it vnordynately
20 and wold rather hate God and passe him in wyrship than love
him, þer-fore I fell as he þat hath his hed downward and his
feet vpwerd.   Bot þu, as ych oþ*er* man, wer made aft*er* my fall
and gatteste a specyall p*r*euelege above me, in as mych as þu
wer bowght wit*h* the blode of the sonne of God.   Þer-fore, for
25 þu haste despised the cherite of God, turne thine hede to my
feete and I shall take thine feet in-to my mowth ; and so be we
Ionede to-geder as they ar wher the one hath a swerde in the
oþ*er*s herte, and the other hath a knyffe in his maly[t]e. [2]   And
for I had an hedde, þat is to sey, vnderstondyng, to wyrship
30 God if I had wold, and þu haddeste feete, that is to sey,
strenghth to goo to God and wold nott, þer-fore my fyerye hede
shall waste thy cold feete, and þu shall be deuored wyth-oute
cesynge, bot not consumed, for þu shalt be reveved ayane to
the same.   Ioyne we vs also to-geder wyth iij ropis, of which
35 the fyrst shall be in the myddes, wit*h* which þi navell and myn
shall be bounde to-geder : so þat when I breth, þu draw my
venym in-to the, and when þu bretheste, I shall drawe thyne

---

[1] ȝaffe me, *catchword.*
[2] MS. malyce ; *Latin* cultrum in visceribus alterius.   *See Glossary.*

entrell*es* in-to me. And worthily, for þu loveste more thy-selfe than thine ayane-byar, as I loved more my-selfe than my maker. Thy hede shal be bounde to my feete w*ith* the secund rope, and wyth the thrid rope my hede shall be bounde to thy feete.   5

After this, I see the same fende hauyng iij sharpe clawes in fol. 48 b ych fote, saynge to the kyng : [1] | for þu, brother, hadeste eyn to see the way of lyf and conscience to discerne be-twyx good and evell, þer-fore my two clawes shall enter and thirlle thyn eyn ; and þe thrid clawe shall enter thy brayne, w*ith* which þu 1 shalt be so strangled þ*at* þu shall be all vnder my feete. For þu wer made to haue be my lord, and I the stole of thy fote. Thu haddest also þoo erres to here the way of lyf, and a mowth to speke þe pr*o*fett [2] of thy sowle. Bot for þu hast dispised to here and speke the helth of thi [sowle],[3] ther-fore ij clawes of 1 myn oþ*er* foote shall enter in-to thyn eres, and the thrid in-to thy mowth, wher-in þu shalt be so tormented þ*at* all thing*es* shall be to the moste bitt*er* þ*at* semede to the before moste swete, when þu offendeste God.

When thes thing*es* wer sayde, anon the hedde and the feete 2 and the navell of the kynge wer Ioyned in maner for-sayde w*ith* þe heed & feete and navell of the fende, and so both bounde to-geder fell dovn in-to hell.

And then herde I a voyce, saynge : O, O, what hath the kynge now of all his riches ? Certenly no thinge bot herme. And 2 what has he now of all hys wyrshipp ? Certes, nott bot shame. And what hath he now of his couetyse, by which he desyred so mych þe kyngdom ? For-soth, right not bot payn. For he was anou*n*ted w*ith* holy oyle and sacrede w*ith* holy wordes and crowned w*ith* kynges crowne, þ*at* he shuld worship þe word*es* 3 and dedes of God, and defende and gou*er*ne the peple of God, know him-selfe vnd*er* þe feete of God, and God his rewarder. Bot he despised to be vncer þe feete of God ; þer-fore he is now fol. 49 a vnder þe feet | of the fende. And for he wold not bye ayane his tyme w*ith* fruytefull werk*es* while he myght, þer-fore from 3 hens-forth he shall haue no fruyte-full tyme.

After this spake ryghtwysnes oute of the boke þat was in the pulpite, saynge to me : all thes thing*es* þat ar thus seriosly

_____
[1] f j.   [2] MS. propfett.   [3] *Latin* animae.

shewed ar do anenste God in a poynte. Bot for þu arte bodely,
þer-fore it is nedefull þat sp[irit]uell [1] thing*es* be shewed vn-to
the [throwgh] [2] bodely lykenes. For þat þe kyng and þe angell
and the fende semede to speke to-ged*er* is no thinge elles but
inspiraci*o*nes of the good & evell sprite made be hem to the
sowle of the kyng, or by hys concellores or frend*es*. That the
fende cried and sayde, 'It is trowth,' it is to mene þat when
the kynge seyde þat he wold hold and kepe all that longeth to
the crowne, how euer it wer I-gott, and nott to reke of ryghtwysnes, then the kyng*es* conscience was thrilled throwgh w*ith*
the irne of the fende, þat is to say, w*ith* the hardnes of synne,
when he wold nott speke and dyscusse which wer tho thing*es*
þat longed rightfully to þe realme, and which nott, and when
he rought nott to examyn what ryght he hadde to the crown.

And then was the hoke pot to þe kyng*es* sowle, when the
fend*es* temptaci*o*n pr*e*valed so mych in his sowle þat he wold
abyde in his vnryghtwysnes vn-to þe deth. Bot þat þer come
an hammer to the kyng*es* bosn aft*er* the hoke, betokeneth tyme
of contrici*o*n yeve to the kynge ; for if the kynge hade had
sych a thought, saynge : 'I haue synned ; I wyll no lenger
wittyngly hold evell goten goodes, bot I wyll amend | me from fol. 49 b
hens-furth,' anon the hoke of ryghtwysnes had be broke w*ith*
the hammer of contrici*o*n, and the kynge had comen to good
lyf and good way. That the fende cryed, 'loo, the kyng ȝeveth
me his tonge,' and anon the snar was putt þer-apon, was
when the kynge wold. not do grace to the man þat he had
defrauded. Þat is thus to vnderstonde, þat who eu*er* wyttyngly [3]
blameth and deffameth his neghtbor for to encrese his own
fame, he is gov*er*ned w*ith* the sprete of the fende, and to be
snared w*ith* a snare of a thefe.

Bot that þer come a sharpe irn to-fore the kyng aft*er* the
snar betokeneth the tyme of chongyng & of correcci*o*n of his
wyll and werke. For when a man corre[c]teth [4] his trespase
w*ith* amendement and with good wyll, sych wyll is an irne
moste sharp, wher-w*ith* the snare of the fende is kytt I-sonder
and remyssyon of synne is gotte. Ther-for if this kynge had

---

[1] MS. spuell ; *abbreviation mark omitted.*
[2] *Latin* tibi per corporales similitudines.
[3] MS. witttyngly.   [4] MS. corretteth.

chonged hys wyll and done grace to the man þat hadde wronge
and was sclandered, anon þe snare of the fende hadde be kytt
away. Bot for he formed his wyll in evell purpose, þer-fore the
rightwysnes of God was þat he shuld be mor harder in synne.
And þat when the kynge thought to pott newe exacciones of
tributes in his realme, þu see venym powred apon his hondes,
betokeneth þat his werkes wer gouerned by the sprite of the
fende and by evell sugesstiones. For as venym makyth cold
fol. 50 a & sekenes in þe body, so was the | kynge labored & vnrested
with wykett suggestiones & thoughtes, sekynge menes how he
myght gette goodes and possessions of oþer men and gold of
hem þat wente by the way. For when wayferynge men slepte
and trowed þat her gold had be in her purse, when they awoke,
they founde þat it was in þe kynges power.

Bot that the vessell of oyntement come after þe venym betokeneth the blode of Ihesu Cryste, by which seke sowle is
quykened. For if the kynge had weyte his werkes in conside-
racion of the blode [1] of Cryst, and prayed God to be his helpe,
and sayde: 'O lorde God, þat haste made me and bowght; I
know þat by thy suffraunce I am comen to þe kyngdom and
crown, þer-fore werre þu þe enmyse þat warr ayanste me, and
pay thu my dettes; for the goodes of the realme ar nott suffi-
ciaunte,' I sothely shuld haue made his werkes and his birthen
more esely to ber. Bot for he desyred oþer menes goodes and
wold be see ryghtfull wher he wyst well þat he was vnrightful,
þer-fore the fende gouerned his herte & stirred him to do ayanste
þe ordinaunce of the church, & to meve werr & defraude Innocentes, till ryghtwysnes oute of the pulpite of Goddes mageste
cried dome and equite.

The whele þat was meved at the [2] kynges brething betokeneth his conscience, which was stirred in maner of a whele, now
to myrth and now to hevenes. The iiij lynes þat war in the
whele betokeneth the fourefold wyll þat ych man oweth to
haue: þat is to say, a perfyte wyll, a stronge wyll, a right wyll,
fol. 50 b & a resonable | wyll. The perfyte wyll is to love God & have
him above all thinges; and this wyll oweth to be in þe fyrst
line above. The secunde lyne is to desyr & to [do] [3] gode to

[1] MS. of the blode of the blode.   [2] MS. at þe at the.
[3] *Latin* facere.

his neghtbour & to him-self for God. This wyll muste be so strong þat it be noþer broke with hate or with covetyse. The thrid wyll is to a[b]stene[1] fro fleshly desyris and to desyre endeles thinges. And this will muste be right þat it be not doo to þe plesaunce of man, bot of God. The fourte will is nott to wyll haue þe werld, bot resonably and only to þe nede.

Þer-fore when the whele was turned, þer appered in the laste lyne goynge vpwarde þat the kynge loved the delytes of the world, & sett nott by the love of God. In þe secunde lyne was write that he loved þe men of the world. In the thrid lyne was write þe love þat he had vnordinately to wordely rechesse & possessiones. In the iiij lyne was write right nott, bott all was voyde wher-in aught to haue be write the love of God. Abofe all thinges, therfor, þe voydenes of the iiij lyne betokenes ye defaute of love and drede of God ; for by drede God is draw in-to the sowle, and by love God is festened in a good sowle. For yf a man had neuer loved God in all hys lyf tyme, and in his laste ende myght say or thinke in his herte, 'O god, me forthinketh with all myn herte þat I haue synned ayanste þe ; yeve me thy love & I shall amende me fro hens-forth ', a man of sych love may nor shall not goo to hell. Bot for the kynge loved him nott whom he aught to haue loved, þer-for he hath now | þe rewarde of his love.   fol. 51 a

After this, I see toþer kyng on the ryght syde of rightwysnes, þat was in purgatorie, þat was lyke to a chyld new bore þat myȝt nott styrr him-selfe, bot onely lyft vp his eyn. & I see that the fende stode on the kynges leeft syde, whos hede was lyke to a payr of belowes with a longe pype, his armys wer as ij serpentes, and his knees lyke a presse, and his feete lyke a longe hoke. On the right syde of the kynge stode an angell moste fayr, redy to help him.

And then I herde a voyce sayng : this kynge apperith now sych as his sowle was disposed when it departed from the bodye.

And a-non the fende cried to the boke in the pulpite, saynge : here is see a merȝelose thinge. This angell and I haue abyden the byrth of this chyld, he with his clennes, and I with my fylth. Bot now the child is bore, nott in bodye, bot from the

---

[1] MS. astene.

bodye, vnclennes in him appereth which þe angell, lothinge, myght not towch the chyld.   Bot I toch him, for he is fall into myn hond*es*.   Bot I wote nott wheder to lede him ; for my derke eyn see him nott, for the lyȝt of a clerenes þat cometh owte of his breste.   The angell seeth him and wote wheder to leede him, bot he may nott towch him.   Þer-fore þu, þat art rightful Iuge, departe our stryfe.

The worde aunswerde oute of the boke þat was in the pulpite, & seyde : tell, þu þat spekys, for what cause this sowle of this kyng come to thine hond*es*.

The fend aunswerd : þu arte rightwysnes, & þu saydest þat non shuld enter heuen that makyth not fyrst restituci*o*n of things*es* vnryghtfully gote.   Bot this sowle is all defowled [1] | of wronge gotten godes.   Secunde, þu saydeste þat þoo tresou*r*s shuld not be gedered þat rusteth and maughtes destrie, bot thoo þat lesteth w*ith*-outen ende.   Bot in this sowle þat place was voyde wher heuenly treso*u*r shuld haue byn gedered & þat place was full wher wormes and [f]rosses [2] wer noryshed. Thride, þu saydest þat a man*es* neghtbor shuld be loved for God.   Bot this sowle loved his body mor then God, & of the love of his neghtbo*ur* he rowght right not ; for he, abydyng in body, was gladd of the takyng away of hys neghtborr goodes. He wonded the hertes of hys sugett*es*, nott takyng hede to the harmes of oþ*er*, so he him-selfe had plente, & he dide what eu*er* him lyste, & comaunded what he wold, and toke litell hede of equite.   Thes ar the p*r*incipall causes, aft*er* which folow oþ*er* innowmm*er*able.

Then aunswerde the worde oute of the boke of ryghtwysnes, saynge to the angell : O þu angell, kep*er* of the sowle, þat arte in lyght and seeste [light],[3] what right or power haste þu to helpe thys sowle ?

The angell aunswerde : this sowle, he sayth, had holy fayth, & byleved and hoped þat all þat he had synned shuld be do away by contrici*o*n & confession.   And he drede the, his God, þof it wer lasse þan h*e* owght.

Then spake ryghtwysnes ayayne and sayde : O þu, myn angell, now it is graunted the to toch the sowle & to þe, þu

---

[1] f iiij.   [2] MS. throsses ; *Latin* ranae.   *See Glossary.*
[3] MS. high ; *Latin* lucem.

fende, to see the light of the sowle. Enquyreth þer-fore both
what this sowle loved when it lyved in body & had all his
membres hole. The angell and the fend aunswerde both : he
loved men & riches.

5　Then seyde rightwysnes ayane out of þe boke : what loved
he when he was aungwyssed w*ith* þe payne of deth ? |

Then aunswerde both : he loved him-selfe, for he was mor fol. 52 a
aungwyssed of the sekenes of his body and of tribulac*i*on of his
herte, than he was of þe passyon of his ayayne-byer.

0　Than spake ryghtwysnes ayane and seyde : yett sekyth and
lokyth what he loved and thought in the laste poynte of hys
lyffe, while he had hole conscience and vnderstondyng.

Onely the goode angell aunswerd : the sowle thought thus,
' Woo ', he sayde, ' vn-to me, for I haue be ou*er*-bold ayanste
15 my ayane-byer. Wold God I had now tyme in which I myght
thonke God for his benefett*es*. For it greveth me more that
I haue synned ayanste God then the payn of my body ; and
þof I shulde neu*er* haue heuen, ȝett wold I serve my God.'

Ryghtwysnes aunswerde oute of the boke : for as mych as
0 þu, fende, mayst nott see the sowle for bryghtnes of his lyght,
and þu, my aungell, may nott towch the sowle for his vnclennes, þer-fore this is the dome : þat þu, fende, purge it ;
and þu, aungell, comforte it tyll it be brought in-to bryghtnes
of blysse. And to the, þu sowle, it is graunted to loke to the
25 good angell & to haue comforte of him ; and þu shalte be p*er*-
tener of the blode of Cryste & of the p*r*ayers of his moder and
of the church.[1]

Then sayde the fende to the sowle : for þu art comen to myn
hond*es* full of metes and evell gote gudes, þer-for I shall now
30 avoyde þe wyth my p*r*esse.

And then the fende putt the brayns of the kyng by-twyx his
kneys, lyke a presse, and streyned it strongly in length and
brede, tyll all the merowth was as thyne as the lefe of a tre.

Secunde, þe fende sayde to the | sowle : for the place is fol. 52 b
35 voyde wher verteus shuld be, þer-for I shall fyll it.

And then he putt the pype of his belowes in the kyng*es*
mouth, and blew strongely, and fylled him myghty full of

---

[1] MS. church of; *but Latin sentence ends with* Ecclesiae.

horrible wynde ; so mych þat all the kyng*es* beyng and synew*es* wer wrechedly broken and breste o-sonder.

Thrid tyme, the fende sayde ayane to the kyng*es* sowle : for þu wer cruell and wi*th*-oute me*r*cy apon thi sugett*es*, which owght to haue be to the as thy sonn*es*, þ*er*-fore myne armes shall bytyngly grype the to-geder ; þat lyke as þu grevest thy suggestes, so shall myn armes, lyke [1] to s*er*pent*es*, all-to rende the wi*th* moste grevouse horror and sorow.

Aft*er* thes iij payn*es*, þat is to say, of the p*r*esse, of the belowes, and of the s*er*pent*es*, when the fende wold haue aggreged the same payn*es* ayane, begynnyng at the fyrst, then I see the angell [of] [2] God putt owte his hond*es* apon the fend*es* hond*es*, that he shuld nott make the peyn*es* so grevouse as they wer at the fyrste tyme. And so att ych tyme, the angell of God esed þe payn*es* ; und aft*er* ych payne, the sowle lyft vp his eyn to the angell, no thing sayng, bot shewyng in his beryng þat he was comforted be him ; and þat he shuld hastely be saved.

Then sayde the worde oute of the pulpyte vn-to me : all thes thing*es* that thus seriosly ar shewed vn-to the ar do anenste God in a poynte ; bot for þu arte bodely, they ar shewed to the be bodely lykenes. Bot this kynge, þof he wer couetouse to haue þe wyrship*es* of the world and for to gete godes þat wer nott his, ʒett, for he dredde God and lefte for that drede some thing*es* þat wer lusty to him, þ*er*-fore þat drede drough him to

fol. 53 a   the love and cherite | of God. For know þu well that mony þat ar entriked wi*th* mony grete synnes gete right grete con-tric*i*on afore her deth, whos contric*i*on may be so p*er*fyte þat not only her synne is foryeve hem, bot also the payn of purga-torie, if they die in the same contric*i*on. Bot the kyng gatt nott cherite till in the laste poynte of his lyf ; for then his strenghthes and his conscience fayling, ʒett he gatt of my grace goddely inspirac*i*on, by whych he sorowed mor of the vnwyr-shipyng of God þan of his own sorow and herme. And this sorow betokeneth that lyght be which the fende was blynded & wyst nott wheder to lede the sowle. ʒett he sayde nott þat he was so blynded for lake of gostely vnderstondyng, bot for he merveled how þat in þat sowle shulde be so grete clerenes of lyght and so mych vnclennes. The angell wyst well I-nogh

[1] MS. the *cancelled*.   [2] *Latin* Angelum Dei.

wheder to lede the sowle, bot he ne my3t towch it till it wer
purged.   As it is write, ' No man shall see þe face of God bot
he be fyrst made clene '.

Then the worde oute of the pulpite spake ayane to me and
sayde : that þu see þe angell putt out his hondes apon the sowle
& [1] of þe fende that he shuld nott aggrege þe peynes betokeneth
the power of the angell above the power of the fende be which
he refreyneth þe fendys malyce.   For the fende shuld haue no
mesur nor ordor in ponyshyng bot if he wer refreyned by þe
vertue of God.   And þer-for God doth mercy in hell; for þough
þer be no redempcion, remission, nor comforte to hem þat ar
dampned, 3ett in als mych as they ar not punyshed bot after
her desertes and after | rightwysnes, þer-for in that is shewed fol. 53 b
grete mercy of God.   Els þe fende shuld haue no temperaunce
ne mesur in his malyce.   That the kyng was see as a child þan
bor be-tokeneth þat who wyll be bor out of the vanite of the
world vn-to the lyf of heven, he muste be innocent, & by þe
grace of God grow in verteus to perfeccion.   That the kyng
lyft vp his eyn to the angell betokeneth þat by the angell, his
keper, he had his comfort ; and of hope he had Ioy, in as
mych as he hoped to come to endeles lyf.   And thes ar spirituall
thinges vnderstonde be bodely lykenes ; for fendes nor angelles
haue non such memberres ne noo such spekyng to-geder, for
thay ar spirites.   Bot by sy[ch]e [2] lykenes her goodenes or
wykednes ar shewed to bodely eyn.

Also the worde spake out of the pulpyte, sayng to me : the
pulpyte þat þu seeste betokeneth þe self god-hed : þat is to say,
fader and sonne and holy goste.   That [3] þu myght nott com-
prehende the lengthh, brede, depnes, and hyghnes of the
pulpite betokeneth þat in God is nott to fynde begynnyng nor
ende.   For God is and was wyth-outen begynnyng, and shall
be with-outen ende.   And þat ych colour of the iij colours seyde
was see in oþer, and yett ych colour was dyscerned from other,
betokeneth that God the fader is endelesse in the sonne and in
the holy goste, and þe sonne in þe fader and in the holy goste,
and the holy gost in hem both, which ar verely one in natur
and distincte in propurte of persones.

---

[1] *Latin* Angelus extendere manus suas super manus Diaboli.
[2] MS. syde ; *Latin* per tales similitudines.   [3] MS. that þt.

That on of the colours semede to be sanguyn and redde be-
tokeneth þe sonne, þat with-oute hurte of his godhed | toke
mannes natur in-to his person.   The white colour betokeneth
the holy goste, be whom is wesshing away of synnes.   The
golden colour betokeneth the fader, þat is the begynnyng and [1]
þe perfeccion of all thinges.   Not that ony perfeccion is mor in
the fadre þan in the sonne, ne þat the fadre is to-fore þe sonne ;
bot þat þu vnderstonde þat þe fader is nott the same in person,
þat is þe son.   For other is the fader in person, & oþer is the
sonne in person, and oþer is the holy goste in person ; bot on in
natur.   Ther-fore iij colours ar shewed vn-to þe boþe departed
and Ionede togeder ; departed for distinccion of persones, and
oned to-geder for oned of natur.

And as in ych colour þu see þe oþer colours, and þu myghtes
nott see one with-oute an-oþer, and þer was nothinge in þe
colours to-fore nor after, more or lasse, ryght so in the trinite
is nothing to-for mor or lasse departed or medeled ; bot one
wyll, one endeles, on power, & on glorie.   And þof the sonne
be of the fadre, and the holy goste of both, ȝett þe fader was
neuer with-oute þe sonne and the holy goste, ne the sone and
the holy goste with-oute the fader.

Also þe worde spake vn-to me & seyde : þe boke þat þu seest
in þe pulpite betokeneth þat in þe goodhed is endeles rightwysnes and wysdom, wher-to no thinge may be added or lassed.
And this is þe boke of lyffe, þat is nott write as the scriptur.
Þat is & was nott ; bot þe scripture of this boke is alway.   For
in þe godhed is endeles beyng and vnderstondyng of all thinges
present, passte, and to come, with-outen any variance or
chaungyng.   & no thing is inuysibile þer-to, for it seeth all
thinges.   That the word | spake it-self betokeneth þat God is þe
endeles word, of whom ar all wordes, and in whom thinges
haue lyf and beynge.   And this same worde spake þan visibly
when the worde was made man and was conuersaunte amongest
men.   Loo, this goodely vision hath the moder of God gote to
be shewed vn-to þe ; and this is the mercy behight to the kyngdom of Sweth, þat men dwellyng þer-in shuld her the wordes
þat procede oute of the mouth of God.   Bot þat few receyve
and beleve thes heuenly wordes I-ȝeve þe from God, þat is nott

----

[1] MS. and to ; *Latin* qui est principium, & perfectio omnium.

Goddes defaute, bot mennes. For they wyll nott leve þe cold
of her aune sowles. Neuer-the-lesse, the wordes of the gospell
wer nott fullfilled with the fyrst kynges of þat tyme; bot the
tymes shall ȝett come when þai shall be fullfylled.

5   How þe fader of hevyn shewed to seynt Birgitt an herde Revela-
dome apon a kynge þat was vnkynde & vnobedient to þe tions,
conselles of God. And how they þat ar in heuen, in erth, VIII,
in purgatorie, & in hell ask wreth apon kynges & princes; Chap. 58.
& how our lady prayeth for hem. Cap. xxiij.

10   God the fader spake to the spouse seynt Birgitt and seyde :
here þu þoo thinges þat I speke, & speke þo thinges þat I byd
the ; not for thy wyrship, ne for thy repreve. Bot onely and
even hold þu in thine herte þe prayser & þe reprever, so þat
neþer þu be meved to ire for reprefe, ne hyued to pride for
15 praysyng. For he is worthi wyrship þat is & was endelessely
in himselfe, which hath made angelles and men only to that
ende, þat | mony shuld be perteneres of his glorie. I am now fol. 55 a
he, & þe same in power and in wyll þat I was than when the
sonne ¹ toke mankynde ; in which sone I am and was, & he in
20 me, and the holy goste in both. And þof it wer preuey to the
world þat he was þe sonne of God, yett it was know to some,
þof it wer fewe. And know þu þat þe ryghtwysnes of God,
þat had neuer begynnyng nor ende, no more than God him-
selfe, was fyrst shewed to angelles as lyght or þei see God ; for
25 they fell nott for ignoraunce of the law of the rightwysnes of
God, bot for they wold nott hold it & kepe itt. For they
vnderstounde þat all þat love God shuld see him and abyde
with him for euer, and they þat hated God shuld be punyshed
endelesly and neuer see him in his glorie. & yitt her ambicion
30 and desyre of wyrship ches rather to hate God & to haue þe
place wher they shall be punyshed, þen to love him þat they
myght Ioy endelesly. And lyke rightwysnes is of a man as of
angelles. For man oweth fyrst to love God and afterwarde see
him,² þat he shuld mowe be see in manhode ; for he myght
35 nott be see in his godhed. And free ches is yove also to man

¹ MS. some ; *Latin* Filius meus.
² *Latin clause omitted*; propterea Filius meus ex charitate nasci voluit
post legem iustitiae.

as to angell, þat they shuld desir heuenly thing*es* & despyce
erthely.   Þer-for I, God, visett mony in mony maner*es*, all
þough my godhed be nott see.   And in mony p*a*rties of the
world I haue shewed to many p*e*rsones how the synne of ych
londe myght haue be amended, and how m*e*rcy myght haue be 5
gotte, or eu*er* I dyde dome & my rightwysnes in t[h]oo ¹ places.
Bot men take non hede to thes thing*es*, ne sett not þer-by.   Þis
ryghtwisnes is also in God, þat all þat ar apon erth first hope
seurly tho thing*es* þat they see nott, & þat they beleve to the
fol. 55 b church of God and to the holy gospell.   And forþer-|mor that 1.
they love God above all thing*es*, that hath yove hem all thing*es* ;
and himselfe he hath yove for hem to deth, þat all shulde
endelessly Ioy w*ith* him.   Ther-for I myselfe, God, speke to
such as me luste, þat it be know how synne owe to be amended,
and how payne may be lessed and blys encresed.   1.

After this I see, sayth seynte Birgitt, as yf all heuenes had
ben on howse, wher-in saate a Iuge in a trone.   & the howse
was full of s*er*uant*es* and p*r*ayseres of the Iuge, ych of hem in
hys voyce.   And vnder this heuen was see a kyngdom.   And
anon þer was herde a voyce þat all myght her it, þat sayde : 2c
come ye, both angell and fende, to the dome ; þat is to say, þu
angell þat arte keper of the kynge, and þu fende þat arte
gou*er*nor of the kyng.

& anon as the worde was spoke, an angell and an fende
stood to-fore þe Iuge.   Þe angell semed as a man trowbled, 25
and þe fende as a man Ioyng.   Þen seyd þe Iuge : O þu angell,
I putt the to be kep*er* of the kyng, when he made couenaunde
of pees w*ith* me and made confession of all his synnes þat he
had do from his younge age, þat þu shuldeste be mor ner to
him þan the fende.   How is he now þer-for so fer from the ? 30

The angell aunswerd : O Iuge, I am brennyng in the fyr of
thi cherite, w*ith* which þe kynge was warmed for a tyme.   Bot
when the kynge lothed & dispised tho thing*es* þat thi frend*es*
sayde to ² him, & it was tediouse to him to do tho thing*es* þat
fol. 56 a þu conc*e*lst him, þan went þe kyng as his own lyst ³ | drowhe 35
him, afer from me, and neghed ych hour vn-to þe enmye.

The fende aunswerde : I am the selfe cold, & þu art the selfe

¹ MS. too ; *Latin* eisdem.
² MS. to to.   ³ drowght him *catchword.*

hete and godly fyre.   Þer-fore lyke as ych þat neghis to the is
mor feruent to gode werk*es*, so þe kyng, neghyng to me, is
made mor cold vn-to thy cherite & more hote to my werk*es*.

Then aunswerd the Iuge: the kynge was stirred to love God
5 above all thing*es*, and his neghtbor as him-self.   Why þer-for
haste þu take from [me]¹ the man þat I bought w*ith* myn own
blode, and makys him to nye his neghtb*our*, not only to his
temp*er*all godes bot eke to his lyf?

The fende aunswerde: O Iuge, now longeth it to me to speke,
10 & þe angell to kepe silence.   For when the kynge went fro the
& fro thi consells & come to me, þan I conceyled him to love
himselfe mor than his neyhtb*our*; & that he shuld nott rech
of the helth of sowles, if he hadde the wyrship of the world;
and that he shuld nott take hede ho wer nedy or defrauded, if
15 his frendis had plente.

Then sayde þe Iuge to the fende: ho so wyll go fro the, they
may; for þu mayst hold non w*ith* vyolens.   Þer-for I shall yett
sende some of my fryndes to the kynge, þat shall warne him
of his p*er*ell.

20 The fende aunswerde: ryghtwysnes is þat ho eu*er* wyll obey
to me, he oweth to be gou*er*ned by me; & þer-fore I shall sende
my concelleres also to the kyng, & it shal be see to hos conceyles
he shall rather gyf stede.

Then sayde þe Juge: goo, for my ryghtwysnes is to deme to
25 þe tormentour þat is his, as well as to him þat hath acc*io*n of
þat þat is dew to him in his cause.

After this, sayth seynt | Birgett, when certen ȝeres wer fol. 56 b
paste, I see ayayn þe same Iuge w*ith* his heuenly hoste, more
moved than he was wonte to be, & as he had be wroth.   & then
30 he seyde to þe aungell & to the fende: telleth, he seyth, whed*er*
of yow hath ou*er*comen.

The angell aunswerd: when I come to the kynge w*ith*
goddely Inspiraci*o*n, & thi frendes w*ith* sp*irit*uell wordes, anon
þe messyngeres of the fende rowned in his eres, and seyde:
35 'Wyll þu spar temp*er*all goodes or thi wyrship or sowles or
bodyes, þat thi frendes whom þu loveste more than thi-self
may haue wyrshipe and p*ro*sp*er*yte?' To this sterryng þe
kynge assented, and to the styrrynges of the freend*es*

¹ *Latin* a me.

90   *The Revelations of Saint Birgitta*

he, saynge, aunswerd:[1] 'I am suffyciaunte I-nogh and wyse I-nowgh of consell with-owte ȝow. Go ȝour wayes fro me with shame.' And so þe kyng torned his bake to the, & his face to the enmye, & putte from him frendes with dishonest repreve and scorne of the frendes of the world.

Then cried the fende and sayde: O Juge, loo, now longeth it to me to gouerne the kynge & to yeve him consell by my fryndes.

The Juge aunswerd: go; and as mych as þu art suffered, punyshe the kynge. For he hath provoked me to indignacion ayaynst him.

Too ȝer after this, the Iuge appered ayane, & the angell & the fende to-for him. Then sayde the fende: O Juge, deme þu now I shall pronownce rightwysnes. Þu art verely the self cherite, & þer-for it longeth not to the to dwell in that herte wher-in Envye and wroth is roted. Thu art also | verry wysdom, & þer-for þu owest nott to be in the herte of him þat desyrith to nye the lyf of his neghtbores, her goodes, and her wyrship. Thu art also verry trouþe, & þer-for it semeth the nott to dwell with þat man þat hath bounde him with oth to do treson & deceytes. Þer-for for this kynge hath spitte þe oute from him as þat thing is spitte owte þat is abhomynable, þer-for suffer me to stirr him and oppresse him, þat he be all oute of his wytt & deede. For my conselles he holdeth wysdom, and thy counsell he takyth for scorne. & with sych mede I desyre to reward him, for he hath do my wyll. Neuer-the-les I may nott do to him with-oute thi suffrance.

And when this was herde, þe Juge semed to haue a mervelouse chongyng; for then he appered bright as the sone, & in that sone wer see three wordes: þat is, vertue, trowth, & rightwysnes. Vertue spake & sayde: I haue made all thinges with-oute merettes goyng to-for. & þer-fore I am worthy to be worshiped of my creatur & not to be dispised. I am also worthi praysing of my fryndes for my cherite. I owe also to be wyrshiped and dred of myn enmyes, for I supporte hem pacyently with-outen her merettes, wher they haue worthely deserued dampnacion. And þer-for, þu fend, it longeth to me to deme all after my rightwysnes and not after thy malyce.

fol. 57 a

---

[1] MS. aunswerd aunswerd.

Then anon spake trowth eke and seyde : I in my godhed
toke manhod of a virgyn, in which manhod I spake & [prech]ed [1]
to peple. I sent also þe holy gost to þe apostoles, & I spake | by fol. 57 b
her tonges. As I speke ych day by spi*ritu*ell infusion to such
5 as me list, *þer*-fore my frendes mote know þat I my-selfe that
am trowth hath sende my word*es* to a kynge, which he hath
dispiced. Þ*er*-for, þu fende, her now ; for I wyll speke þat it
be know whed*er* the kyng hath obeyde to my concell or to my
stirryng*es*. For I wyll tell all the concell I ȝove to the kynge,
10 rehersyng now in few word*es* þat I exp*re*ssed to-for mor largely.
For the kynge was sterred & concelled to be-war of all synnes
forbode of holy church, & to haue moderate fastyng*es*, so þat
he myght her and aunswer his sugett*es* compleynt*es*, & be redy
to do right to rich and poor þat aske it ; so þat for mych
15 abstinence þe goode of þe comynte of the peple of the realme
and þe gou*er*nance of the comyn p*ro*fett be nott lassed, ne þat
he shuld nott be þe mor sleuth for ou*er*-mych excesse to yeve
audience to all. Also the kynge was conceyled & stirred how
he shuld s*er*ue God & p*ra*y, and which dayes and tymes he
20 shuld lefe oþ*er* occupaci*ones* & entente to the comyn p*ro*fett of
his realme. Also þe kynge was concelled which days he shuld
ber þe kyngely crown to the wyrship of God ; & þat he shuld
treete all his conceylles wi*th* men þat loveth trowþe & wi*th* the
frend*es* of God ; and þat he shuld neu*er* wyttyngly passe trouth
25 ne law ; & þat he shuld nott putt non vn-wounte greuaunce to
þe comyn peple of his realme bot for defence of the same, & for
werr ayaynest the paynem*es*. Also the kynge was conceyled
to haue an nowmbre of seruaunt*es* in howsehold, acordyng to
þe faculte of lyfelod and rent*es* of the cheker of his realme.
30 & all þat left ov*er*, he shuld departe wi*th* his | knyght*es* and fol. 58 a
frend*es*. Also the kyng was conceyled wysely to monysh hem
þat wer insolente & lewde wi*th* cheritable word*es*, and manfully
to correkke hem ; & þat he love in goodely cherite hem þat
wer prudente and sadde ; & that he shuld defende þe peple
35 dwellyng in his realme and yiff his yiftes wi*th* discrecion ; & all
tho thing*es* þat longe to the crown he shuld nott lessen nor
alyene ; that he shuld deme rightfully both men of the lond
and strangeres ; þat he shuld love the clergye, & cheritably

---

[1] *Latin* praedicabam ; MS. purchesed.

gadre to him his chyualrye, and norish in peece þe comen peple
of his realme.

When thes thing*es* wer herde, The fende aunswerde to the
Iuge & sayde : and I conceyled the kynge to do some synnes
p*r*iualy which he durst nott do in open.   I conceyled him also 5
to say longe & mony p*r*ayers and psalmes w*ith*-oute attendaunce
and deuoc*i*on of herte, þat so [1] he shuld p*r*olonge & occupie þe
tyme in vayne, & nott her anye þat wold compleyn, ne do any
ryght to such as suffered wronge.   Also I styrred þe kynge to
leve & despice oþ*er* goodemen of the realme ; & to lyft vpp and 1
p*r*eferr oo man above all oþ*er* ; & to love him w*ith* all his herte,
mor than him-self ; and to hate his one sonne ; & to greve the
comyn peple of the realme in his exacc*i*ones ; & to slee men
& spoyle churches.   I stirred the kynge also to dissimile
rightwysnes ; and to suffer ych man to nye oþ*er*, þat he shuld 1
aliene & yeve londes longynge to his crown to a grete p*r*ince of
a noþ*er* realme, my swor brother ; and this I conceyled to þat
ende þat treson and werr shuld be arered ; þat goodemen &
rightfull shuld be caste done ; wyked peple shuld be drowned
þe depper in hell ; & thay that shall be purged in purgatorie 2
fol. 58 b shuld be the | more grevously tormented ; women shuld be
defowled ; shippes in the see shuld be robbed ; sacrament*es* of
the church shuld be dispiced ; lecherouse lyf shuld þe mor
boldely be contynued ; and all my wyll mor frely fulfilled.
And thus, þu Juge, be thes synnes, & mony oþ*er* now I-do 2
& fulfilled be the kynge, it may be p*r*eved & know whed*er* the
kyng hath obeyde to thi concele or myne.

After this spake rightwysnes, aunsweryng, & seyde : for the
kynge hath hated verteu & dispised trowth, þer-for it longeth
now to þe to encrese some of thyne conceyles ȝove to the kyng. 3
& I owe aft*er* rightwysnes to lassen & w*ith*-draw from him
some of my graces I ȝove to him.

The fende aunswerd : O Iuge, I shall multiplie & mor my
ȝift*es* to the kynge.   & first, I shall sende him necligence, þat
he take non hede of the werk*es* of God in his herte, & þat he 3
thenke nott on the werk*es* & exsamples of thy frendes.

Ryghtwysnes aunswerd : & I shall lasse vn-to him þe Infu-

----

[1] MS. longe *cancelled*.

*ci*ones of the holy gost, & I shall wi*th*draw from him the goode
thoughtes & comfortes þat he had to-for.

Þan seyde þe fende: I shall sende him boldenes to thinke &
to do dedely synnes & venyall wi*th*-out bashment or shame.

5 Ryghtwysnes aunswerd: I shall lessen his reson & discre-
*ci*on þat he discerne nott ne discusse þe rewardes and domes
of dedely synnes & venyall.

The fende sayde: I shall yeve him drede þat he dar nott
speke ne do right ayanste þe enmyse of God.

0 Ryghtwisnes aunswerde: I shall lessen his prudence &
knowyng*es* of thing*es* to be do so lewdly, þat he shall seme
mor like a foole & a Iap*er* in wordes & dedes than a wyse man.

Then seyde the fende: I shall putt to him angwysse and
tribula*ci*ones of herte, be-cause he hath not pr*osper*yte | after fol. 59 a
5 his wyll.

Ryghtwysnes aunswerde: I shall lesse to him gostely comfortes, which he had some tyme in p*ra*yeres & in his dedes.

Þe fende sayde: I shall put to him fellnes to thinke sotell
inven*ci*ones, by which he may begyle and disceyve hem whom
20 he desyrith to destrie.

Ryghtnes aunswerd: I shall lesse his vnderstondynge so
mych þat he shall take non hede of his own wyrship ne of his
own p*ro*fyte.

The feende sayde: I shall putt to him such Ioy of herte þat
25 he shall nott reke of his own shame, ne of the herme and
p*er*ell of his sowle, while he may haue temp*er*all p*ro*sp*er*ite
aft*er* his wyll.

Ryghtwysnes aunswerde: I shall lessen his thinking to-for
& þat consyderac*i*on that wysemen have in her word*es* & dedes.
30 Then seyde the fende: I shall yeve him a womannes boldenes, & an vnsemely drede, and sych beryng þat he shall seeme
mor lyke a ribold or an harlott than a crowned kynge.

Ryghtwysnes aunswerd: sych dome is he worthy, þat
dep*ar*teth him frome God. For he oweth to be despised of
35 his frendes, & to be hated of the comentye of his peple, & to
be caste down of Godd*es* enmys; for he hath myssevsed þe
ȝeft*es* of Godd*es* cherite, both gostely and bodely.

Than spake verteu [1] ayane and seyde: thes thinges þat ar

---
[1] *Latin* veritas.

shewed to the ar nott for the merett*es* of the kynge, hos sowle
is nott ȝett demede ; bot it shall be demed in the laste poynte
of his lyfe.

After thes thing*es* wer sayde, I see þat tho iij, þat is to say,
verteu, trowth, & rightwysnes, wer lyke to the Iuge þat spake 5
to-for.

& then I herde the voyce, as it had be of a bedell saying :
O ye, all heuenes w*ith* all planett*es*, yeveth silence ; & all ye
fol. 59 b fendes þat | ar in derknes, listeneth ; and all ye other þat ar in
derkenes, hereth ; for the sou*er*ayne emp*er*our p*ro*poseth to here 10
domes apon the princes of erth.

And anon the kynges that I see wer nott bodely bot
sp*iri*tuell. & my gostely eres and eyne war opned to her and
see. And than I see Abraham come w*ith* all sayntes þat war
bor of his gen*er*acion. Than come all p*atriark*es and p*ro*fett*es*. 15
& aft*er*warde I see the iiij euangelistes, hos shapp was lyke to
iiij bestes, as they ar paynted apon wallys in the world,
save they appered quyk and nott dede. After this, I see
twelfe seet*es*, & in hem the xij appostoles, abydyng þe comyng of the power. Then come Adam and Eve w*ith* mar- 20
tires & confessores and all oþer sayntes þat come of hem. Bot
the manhod of Criste was nott yett see, ne the body of his
blessed moder ; bot all abode her comyng. The erth and the
water s[e]med[1] to be lyft vp to heven, & all thing*es* þat wer
in hem meked hem, & w*ith* reu*er*ence bowed hem to the power. 25

Then, aft*er* this, I see an awt*er* þat was in the seete of the
maieste, & a chalesse w*ith* wyne and wat*er* and brede in lykenes of a hoste offered apon þe auter; and then I see how in a
church of the world a p*re*este be-gan masse, arayd in a p*re*stes
araye. & when he had do all þat longed to the masse, & come 30
to the wordes w*ith* which he shuld blesse the hoste, I see as if
the sone and the moone & þe sterres w*ith* all oþer planett*es*,
& all heuenes w*ith* her courses and mevynge, sownede w*ith*
swetteste noote and w*ith* sondery voyces. And all the songe[2]
and melodye was herde, and semed as it had be vnnowmmer- 35
fol. 60 a able maners of musyk, whos most swete sowne was impossible
to be comp*re*hended of mann*es* wytt | or to be spoke. They
þat wer in lyght be-held the p*re*ste & enclyned hem to the

---

[1] MS. somed.   [2] MS. and all the songe and all the songe.

power w*ith* reu*e*rence and wyrship, and they þat wer in derkenes horred and dredde.

Bot when the wordes of God wer sayde of the prest apon the
hoste, it semed to me that the same sacred hoste was in the
5 seete of the maieste in iij fygures, abydynge neu*er*-the-lesse in
the honde of the p*r*este. And the same holy hoste was made a
quyke lombe, and in the lomb appered a face of a man. And
a brynnyng flawme was see w*ith*-in & w*ith*-owte the lombe and
the face. And when I festened my syght besyly in by-holdynge
10 the face, I se the lombe in the face. And when I behold the
lombe, I see the same face in the lombe. & the virgyn sate
crowned by the lombe, and all angelles se*r*ued hem, which wer
of so grete multitude as þe motes in the sonne. And a
mervelouse shynyng proceded fro the lombe. Ther was also
15 so grete multitude of holy sowles, that my sight myght nott
behold hem in length, brede, heght, and depnes. I see also
some places voyde, þat ar ȝyt to be fulfilled to the wyrship of
God.

Then herde I a voyce oute of the erth, of vnnowme[ra]ble [1]
20 thousaundes, crying & seying : O lorde God, rightful Iuge,
ȝeve dome apon our kynges and princes, and take hede to the
shedyng of o*ur* blode, and be-hold the sorowes and wepynges
of our wyfes and children. Be-hold our hungre & shame, o*ur*
wound*es* & our p*r*isonment*es*, brynnyng [2] of our howses, & the
25 vyolac*i*on of the chaste maydens [3] & women. Be-hold the
wronge doo to churches and to all the clergye. & se þe false
byhest*es* and deceyt*es* of kyng*es* & of princ*es*, & the pillage þat
they wrayste to hem w*ith* vyolence & Ire. For they reke nott
how mony thousaundes die, so they may spred o-brode her
30 pride.

Þan cried ther oute of hell as it had be vnnowme*r*able thou- |
sandes, saynge : O Iuge, we know þat þu art maker of all fol. 60 b
thing*es*. ȝeve dome þer-for apon the lordes whom we se*r*ued in
erth. For they haue drowned vs in hell depper than we shuld
35 haue be, and þowghe we wyll the harme, ȝett ryghtwysnes
compelleth vs to compleyn & say trouth. For our erthely
lordes loved vs w*ith*-oute cherite ; for they roght no more of

---

[1] MS. vnnowmeble.   [2] MS. brymnyng (*five strokes*).
[3] MS. n *above line*.

our sowles than of doggis.　& it was allon to hem wheder we
loved þe, our maker, or noo, desyringe eu*er* to be beloved &
served of vs.　Þ*er*-for thay ar vnworthi heuen ; for they reke
nott of the.　& they ar worthy hell, bot thy grace helpe hem.
For they haue deceyved vs ; & þ*er*-for we wold suffer mor 5
grevous paynes þan we suffer, that her payn shuld neu*er* haue
ende.

Aft*er*ward, they that wer in purgatorie, spekynge be lykenes,
cryed & sayde : O Juge, we ar demed to purgatorie for contrici*on* & gode wyll þat we had in þe end of o*ur* lyf.　And þ*er*- 1
for we compleyn apon the lordes þat ȝyt lyff in erth.　For they
aught to haue gou*er*ned vs, & to haue warned vs w*ith* word*es*
& blamyng*es*, & to haue taught vs w*ith* holsom conseyles &
exsamples.　Bot they comforted vs rather, & pr*o*uoked vs
rather to evell dedes and synnes.　And þ*er*-for our payn is now 1
the mor grevouse for hem ; & the tyme of payne is þe larger ;
& our shame & tribulaci*on* is the mor.

Then spake Abraham w*ith* all þe p*a*triarch*es*, and seyde : O
lorde, amongest all thing*es* desiderable, we desyre that thy[1]
sone shuld be bor of o*ur* lynage, þat is now despised of þe 2
princes of erth.　Þ*er*-for we aske dome apon hem, for they take
no hede to thy m*er*cye, ne they dred nott thy dome.

Then spake the pr*o*fett*es* and seyde : we pr*o*fecyed of the
comyng of the sonne of God ; and we seyde þat for the delyu*er*-
aunce of þe peple was nedefull that he shuld be bor of a virgyn 2
fol. 61 a & suffer tre-|son and be take and be scorged & be crowned
w*ith* thornes & att laste dye on the crosse, that heven shuld be
opened & synne do away.　Wher-for thoo thing*es* ar now fulfilled þat we seyde ; þ*er*-fore we aske dome apon the princes of
the erth þat despyce thy sonne þat of thy cherite dyed for hem. 3

The[n][2] spake the euangelystes & sayde : we ar wyttnes þat
thi sone hath fullfylled in him-selfe all thing*es* þat wer for-
sayde of him.

Also the appostoles spake and seyde : we ar Iuges, þ*er*-for it
longeth to vs to deme aft*er* trowth.　Wher-for he that despices 3
the bodye of God & his pr*e*cept*es*, we deme to perdici*on*.

After all this, þe virgyn that saatt by the lombe sayde : O
moste swete lorde, haue m*er*cy apon hem.

---

[1] MS. they ; *Latin* Filius tuus.　　　　　[2] MS. the ; *Latin* tunc.

To hir the Iuge aunswerd : it is nott right, he seyth, to
denye the eny thing. Ther-for they that sesen from synne and
do worthy pennaunce shall fynde me*r*cy ; and dome shall be
torned away from hem.

After this I see that the face þ*at* was see in the lambe spake
to the kyng and seyde : I haue do grace w*ith* the, for I haue
shewed the my wyll : how þu shuldest ber and demene the in
thy goue*r*naunce, & how þu shuldest goue*r*ne thi-self honestely
and worthely.   I cheresed the also w*ith* swete word*es* of cherite
as a moder, & I fered the w*ith* warning*es* as a pitevos fad*er*.
Bot thu, obeyng to the fende, hast cast me from the, as a
moder casteth away a dedebor chyld whom she deyneth noþer
to touch ne putt her tet*es* to his mouth.   & þ*er*-for all þe goode
þat is byhyght þe shall be take from the & yove to one þat
shall come aft*er* the.

After this, the virgyne þ*at* saate w*ith* the lambe spake to me
and sayde : I wyll tell the how vnde*r*stondyng*es* of sp*iritu*ell
visiones is yeve vn-to þe ; for the | sayntes of God receyve the fol. 61 b
holy goste dyue*r*sely.   For some of hem knowe to-fore the
tyme when tho thing*es* shuld fall þ*at* wer shewed to hem, as
holy p*r*ofett*es*.   Other knew to-fore what ende any batell shuld
haue, or eu*er* they that shuld fyght entered bateyle.   Oþ*er*
knew in spirett what they shuld aunswer to p*er*sones that
comen to hem when any thing*e* was asked of hem.   Oþ*er*
knew wheþ*er* they wer dede or quyke þ*at* wer fer frome hem.
Bot it is not lefull to the to know other thing*es*, bott to her and
see gostely thing*es*, & to write þe thing*es* þa þu seeste, & to tell
& say hem to such p*er*sones as þu [art] [1] bode.   And it is nott
lefull to the to wete wheþ*er* they be olyve or dede, to whom þu
art bode write ; or wheþ*er* they shall obey or nott to the conceyles of thy wrytyng I-yeve to the from God in sp*iritu* ell
vision for hem.   Bot þough this kyng haue dispiced my
wordes, ȝyt þer shall [come] [2] anoþ*er* þat shall receyve hem
w*ith* reue*r*ence and wyrship and vse hem to his helth. Amen.

Our lorde Ihe*su* Cryst blameth & treteth herde sentenc*e* Revela-
apon all maner of peple, of what state or degre eu*er* they be, tions,
for her synnes & vnkyndenes, be-hotyng me*r*cy if they wyll Book VII,
Chap. 30.

---

[1] *Latin* quibus tibi praecipitur ; *and cf. below.*   [2] *Latin* veniet.

H

amende hem. & this revelacion our lord bad seynt Birgitt write laste of her revelaciones, affirmyng þat his dome shall be fullfylled apon all peple þat torne not to him with wery mekenes, like as it is shewed in this same revelacion. Cap. xxiiij.

I see a grete pales like to a bryght heuen, wher-in was an hoste of heuenly chevallrye, vnnowmerable as motes of the sonne, shynnyng bright as the sonne bemes. Ine this paleys þer satt fol. 62 a in a marvelouse trone, as it wer | a person of a man of incomprehensible feyrenes, & as lord of grete power, whos clothes were mervelouse and of vnspekeable clerenes. And a virgyn stode to-fore him þat sate in the trone þat was brighter than the sonne, whom all they that wer ther of heuenly chevalrye wyrshoped reuerently as the quene of heyvenes.

Then he þat sate in the trowne opned his mowth and sayde : her ye, all my enmyes lyvyng in the world ; for I speke not now to my frendes þat foloweth my wyll. Her ȝee, all clerkes, archbysshoppes, bishoppes, and all þat ar of lowr degre of the church. Here ȝe eke, all religiose peple of what-euer order ye be. Hereth eke, ȝe kynges, princes, and Iuges of the erth, and all soueraynes and seruantes. Hereth eke, ȝe women, princesses, ladies, wyves, maydenes, and all peple of what euer condicion or degre þat ȝe be, grete or smale, þat dwell in the world. Here thes wordes which I my-selfe þat made yow speke now vn-to yow. I compleyne, for ȝe ar go a way fro me, & ye haue yeve fayth to the fende, myn enmye. ȝe haue forsake myn comaundementes, & ȝe follow[1] the wyll of the fende and of his sugestyones. ȝe take non hede þat I, vnchaungeable & endeles God, your maker, come downe from heven vn-to a virgyn, takyng of hir a body, and was conuersaunte with yow. & I be my-selfe opned yow þe way & shewed yow concelles be which ȝe shuld go vn-to heuen. I was naked, scourged, and fol. 62 b crowned with thornes, & so strongly | streched o-brode and lenghth on the crosse þat all ȝe synowes & Ioyntes of my body wer as they had bene lewsed in sounder. I herde all repreves and suffered moste despisable deth & bytter sorow of herte for your helth. O ȝe myne enmyes, of all thes thinges take ȝe no hede, for ye ar deceyved. & þer-for ye ber the yoke

[1] MS. fololow.

and the byrden of the fende with disseyveable swettenes, & ʒe
knowe nott nor fele not thoo thinges, tyll endeles sorow neghe
apon yow ; & ʒytt þese thinges suffice nott to yow. Bot þer-to
your pride is so mych þat yf ʒe myʒt ascende above me, ʒe wold
gladely do it ; and the luste of your flesh is so mych þat ye
wold rather be with-owte me þan ʒe wold leve your inordinate
delyte. And also your couetyse may nott be fylled, as a sakke
þat is open att both endes ; for þer is nothing þat may fyll
your couetyse. Þer-fore I swer in my godhed þat if ye dye in the
state þat ʒe ar ine now, ʒe shall neuer se my face, bot for your
pride ye shall be drowned so depe in hell þat all fendes shall
be above yow & torment yow with-outen comforth. For your
lecherye ʒe shall be fylled with horrible venym of the fende,
and for your couetyse ʒe shall be fylled with sorow and
angwysse and be parteners of all evells þat is in hell. O ye
myne Enmyes, abhomynable, vncurteys, and vnkynde, I seme
to yow as a worme dede ine wynter ; and þer-for ye do what
ye wyll, and haue prosperyte. Bot I shall aryse in Soumer,
and then ʒe shall be stylle ; and ye shall nott flee myn
honde. Nethlesse, O ʒe Enmyes, for I haue bowght yow with
my blode, and I seke right noght bot your sowles, þer-for
torneth yett aʒayne to me with mekenes, & I | shall receyve fol. 63 a
yowe gladely, as my children. Shakyth from yow the grevouse
yokke of the fende and hath mynde on my cherite ; and ʒe
shall see in yowr conscyence that I am esy and myld. Amen.

Assint laudes deo.

[The rest of fol. 63 a and fol. 63 b blank ; another hand com-
mences at the top of fol. 64 a.]

How oure blissid lady is redy to helpe alle, bothe fol. 64 a
wyues, widowes, and maydens. Revela-
tions,

Here thou,[1] saith the modre of God to seint Birgitte, that Book IV,
prayest God with all thyne herte that thi children may please Chap. 53.
God. Truely, suche prayer is plesyng to God. For there is
no modre that loueth my son aboue all thynges and askith the
same to hir children, but þat I am anone redy to helpe hir to

---

[1] MS. what *incorrectly inserted above line between* thou saith ; *Latin* audi tu
(inquit) mater Dei, quae toto corde rogas Deum.

þe effect of hir askyng.   There is also no widowe þat stably prayeth aftir the helpe of God to stonde in widowhod to þe worship of God vn-to hir deth, but that anone I am redy to fulfille hir wille with hir.   For I was as a widowe, in þat I hadde a sone in erthe that had no bodily fadre.   There is also no virgyn that desireth to kepe hir maydenhode to God vn-to hir deth, but þat I am redy to defende hir and to comforte hir. For I myself am verrayly a virgyn.   Nor thou owest not to meruaile whi I say these thinges.   It is write that Dauid desyred kyng Saules doughter, whan sche was mayde.   He resceyued hir also, whan sche was widowe.   He had also the wyf of Vrye, while hir husbonde lyued.   Neuirtheles, the desyre and lust of Dauid was not with-oute synne.   But that gostly dilectacion of my sone, which is lorde of Dauid, is with-oute all synne.   Therefor, as these thre lyves, that is, mayden-hod, widowhod, and wedlok, plesed Dauid bodily, so plese it my sone to haue hem in his moost chast delyt gostly.   Therefor no meruail though I helpe hem and drawe her gostly delyte in-to the delyt of my sone, for his delyt is vn-to hem.

The mantelle of mekenes.

Revela-
tions,
Book II,
Chap. 23.
Oure lady seint Mary spekith vn-to the spouse of Crist, seint Birgitte, and saith : many meruaillen why I speke to þe.   Certayne therefore it is that my meknesse be schewed, for as þe hert ioyeth not of a membre of the body þat is seeke to-fore it resceyue helthe ayene, and whan it is hole, the herte is more glad ; so I, synne a man neuer so moche, yf he turne ayene to
fol. 64 b me with[1] alle his herte | and with veray amendement anoon, I am redy to resceyue hym.   And I take noo kepe how moche he hath synned, but with what entent and wille he turneth ayene.   I am cleped of alle modir of mercy.   Forsothe, doughtre, the mercy of my sone made me m[e]rcifull,[2] and þe disese of hym made me to haue compassion.   And therefor schall he be wreched þat cometh not to mercy while he may. Therefor, thou my doughter, come and hide the vndir my mantell, whiche is dispisable outward, but ynward it is profit-able for thre thinges.   First, it schadowith from tempest of wyndes.   Seconde, it kepith from bytyng colde.   Thridde, it

---

[1] MS. of *cancelled, and* with *inserted above line.*   [2] MS. mrcifull.

defendith fro reyne. This mantel is my mekenes. This semeþ
to þe louers of the worlde full despisable and veyn to folue.
What is more despisable þanne to be cleped a foole, and not be
wroth nor speke ayene ? What is more despisable þanne to
leue and forsake alle thinges, and to be nedy in all thinges?
What is more sorowful amonge wordly peple than a man to
suffre and dissimile wronge doon vn-to hym, and to bileue and
holde hym-selfe lower and more vnworthy þan alle othir?
Suche, doughtre, was my mekenes. This was my ioye, this
was all my wille, that [I] [1] wolde plese noone but my sone.

And this, my mekenes, is vaylable vn-to thre thinges. First, [2]
for tempest of wynde and wedir ; þat is, for þe repreef and de-
spyt of men, for as wynde and wedir that is full of tempest and
stronge greueth a man on eche syde and makith hym colde, so
repreues beren donne lightly a man that is vnpacient, and
thenkith not on þe tyme and thinges þat arne to come and
maken his herte colde from charitee. But who euer take kepe
besily to my mekenes, he most thenke what I, lady of alle,
herde, and seche my praysing and not his, and considre þat
wordis arne but wynde ; and anoone he schall haue refresshyng
and fynde eese. For why are wordly peple so vnpacient to
suffre wordes and reproves, but for þey seche more their owne |
praysing than the praysing of God ? And there is no mekenes fol. 65 a
in hem, for they haue their eyen sperde from biholding of hir
synnes. Ther-for, though the rightwysnes that is write say
that a man is not bound to suffre or to here repreuable wordes
withoute cause, it is vertue and worthy reward to here and to
suffre paciently contrarious thynges seyde or doo vn-to hym.

Seconde, [3] my mekenes defendith from bytyng colde, þat is
to say, from carnal frenschip and fleschly loue. There is a
manere of frenschip and loue by which a man is loued oonly
for these thinges that arne present, as þei that seyen thus:
' Fede thou me, and I schall fede the in this lyf. For I recke
not who fede the aftir thi deth. Worship þou me & I schall
worship the, for I charge litil what worship folue here aftir.'
This frenschip is colde and with-oute hete of þe loue of God.
And it is as snowe frore in the loue and compassion of his

[1] *Latin* cogitabam.   [2] MS. j *in margin.*
[3] MS. ij *in margin.*

neighburgh that hath nede. And vnfruytfull to rewarde, for
whan hir felaschip is departid and þe table layde doune, anoone
all the profyt of hir frenschip and loue is dissolued and þe fruyte
there-of agoo.   But who euere folue my mekenes, he doth wele
to alle for God, bothe to enmyes and to frendes. [To frendes],[1]
for they abyde stablely in the worship of God ; and to enemyes,
for they arne the creatures of God, and in happes they schullen
be-come goode.

Thridde[2] is the beholdyng of my mekenes defendith from
reyne and from vnclennesse of water that cometh of cloudes.
Whereof cometh cloudes or skyes, but of humours and mois-
ture goyng oute of the erthe, and arne lifte up in-to þe firma-
ment, and there waxe thicke ?   And so comen thre thinges of
hem : rayne, hayle, and snowe.   This cloude betokeneth
mannes body, þat cometh of vnclennesse.   This body hath
thre thinges with it, as hath the cloude : for the body hath
heryng, seyng, and felyng.   In that þat the body hath sight, it
desyreth tho thinges þat it seeth ; it desyreth goode thinges
and fayre faces, and | it desyreth large possessiouns.   And
what arne alle thise thinges but as reyne comynge of cloudes,
defoulyng the herte in desyre and loue to gadre goodes to-
gedre, vnrestyng the herte by many besynesses, disperplying
the herte by many and vnprofitable thoughtes, and troublyng
it in leuyng of tho thinges þat it hath gadrid to-gidre.   In þat
that the body hath heryng, it herith gladly the owne worschip
and loue and frenschip of the worlde.   It herith also all þat is
delitable to þe body and noyous to þe soule.   And what arne
all thise thinges, but as snowe þat sone is dissolued and makith
þe soule colde to God and harde to mekenes ?   In that that the
body hath felyng, it felith gladly þe owne lust and eese of þe
flessh.   And what is this but hayle frore to-gidre of waters of
vnclennesse, makyng þe soule vnfruytfull to gostly þinges,
stronge to wordly thinges, and softe to þe desyre of þe body?
Therefor who euer desyre to be defendid from this cloude, fle
he to my mekenesse and folue it ; for by þat he schall be
defended from couetise of sight, that he desyre not vnleful

fol. 65 b

---

[1] *Latin* amicis. Amicis. *The MS. has omitted the second* Amicis, *which is
necessary for the sense.*

[2] MS. iij *in margin.*

thing*es*; and from delyt of hering, that he here not ayenst
trouthe ; and fro lust of the flessh, that he be not ouercome in
vnlefull steringes.

Forsoth, I say to þe that the beholdyng of my mekenes is as
5 a good mantell, makyng hote hem þat bere it.   That is to say,
not hem that bere it only in thought, but also in dede ; for a
bodely mantell makith not a body hote bot if it be bore, nor
my mekenes pro*f*iteth not hem to thenke it, but yf eche of hem
studie to folue it in dede to her power.   There-for, my dough-
10 t*er*, doo vp-on the this mekenes to þy power ; for wy*m*men of
þe worlde bere mantels that haue moch pryde outward and
with-in, but litil pro*f*yt.   Suche clothinge fle þou in all wyse ;
for but yf þe luf of the worlde be first foule [1] | and lothsom vn- fol. 66 a
to þe ; and but yf þou thinke continuelly the m*er*cy of oure
15 lorde God schewed vn-to þe, and thyne vnkyndnesse ayen to
hym ; and but yf thou thinke alwey tho thinges þat þou hast
doo and þat þou doest, and what sentence of dome þou deseruest
ther-fore, thou maist not gete the mantel of my meken es.   For
where-to meked I me so moche, of where-of deserued I so
20 moche grace, but for I thought and knewe wele þat I was right
nought nor had right nought of my-self ?   There-for I wolde not
myn oune preysyng, but þe p*r*aysyng and worschip of hy m
only that was yeuer and maker of all.   Therefor, dought*er*,
flee þou to þe mantel of my mekenesse, and thenke and holde
25 thy-self a synner aboue all othir.   For þough thou see ony
wykked, thou wost not what schall come vn-to hem to-morowe .
Also þou wost not wi*th* what entent nor with what knowyn g
thei do it, wheþ*er* it is of freelte or of purpos.   Therfore p*re*-
ferre thi-self to-fore none ; and thou owist to deme none in
30 thyn herte.

Oure lorde Ih*es*u Cryst techith vs to meke vs in foure
man*er*s.

The sone of God spekith vn-to seint Birgitte and saith :
Thou owest to meke the in foure man*er*e wyse.   First,[2]
35 anempst hem that haue power by estat or by office in þe

---

[1] *Marg. gloss* : A schort lesson : | how þou schalt arraie the in þe mantel of
mek[e]nesse.

[2] MS. j *in margin.*

worlde. For sithe man despisid and lefte to obeye God, it is
worthie þat he obbeye to man. And for folke mowe not be
with-oute gouernours, therefor reuerence and worschip most be
youe to þe power. Seconde,[1] þou most meke the anempst hem
that bene poure gostly, that is to seye, anempst synners, 5
prayeng for hem and thonkyng God for in happes thou art not
ne hast be noon suche. Thridde,[2] anempst hem that bene riche
gostly, that is to say, anempst þe frendes of God, thenkyng
thy-self vnworthy to serue hem or to be conuersaunt amongst
hem. Fourthe,[3] anempst þe pore of þe worlde, helping hem 10
and clothing hem and wasching her feet. |

This is a reuelacion sende to the holy spouse of Crist,
saint Birgitte, in whiche oure lady saint Marye repreueth
the pryde of wymmen in her porte, beryng, speche, array,
and oþere gouernaunce, by example of thre wrecched 15
wymmen; of whiche one was in helle, anothir in purgatorye, and the thridde alyue.

The[4] holy spouse of Crist, saint Birgitte, spekith vn-to oure
lorde Ihesu Crist wordes of louyng and praysyng for the grete
grace þat he wrought with hir, and saith : praysing be vn-to þe, 20
almyghty God, for all thinges þat bene made, and worschip for
alle thi vertues. Seruice be youe vn-to þe of all creatures for
thi grete loue and charitee. I, ther-fore, vnworthy and sinfull
euer fro my youthe, thonke þe, my God, that thou denyest
grace to no synners that asken hit ; but thou sparist and hast 25
mercy on alle. O my suettest God, it is full meruellous that
thou workist with me ; for whan it plesith the, thou bringist
my body in a spiritual slepe, and than þou excitest and rerist
vp my soule to see and here and fele gostly thinges. O my
God mooste swete, how suete bene thy wordis to my soule, 30
which sualwith hem as mete althir suettist. And thei entren
with ioye in-to myn herte, for whan I here thy wordes, I am
bothe full and hungry ; fulle, for me delitith no thinge but thi
wordes ; hungry, for the more I here hem the more feruently
I desyre hem. Ther-for, blesful God, yeue me helpe euere to 35
do thy wille.

[1] MS. ij *in margin.*   [2] MS. iij *in margin.*   [3] MS. iiij *in margin.*
[4] *Marg. gloss* : Oure lorde appering vn-to saint Birgitte.

and lothsom vn to þe · and but yf þou thinke contynuelly the mcy
of oure lorde god schewed vn to þe · and thine vnkyndnesse ayen
to hym · and but yf þou thinke alwey tho thinges · þt þou hast
doo · And þat þou doest · And what sentence of dome þou deser-
nest þerfore · thou maist not gete the mantel of my mekenes
ffor where to meked y me so moche · or where of deserued y
so moche grace · but for y thought · and knewe wele þt y
was right nought · nor had right nought of my self · þerfore y wolde not · myn owne preysing · but þe preysing and
worschip of hym only that was euer and maker of all
þerfor ought flee þou to þe mantel of my mekeneſſ
and thenke and holde thy self · a synner aboue all othyr
for þough þou see ony wykked · þou wost not · what
schall come vn to hem to morowe · Also þou wost not wt
what entent · nor wt what knowyng · thei do it · whey
it is of feeble · or of purpos · þerfore preyse thi self to
fore none · and thou ouest to deme none in thyn herte
¶ Oure lorde this gyft techith vs to meke vs in foure maū
¶ þe sone of god spekith vn to eu't synggite and saith
þou ouest to meke the in foure mane wyse · first
anempst hem that hane power by estat · or by office in þe
worlde · for elthe man desirid and lefe to obeye god · it
is worthie þat he obeye to man · And for folke molle not
be wt oute gouernonis · þerefor reuerence and worschip
most be yone to þe power · Seconde þou most meke the -
anempst hem that bene powre gostly · that is to seye · anempst
synneres prayens for hem · and thonkyng god · fer in happes
þou art not · ne hast be noon suche · Thyrde anempst hem
that bene riche gostly · that is to say · anempst þe frendes of god
thenkyng thy self · vnworthy to serue hem · or to be conuersant
amongst hem · fourthe anempst þe pore of þe worlde helpyng
hem and clothyng hem · and waschyng her feet ·

Oure lorde Ihesu Crist ansuerith and seith : I am with-outen
begynneng and withouten ende. And alle thinges that are
arne made by my power ; all thinges arne disposed by my
wisdom and all thinges arne gouerned be my doome and wille ;
and alle my workes arne ordeyned by charitee. Ther-fore to
me is right nought impossible. But that herte is ouer-harde
that nothir loueth me ne dredith me, sith I am gouernoure of
all þinges, | and Iuge. And ȝit man fulfilleth rathir the wille fol. 67 a
of þe deuell, whiche is my turmentour and a deceyuour, whiche
yeueth oute venym largely by the worlde, for which soules
mowen not lyue, but thay arne drouned doune in-to the deth
of helle. This venomos synne, which, though it be bitter vn-to
þe soule, ȝit to many it sauoreth swetly, and eche day it is
drowe oute of þe deuels honde vpon moche people. But whoo
herde euere ony¹ suche thingis, that lyf is offred vn-to alle,
and thai chesen rathir deth þan lyf. Neuertheles I, God of
alle, am pacient and haue compassion of her wrecchidnesse.
For I doo as a kyng þat sendith wyne vn-to his seruantis and
saith : 'Brille it forth to many, for it is holsom. It yeueth
helthe vn-to þe syke, myrthe vn-to hem þat bene heuy, and
a manful hert to them þat bene hoole.' Bot ȝit þe wyne is not
sente but by an able vessell. So I haue sent my wordes,
whiche arne likned to wyne, vn-to my seruauntes by the, that
art my vessell, whiche I wille fille and drawe oute aftir myn
owne wille. Myne holy spirit shall teche the wheder thou
schalt goo and what þou schalt saye. Ther-fore speke thou
ioyfully and with-oute fere tho thinges that I bidde the ; for
there is none that schall preuayle ayenst me.

Thanne ansuerde the spouse, seint Birgitte : O king of all
glorie and blisse, yeuer of all wisdom and graunter of all
vertues, why takist thou me to suche a werk, that haue wasted
my body in synnes ? I am as an asse, lewde and vnwyse and
defectif in vertues ; and I haue trespassid in alle thinges and
no thyng amendid.

Oure lorde Ihesu Cryst answerde : if money or othir metall
be presented vn-to a lorde, who schulde meruaille, though
he | made hym there-of crounes or ringes or peces to his owne fol. 67 b
profite ? So is it not to meruaille though I resceyue þe hertis

¹ MS. ony *inserted above line.*

of my frendes presented vn-to me, and doo my wille in thaym.
And for as moche as one hath lesse vndirstonding and anothir
more, there-for I vse the conscience of eche as is expedient to
my worschip.   For the herte of a rightfull man is my money ;
therfor be thou stable and redi vn-to my wille.

Than [1] spak the modir of God to seint Birgitte, sayeng :
What sayen þe proude wommen in thy kyngdome ?

Saynt Birgitte ansuerd : O lady, I am one of thaim, and
ther-fore I am aschamed to speke in thy presence.

Than sayde the modir of god : though I knowe it better þan
thou, ȝet I wole here it of the.

Saynt Birgitte ansuerde : whanne, sche saith, verray mekenesse was prechid to vs, we seide that oure progenitours
enherite vs, and yaue vs in heritage large possessions and fayre
nortur of maneres and condicions.   Why ther-fore schulde I not
folue them ?   My modir saat with the first and the highest and
was clad and arrayed noblely, hauyng right many seruauntes
and norsshyng thaim with worschip.   Why schulde I not also
enherite suche thinges to my doughter, whiche hath lerned to
bere hir noblely and to lyve with bodily ioye and to die with
grete worschip of the worlde ?

The modre of God ansuerd : iche womman that hath thise
wordis and sueth hem in dede gooth by the verry way vn-to
helle.   And ther-for suche ansuere is full harde.   What pro-
fiteth to haue suche wordis, whan the maker of all thinges
suffred his body to abyde and duelle in erthe with all mekenesse fro the tyme of his birthe vn-to his deth, and there come
neuere cloth of pride vpon hym.   For-sothe, suche wommen
considren not his face, how he stoode lyving and dede vpon | the
crosse, blody and pale for paynes ; nor that rekken not of his
repreues whiche he herde, nor of his despisable deth whiche he
chees ; nor thei haue not in mynde the place where he ȝaaf vp
the spiryt, for where theues and robbers had resceyued many
woundes, there was my sone wounded.   And I, that to-fore all
creatures am moost dere vn-to hym, and in me is all mekeness,
was there present.   And there-fore thay that done such proude
and pompous thinges, and yeuen othir occasion to folue thaim,
bene liche vn-to a sprenkle ; whiche, whanne it is put to

fol. 68 a

---

[1] *Marg. gloss* : Oure lady and saint Birgitta.

a brennyng licour, it brenneth & defouleth alle theim that it
sprenklith. Right so the proude ȝeueth ensample of pryde,
and full greuously they brenne soules by euel exsamples.

And ther-fore I wil now doo as a good modre whiche, fering
5 hir children, makith hem to see þe rodde, whiche the seruauntes
seeth also. But the children, seyng the rodde, dreden to offende
hir modre, thonkyng hir that sche wolde threten hem and not
bete thaim. The seruauntes dreden to be beten yf thay tres-
passe. And so of þat drede of the modre the children doon
10 moo good dedes than they dedyn to-fore, and the seruauntes
doon lasse euell. So sothly, for I am modre of mercy, ther-for
I wole schewe to the the rewarde of synne, that the frendis of
God may be more feruent in the charitee of God. And synners,
knowyng thaire perell, flee synne, atte leest, for drede. And
15 on this manere wyse I haue mercy bothe of good and euel; of
the good peple, that thay obtene and gete more croune and
reward in heuen; of the wicked, that thay suffre lasse payne.
And there is none so moche a synner, but þat I am redy to
helpe hym; and my sone to yeue hym grace, yf he aske mercy
20 with charite.

Aftir this, there appered three wymmen:[1] that is to sey,
the modre, and the doughter, and the nyfte, that is, the
doughteris doughter. But the modre and the nyfte appered
dede, and the doughtir aperid o-lyve. The saide deed modre
25 se-|med to comme crepyng oute of a foule and derke clay diche; fol. 68 b
whos herte was drawe oute of hir body, hir lippes kut of, and
hir chyn tremeled; hir teth, schynyng, white, and longe,
grinted and chatred to-gidres; hir nose thrilles weren all-to
gnawe; hir eyghen put oute, hangyng doune on hir chekes
30 betwene senowes; hir forhed was holowe; and instede of hir
forhed was there a grete and derke depnesse. In hir hede the
hede panne faylled and was away, and the brayne boyled vp as
it had be leed, and flowed oute as blak picche. Hir nek turned
a-boute as a tree that is turned in the instrument of a turnour,
35 ayenst whiche was sette an Irne alther sharpest, kittyng and
shaving away with-outen ony comfort. Hir breste was open
and full of wormes longe and smale; and eche of thaim
walowed hider and thider vp-on othir. Hir armes were liche

[1] *Marg. gloss* : the apperin[g] of thre wym[men].

vn-to the haftes or handlis of a grynding stone.   Hir hondes
weren as keyes full of knottes and longe.   The chynes of hir
bak weren alle dissolued, eche from othir ; and one goyng vp,
anothir goyng doune, they cessed neu*ere* of mevyng.   A long
and a grete serpent come forthe by the nethir p*artie* of hir
stomak vn-to þe ou*erparties ; and ioyneng the heed and taylle
to-gidre as a rounde bowe, wente rounde aboute hir bowels
continuelly, as a wheel.   Hire hippes and hir legges semed as
two roughe staues of thorne full of prickes moost sharpe.   Hir
feet weren as it hadde bene toodes.

   Thanne [1] this dede modre spak vn-to hir dought*er* þat was
o-lyve, sayeng : here thou, alto torne and my venomos doughtre.
Woo to me that eu*ere* I was thy moder.   I am sche that sette
the in þe nest of pryde, in whiche thow, maad hoo[t],[2] waxist
til thou come to age.   And þan it was plesyng to the that thou
haddist spe*nt* thyne age in that nest.   Therefor I say to the
that as often as thou turnest thyn eyhen with lokyng, or sight
of pryde whiche I taught the, so ofte castist thou boyling
venom in my*n* | eyghen w*ith* vnsuffrable brennyng hete.   As
often as thou spekest wordes of pride whiche thou lerndest of
me, so often swalowe I moost bitt*er* drinke.   As often as thyne
eren arne fillid w*ith* wynde of pryde whiche the wawes of
arrogance and pryde exciten and stiren vp in the, that is to
say, to here p*raysinges of thyn owne body and to desyre
worschippes of the worlde, whiche thou lernedest of me ; so
often cometh to myn eres a feerful and dredfull soune, with
wynde blowyng and bre*nnyng.   Woo there-fore to me, poure
and wrecched : ther-fore poore, for I haue nor fele right nought
of good, and ther-for wrecched, for I haue habundaunce and
plentee of all euell.   But thou, doughtir, art liche vn-to the
taille of a cowe whiche, goyng in foule claye, as often as sche
moeueth hir taille, so often sche defouleth and bys[p]renglith [3]
thaim that been nye aboute hir.   So thou, doughtre, art lyke
vn-to a cowe ; for thou hast not no goodly wisdom, and thou

fol. 69 a

----

[1] *Marg. gloss* : the dede modre and the dought*er* o-lyve.
[2] MS. maad hood ; *Latin* in quo calefacta crescebas, donec ad aetatem
pervenisti.
[3] MS. bystrenglith ; *Latin* aspergit.   *Cf. N.E.D.* bespringild (*c.* 1440) ;
the g *is influenced by M.E.* besprenge[n], *to besprinkle.*

goest aftir the werkes and steringes of thy body. Ther-for as
often as thou foluest the werkes of my custome, that is to say,
tho synnes which I taught the, so often is my payne renewed,
and the more greuously it brenneth vp-on me. Ther-fore, o þu
5 my doughtre, why art thou proude of thy generacion and
kynne? For it be honour and worschip vn-to the that the
vnclennesse of my bowelles was thyne pilowe, my schamefull
membre was thyne oute goyng, and the vnclennesse of my
bloode was thy clothinge whan thou were bore? Ther-for now
10 my wombe, in which thou lay, is alto eten with wormes. But
why, doughtir, playne I vp-on the, whych I aught more to
playne vpon myself? For thre thynges ther arne that turmenten
me moost greuously in myne herte. The first is that I, maad
of God to heuenly ioye, mysvsid my conscience and haue dis-
15 posed me vn-to the sorowes of helle. The seconde is that God
made me fayre as an aungell, but I deformed and haue forschape
my-self so that I am more | liche vn-to the deuel than to an   fol. 69 b
aungel of God. The thridde is þat in the tyme youen to me,
I made a full euel chaunge. For I resceyued a litil thing
20 schort and transitorie, that is to say delectacion of synne, for
whiche I fele now endles euel, that is, þe payne of helle.

Thanne [1] saide this deed modre vn-to the spouse of Cryst,
saint Birgitte: thou, sche saith, that seest me, seest me not
but by bodily liknesse. For yf thou schuldest se me in that
25 fourme in whiche I am, thou schuldest dye for drede; for alle
my membres arne deuels. And there-for the scripture is trewe
that saith that as rightfull men arne membres of God, so
synners arne membres of the deuel. Right so haue I now in
experience that deuels arne fastned vn-to my soule; for þe
30 wille of my herte hath disposed me vn-to so moche filthe,
deformyte, and myschap. But here now furthermore. It
semeth to the that my fete arne as toodes. That is for I stode
stablely in synne; there-for now fendes stonden stablely in
me. And alwey bytyng and gnawyng me, thai arne neuere
35 full. My legges and my thyes arne as staues fulle of prickyng
thornes, for I hadde a wille aftir flesshly delectacion and myn
own lust. That iche chyne of my bak is loose, and eche of
hem moued ayenst othir; that is therfor for the ioye of myn

---

[1] *Marg. gloss* : [t]he dampned [m]oder spekith to [S]aint Birgitte.

herte sometyme went vpward ouermoche for wordly solace and
comfort, and somtyme ouermoche dounward by to moche
heuynesse, grucchyng, and wratthe for aduersitee and disease
of the worlde.   And therefor as the bak is moued and sturid
after þe moeuyng of þe hede, so aught I to haue be stable ʒ
and moeuable aftir þe wille of God, which is heed of all good.
But for I did not soo, there-for I suffre rightfully these paynes
that þou seest.   That a serpent crepeth forthe by the lower
fol. 70 a   parties of my | stomak vn-to the hier parties, and standyng as
a bowe turneth aboute as a whele, there-for it is for my lust ɪ
and delyte was inordinat ; and my wille wolde haue had alle
worldes goodes in possession, and in many wyse to haue spent
hem, and vndiscretly.   Ther-for now the serpent serchith
aboute myn entreils withoute comfort, grawyng and byting
with-outen mercy.   That my brest is open and alle-to gnawe ɪ
with wormes, that schewith the verray rightwisnesse of God ;
for I loued foule and roten thinges more þan God ; and þe loue
of myn herte was all youen to transitori and passing thinges
of the flesshe and the worlde.   And there-for as of smale
wormes arne brought forthe lenger wormes, right soo my 2
soule ; for the foule stinking thinges that I loued is fulfilled
with deuels.   Myn armes semen as they were haftes ; that is
for I hadde my desyre as two armes ; þat is to say, for I desyred
long lyf, that I myght haue lyued longe in synne.   I wolde
also and desyred that the dome of God had be more esy than 2
the scripture saith.   Neuertheles, my conscience tolde me wele
that my tyme was schorte and þe doome of God vnsuffrable.
But ayenward my desyre and delyt that I had to synne stired
me to thenke that my lyf schulde be longe and the doome of
God suffrable.   And of suche suggestions my consciens was 3
subuerted and turned vp so doune, and my wille and reson
folued lust and delectacion.   And ther-for now the deuell is
moeued in my soule ayenst my wille, and my conscience
vndirstondith and feleth þat the dome of God is rightfull.   My
hondes arne as longe keyes.   And þat is for the preceptes and 3
comaundementes werne not delitable to me ; and therfor myn
handis arne to me now grete birden, and to noon othir vse.
fol. 70 b   My necke is turned aboute as a tree | that is turned ayenst
a scharpe yren ; that is for the wordes of God weren not swete

vn-to me to swalue and taste thaym in the charitee and loue
of myn herte; but thay weren ovir bitter, for thai argued and
repreued the delectacion and wille of myn herte; and therfore
now a scharpe Iren stondith ayenst my throte.   My lippes
5 arne cutte of, for they werne redy to wordes of pride, vayne,
gameful, and vnhonest; but naughtfull they weren and full
irkesom to speke the wordes of God.   My chynne apperith
tremelyng, and my teeth grintith and betith to-gidre; that is
for I was of full wille to yeue mete vn-to my body, þat I myght
10 seme faire and desirable, hoole and stronge to alle the delites
and plesaunce of the body.   And there-for now my chynne
tremlith and quaketh with-oute comforte, and my teth beten
to-gidre; for all þat thay wasted was but an vnprofitable
labour as to þe fruyt of the soule.   My nose is cutte of; for as
15 amongest you it is wonte to be do vn-to thaym that trespassen
in suche a caas to thaire more schame, right so is the mark of
my shame sette vpon me endelesly.   That myn eyghen hange
doune bytwene senowes vp-on my chekes, it is rightfull that
right as the eyghen ioyed of the fairnesse of my chekes for
20 ostentacioun and schewyng of pryde, so now of moche wepyng
thay arne putte oute and hange doune to my chekis with
schame and confusion.   And right wisly is my forhed holowe,
and in-stede of it there arne grete derknesse.   For aboute my
forhed was sette the veyle and the arraye of pryde; and I wolde
25 appere gloriouse, and be seen of fairnesse, and seme fayre.
And ther-for my forhed is now derke and foule, deformed and
misseshape.   That my brayne boyleth vp and flowith oute as
leede and picke, it is wel worthy.   For as lede is softe and
may be bowed aftir the wille of hym that vsith it, right so my
30 conscience, whiche lay in my brayne, was bowed to þe wille of
myn herte, although I vnderstode wele tho thinges þat | [1] I fol. 71 a
schulde haue doo.   And the passion also of the sone of God
was no thinge fastned in myn herte, but it flowed owte as
a thynge that I knewe wele and toke none hede of.   And
35 furthermore, of þat holy blood that flowed oute of the membres
of þe sone of God, I toke no more kepe than of picke, and
fledde as picke þe wordes of charitee and of the loue of God,
lest they schulde turne me or trouble me from the delites of

---

[1] I schulde haue *catchword*.

the body.   Neuertheles, oþere while I herde the wordes of God
for schame of man; but as lightly as thay entrid, so lightly
thay went oute of myn hert ayene.   And therfor now my
brayne flowith oute as brennyng picke, with moost hoot
boylyng.   My eres arne stopped with harde stones, for woordes
of pride entrid in thaim ioyfully, and softly and suetly they
wenten doune in-to the herte, for the charitee of God was sperd
oute of my herte.   And for þat I did all that I myght for pryde
and for the worlde, ther-for now ioyfull woordes bene sperd
oute from myn eeres.

　But thou may aske yf I did ony meritorie or goode dedes.
And I aunswere the I did as doth a chaunger of money, which
clippeth or kitteth the moneye; and sith resigneth or taketh it
ayen to the lorde þat oweth it.   So I fasted and did almes and
suche othir goode werkes; but I did hem for drede of helle, 1
and for to escape thaduersitees and disease of the body.   But
for the charite and the loue of God was kutte of from my
workes, therfore such workes werne not vaillable to me for to
geten heuen, although thay ware not with-outen reward.
Thou myghtest also aske hou I am with-inforthe in my 2
wille, whan so moche foulnesse and mysshappe is with-oute-
forthe.   I answer: my wille is as the wille of a mansleer or of
hym that wolde gladly slee his owne modre.   So I coueyte and
desyre the worst euel vn-to God, my maker, which hath be to
me best and moost swete.   2

fol. 71 b Thanne the dede | nyfte,[1] þat is, the doughtres doughter of
the same deed Beldame, spak vn-to hir owne modre that was
ȝit than o-lyve, sayeng: here, thou scorpion my mooder, woo
to me, for thou haste euel deceyued me.   For thou scheudest
me thy mery face, but thou prickedest me ful greuously in 3
myn herte.   Thre counsails thou yaf me of thy mouthe, thre
thinges I lerned of thy workes.   And thre wayes thou scheudest
me in thy processe and forth goyng.   The first counseill was to
loue flesshly for to gete carnall loue and flesshly frenschip.
The second was to spende temporall goodes ouere largely for 35
worschip of the worlde.   The thridde was to haue reste for
delectation and delyte of the body.

　These counsailles weren to me ful noyous and grete hind-

[1] *Marg. gloss*: [s]pekith vn-to hir modre.

ringe. For I loued carnally, ther-fore haue I now shame and spirituel enuye. And for I spent wastfully temporell goodes, therfor was I pryued of grace and the yeftis of God in my lyf, and aftir my deeth I haue goten me grete confusion and shame. For I delited in the quyet and rest of the flesshe in my lyf, therfore in the houre of my dethe began vnrest of my soule with-outen comfort.

Thre thinges also I lerned of thy workes. The first was to doo somme goode dedes, and neuertheles vse forthe and not to leue þat synne that delyted me : as a man shold doo that delid hony with venym, and offerd it vn-to a Iuge ; and he, therby moeued to wratthe, shedde it vp-on hym that offerid it. So am I now experte in many-folde anguysshe and tribulacion.

The seconde is þat I lerned of the a merueillous manere of clothinge me ; that was to hille myn eyghen with a kerchif, to haue sandales on my | feet, gloues on my hondes, and the necke fol. 72 a all nakid with-out-forthe. This kerchif hilling myn eyghen betokeneth fairnesse of my body, which so beschadowed my gostly eyghen that I toke none hede nor see not the fairnesse of my soule. The sandals whiche kepen the fete vndirnethe and not aboue betoken the holy faith of the chirche, whiche I helde faithfully, but there folued it no fruytfull workes. For as sandals furtherne my fete, right so my consciens, stondyng in faith, promoted my soule. But for good workes folued not, therefor my soule was as naked. The gloues on the hondes bitoken a veyne hoope that I hadde ; for I extendid my workes, whiche arne tokened in the handes, in-to a so greet and large mercy of God, which is noted in the gloues, that,[1] whanne I groped the rightwisnesse of God, I felte it not nor toke none hede there-of. There-fore I was ouer bolde to synne. But whan deth cam, than fille doune the kerchef from myn eyghen vp-on the erthe, that is to say, vp-on my body. And thanne the soule see and knewe it-self that it was naked, for fewe of my dedes weren goode, and my synnes weren many. And for schame I myght not stonde in the paleys of the endles kyng of blisse, for I was schamefully clothed. But þanne deuels drowe me in-to harde payne, where I was scorned with schame and confusion.

[1] *Latin* quia.

I

The thridde thinge, modre, that I lerned of the was to clothe the seruaunt in the lordes clothes, and to sette hym in the lordis seete, and to worschip hym as a lorde, and to ministre vn-to þe lorde the releefs of the seruaunt and alle thinges that weren despisable.   This lorde is charitee and the [5] loue of God.   The seruaunt is a wille to synne.   Sothly in my

fol. 72 b herte, where owed to haue regned godly charitee was sette þe | seruaunt, that is, dilectacion and lust of synne, whomme I clothid thanne whan I turned vn-to my wille all temporall thing that is maad.   And the releefs and the parynges and moost abiect [10] thinges I yaue vn-to God, not of charitee, but of drede.   So ther-for was myn hert glad of fulfilling and dilectacion of mine own wille, for the charite and the loue of God was excluded frome me, and the goode lorde spered oute and the euel seruaunt closid with-inne.   Loo, modor, þise thre thinges lerned [15] I of thy workes.

Thre wayes thou scheudest me also in thy forthegoyng.   The first was bright.   But whan I entred in it, I was blendid of þe brightnesse there-of.   The seconde was compendiouse and sleper as Ise, in whiche, whan I wente oo stappe forward, I [20] sloode ayene bakward an hool paas.   The thride way was ouer longe, in whiche, whan I wente forthe, ther come aftir me a scharpe rennyng floode and baar me ouer vnder an hille in-to a depe diche.

In the first way is noted the forth-goyng of my pryde, which [25] was ouere bright ; for the ostentacion and schewyng which proceded of my pride shined so moche in myn eyen that I thought not the ende of it, and ther-for I was blynde.

In the seconde way is noted inobedience [1] in this lyf is not longe ; for aftir deth a man is compellid to obbeye.   Neuerthe- [30] les, to me it was longe, for whan I went oo stappe forward in mekenesse of confession, I slood bakward a paas.   For I wolde þat the synne confessid schulde haue be foryoue, but aftir confession maade, I wolde not flee þe synne.   And therefor I stode not stably in the steppe of obedience, but I slode ayene [35] in-to synne, as he þat slideth vpon yse ; for my wille was coolde and wolde not aryse and flee froo tho thinges þat delited

fol. 73 a me.   So therfor whan I went | a steppe forward shryuyng of

[1] MS. in obedience.

my synnes, I slood a paas bakward ; for I wolde falle ayene to thoo synnes and dilectacions that delited me, of whiche I was confessid.

The thridde way was that [I]¹ hooped a thinge which was
5 impossible ; that is, to mow do synne and not to haue longe payn ; to mowe also lyue longe, and the hour of deth not to nyghe. And whan I went forthe by this way, þere cam after me an hasty rennyng floode ; that is to say, deth, whiche froom oo yere to anothir caught me and turned my feete vp so doune
10 with payne of syknesse. What were these feete, but, whan syknesse come vp-on, I myght litill take hede to the profyt of the body and lasse to the helthe of the soule ? Ther-for I fille in-to a deepe diche, whan my herte that was high in pride and harde in synne braste, and the soule fille doune lowe in-to the
15 diche of peyne for synne. And therfor this way was longe ; for aftir þe lyf of the body was ended, anoon ther began a longe peyne. Woo, therfor to me, my modre ; for alle thoo thinges that I lerned of the with Ioye, nowe I wayle hem with wepyng and sorowe.

20 Thanne spak this same deed doughter² vn-to the spouse of Cryst, saint Birgitte, whiche sigh all þise thinges, sayenge : here thou that seest me. To the it semyth that myn hede and my face is as it were thondre, thondring and leuennyng with-inne and with-oute ; and my necke and my breste as it were putte
25 in an harde presse, with longe sharpe prickes ; myn armes and my feete arne as it were longe serpentes ; and my wombe is smyten with harde hamers ; my thyes and my legges arne as it were flowing water oute of the goters of a roof ; and my fete allto frore to-gidre. But ȝet ther is oo payne with-inneforthe |
30 that is bitter³ to me than alle thise. Right as yf ther were ony **fol. 73 b** persone of whom alle the brethes of his leving spiritis weren stopped and alle the veynes, fulfilled with wynde, arted hem vn-to the herte, whiche for violence and strengþe of thoo wyndes schulde begynne to breste ; so am I disposed with-
35 inneforth ful wrecchidlye for the wynde of my pryde, whiche was to me full dere beloued. Neuertheles, ȝit I⁴ am in the waye

---

¹ *Latin* sperabam.
² *Marg. gloss* : The deed nyfte spekith to saynt Birgitte.
³ *Latin* amarior.   ⁴ MS. I I.

I 2

of mercy, for in my moost greuous syknesse I was shryve in the best wyse I coude, for drede of peyne. But whan deeth came neer, than com to my mynde the consideracion and beholding of the passion of my God, hou that was moche more greuous and more bitter than all that I was worthy to suffre for my synnes and demerites. And with suche consideracion, I gate teeres and wepte waylled that the charite and the loue of God was so moche to me and myn so litil to hym. Than I behelde hym with the eyghen of my conscience and saide: 'O lorde, I beleue the, my God. O thou sone of the virgine, haue mercy vp-on me for thy bitter passion ; for now from hens-forward wolde I amend my lyfe, yf I hadde tyme, full fayne.' And in that poynte of tyme was ther accendid and kyndelid in myn herte a sparcle of charitee, by whiche the passion of Cryst semed more bitter to me þan myn owne deth. And so than brast my herte, and my soule come in-to the hondes and pow er of deuels to be presented in the doom of God. Therfor it come in-to þe hondes of deuels, for it was not worthy that the aungels of fairnesse schulde come nere the soule of so moche foulenes. But in the doome of God, whan the deuels cryed and asked that my soule schulde be dempte and | dampned vn-to helle, the Iuge ansuerde : 'I see, he saith, a sparcle of charite in the herte whiche owith not to be quenched, but it most bee in my sight. Therfore I deme the soule vn-to purga-cion, vn-to þe tyme that it be so worthely purged and made clene that it deserue and haue foryefnesse.'

But now myght thou aske yf I schall haue parte of all the goodes and goode deedes that be done for me. I aunswere the by a lyknesse. Right as yf þu see two balaunces hange, and in that one were naturelly bering dounward and in the tothir were some light þing goyng vpward, the gretter thinges and fayre that were put in the voyde balaunce, so moche the rathir scholde þai lifte vp the tothir balaunce þat is hevy and of grete weight. Right so is it with me ; for the depper that I was in synne, the more greuously am I goo doun into payne. And therfor what euere be doo to the worschip of God for me, it liftith me vp from peyne ; and specially that prayer and good that is doone be rightfull men and the frendes of God, and benefetes þat be doon of wele goten goodes and dedes of

charitee.   Such thinges, sothly, thay bene that maken me eche
daye to nygh more nerre to God.

Aftir this spak the holy modre[1] of God vn-to the spouse of
Cryst, saint Birgitte, and saide : Thou meruaillest how I that
am Quene of heuen and thou that lyuest in the worlde and that
soule that is in purgatorye and that othir that is in helle
speken to-gidre.   This schall I wele tellen the.   I, sothly, goo
neuere from heuen, for I schall neuere be departid from the
sight of God.   Nor that soule þat is in helle schall not be
departed from payne.   Nor that soule that is in purgatorie,
nothir, til it be clene purged.   Nor thou schalt not come to vs
to-fore the departyng of thy bodily lyfe.   But thy soule with
thyn vndirstonding, by vertue of the spirit of God, is lyfte vp
to here the wordes of God in heuen ; and thou arte suffred to
knowe som paynes in helle and in purgatorie, for warnes | and fol. 74 b
amendement of euel lyuers and to the comforte and profyte of
thaim that bene good.   Natheles, knawe thou that thy body
and thy soule arne Ioyned to-gidre in erthe, but the holy gooste
that is in heuen yeueth the vndirstonding to vndirstonde his
wille.

Aftir this, this thridde womman that was o-lyue lefte all the
worlde and entred in-to Religion, and lyued all hir lyf aftir in
grete perfeccion and holynesse.

How our lady tellith saint Birgitte of the doome of Sir Revela-
Charles hir sone ; and what allegeaunce oure lady and his tions,
good aungel made to-fore Cryste for his soule ; and what Chap. 13.
the feende allegged ayenst the soule ; and of the sentence
that Cryst yaf for deliueraunce of the soule.

Owre lady saint Marye speketh vn-to saint Birgitte and saith :
I wole tell the hou I did to the soule of Charles thi sone.
When it was departid from his body, I did as a womman that
standith by another womman whan sche childeth, to help the
chylde that it dye not of flowyng of bloode ne be not slayne in
that streight place were it cometh oute ; being also ware that
the childes enemyes that bene in the hous slee it not.   On
the same wyse did I ; for I stode nygh the saide sone a litel
to-fore he yaf vp the spirit, that he schulde not haue no flesshly

---

[1] *Marg. gloss* : Oure lady a[pperith] ayene vn-to s[aint] Birgitte.

loue so in mynde that it schulde cause hym to thenke or say
onythinge ayenst God ; nor that he schulde wille leeue [1] ony
thinges that weren plesing to God ; nor wille to do tho þinges
that myght in ony wyse be contrarie to the wille of God and
hindring to his soule.   I halpe hym also in that straite place
þat is in the goyng oute of the soule from the body ; so that
he schulde not suffre so harde payne in deeth that schulde
cause hym to be vnstable or to dispeire in ony wyse, ne þat he
schulde not foryeten God in his dyeng.   I kepte also his soule
in suche wyse from his dedly enmyes, that is to say, from
fendes, that none of hem myght touche it.   But anoone as it
was goo oute from the body, I toke it in-to my keping and |

fol. 75 a defence.   And than alle the company of feendes hastely fledde
and wente awaye, which of thaire malice desireden to haue
worwed the soule and euerlastyngly to haue putte it in torment.   But how the doome was of the soule of the same
Charles after his deeth, it schall be schewed the plainly whan
it pleseth me.

Thanne, aftir a fewe dayes, oure lady saint Marie appered
vn-to saint Birgitte wakyng in prayer, and sayde : now it is
leeful vn-to the, by the goodnesse of God, to see and to here
how the doome was doo vp-on the saide soule whan it was
departid from the body, and that that was done thanne in a
momente of tyme, that is, in a right schort whyle, to-fore the
vnspecable magestee of God schall be schewed vn-to the by
order and by layser, by bodily liknesse, so that thyne vndirstonding may conceyue it.

Thanne anoone saint Birgitte was rauysshed into a grete and
fayre paleys, where sche sigh oure lorde Ihesu Crist sitting to
deme as a crouned Emperour, with vnnumerable company of
aungels and sayntes seruyng hym.   And by hym sche sigh
standing his moost worthy moder, listnyng vn-to the doome.
It semed also that a soule stoode a-fore that Iuge in grete feere
and dreede, and naked as a childe than bore, and as it had be
blynde in all wyse, so þat it sigh nothinge in conscience.   But
ʒit it vndirstode what was saide and done in the paleys.   There
stode also an aungel on the right syde of the Iuge by the soule,

---

[1] *Latin* vellet omittere.

and a feende on the lefte syde.   But neither of hem touchid the
soule nor come nye it.

Aftir this the feende cried and saide : here tho, almyghty
Iuge.   I playne to-fore the that a womman, which is bothe my
5 lady and thy moder, whom thou louest so moche that thou
haste made hir myghty a-boue heuen and erthe and a-boue vs
alle feendes of helle ; for sche hath do me wronge and vnright
of this soule that stondeth now here.   For I aught of right to
haue take this soule to me anoone aftir it was | goo from the fol. 75 b
10 body, and with my felaschip to haue presented it vn-to thy
doome.   And loo, thou rightfull Iuge, that womman, thy
modre, toke this soule in-to hir stronge keping or it was fully
oute of his mouthe, and hath brought it vn-to thi doome.

Thanne the holy virgine, oure lady saint Mary, modir of
5 God, aunsuerd thus : here myne ansuere, thou deuel.   Whan
thou were maade, thou vndirstode that rightwisnesse þat was
in God euerelastingly with-outen begynnyng.   Thou haddist
also free choys to do what the list beste.   And though thou
chees rathir to hate God than to loue him, yet thou vnder-
10 stondist welle alwaye what owith to be doo aftir rightwisnesse.
Therefor I say to the that it longed more to me than to the to
presente this soule to-fore God, verray Iuge.   For while this
soule was in the body, it hadde grete charitee and loue vn-to
me, thenkyng ofte in his herte that God vouched sauf to make
25 me his modre, and þat he wolde enhaunce me hye a-boue alle
thinges that he made.   And for this cause he began to loue
God with so moche charitee that he said thus in his herte : ' I [1]
ioye so moche that God loueth the virgen Marie his modre
a-boue alle thinges that there is no creature nor bodily delite
30 in this worlde that I wolde chaunge for that ioye ; but I schuld
preferre that ioye to-fore alle erthely delytes.   And yf it were
possible that sche myght be hindrid in the leest poynte from
that worthynesse that sche is inne anempst God, I schulde rathir
chese to me in letting there-of to be tormentid euerelastingly in
35 the depnesse of helle.   And therefore endles thonkyng and
euirlasting blisse be vn-to almyghty God for þat blissid grace
and grete glorie that he hath youe vn-to his moost worthy

[1] *Marg. gloss* : (*in different hand*) ; [marke] how thu shall [loue o]wre
lady.

modre.' Ther-for, thou deuel, see now with what wille this knight dyed. And what semeth the ; whethir was it more

fol. 76 a right that his soule scholde come in-to my | defense to-fore the doome of God, or to thyne hondes, wikkedly to be tormentid ?

The feende aunsuerde : it is not my right that that soule ᷓ that loueth the more than it-selfe schulde come to myn hondes or than the doome be youe. But though thou haue oo right to doo this grace with hym to-fore the doome, yet aftir the doom be youe, his werkes schulle deme hym to myne hondis to be punisshed. Now, thou Queen,[1] I aske of the why thou drofe ᷓ so alle vs fendes from the presence of his body in the passing of the soule that none of vs myght make there ony horrour, ner bringe hym in no feer ne drede. The virgin Mary aunsuerde : that did I for that brennyng charite and loue that he hadde vn-to my body and for the ioye that he hadde that I was the ᷓ moder of God. Therfor I gat hym that grace of my sone that none euel spirit schulde come nerre hym where euere he were, nor ȝit where he is now.

Aftir this, the feend spake vn-to the Iuge and saide : I know wele that thou arte rightwisnesse and power. Thou demest ᷓ nomore vnright to the deuell than to an aungel. Deme þou ther-fore and dampne this soule to me. In that wisdome þat I hadde whan þou madist me, I haue write alle his synnes. I haue also kepte alle his synnes in that malice þat I hadde whanne I felle from heuen. For whan this soule come first to ᷓ suche age of discrecion that it vndirstode wele that it was synne that it dide, than his owne wille drow hym more to lyve in wordly pryde and flesshly delite than to withstonde suche thinges.

The aungell aunsuerde :[2] whanne his modre vndirstode firste ᷓ that his wille was flexible and redy to bowe to synne, anoone she socoured hym with workes of mercy and longe prayers that God scholde vouche sauf to haue mercy vp-on hym, that he fille not ferre from God. And by[3] thise[4] workes cf his moder

[1] *Marg. gloss in different hand* ; marke this qu[estion] of þe feende [and owre] ladysse aw[nswere] þer to.

[2] *Marg. gloss in later hand* ; Marke how þe [modres] prayers purchesyth /disposicion to [contri]cion of hyr [sone].

[3] for *cancelled, and* by *written above by hand that made marginal glosses.*

[4] i *changed to* o *by same hand that made marginal glosses.*

he gat the drede of God, so that as often as he felle in-to synne,
anone he hastid | hym to schryve hym therof.　　　　　fol. 76 b

The feende ansuerde : me behoueth to telle his synnes. And
anone as he wolde haue be-gonne to telle, he began to crie and
5 waille and to seke besyly in hym-selfe, bothe in his heede and
in alle the membres that hym semed to haue. And it semed
that he alle-to trembled and schoke, and of grete trouble he
cryed : allas and woo vn-to me, wrecche. How haue I loste
my long labour ? For not onely I haue loste the texte, but
10 also all the matere is brente where-inne alle thinges werne
writen. The matere betokneth the tymes in which he synned,
where of I haue nomore mynde than of the synnes þat weren
writen there-inne.

The aungell aunsuerde : this haue wepinges and longe labour
15 of his modre and many prayers doo ; so that God, hauyng compassion of hir wailinges, yaue hir sone suche grace that for eche
synne that he did, he gat contricion and made meke confession
of godly charitee. And ther-for tho synnes arne foryete and
putte oute of thy mynde.

20 The deuel aunsuerde, affermyng that he hadde yet a sak full
of writinges of suche synnes as the knyght hadde purposid to
haue mendid, but after he tooke no kepe thereof. And ther-
fore he most be tormentid til he haue I-done satisfaccion by
payne for suche synnes as he amendid not in his lyfe.

25 The angell ansuerd : open thy sak and aske me dome of tho
synnes for whiche thou moste chastice hym.

Thanne the feende cryed as he hadde be woode, and saide : I
am spoiled in my power ; for not only my sak is taken a-weye
from me, but also the synnes that weren ther-inne. This sak
30 was slouþe, where-inne I putte alle his synnes that I most haue
punished hym fore. For for slouthe he lefte many goode dedes
vndone.

The aungell aunsuerd : The teres of his modre haue spoiled
the and broken thy sak and distroied thy wryting, so moche
35 hir teeres plesed God.

The fende ansuerde : yet haue I here some thinges to say
ayenst hym ; that is to say, his venyal synnes.

The aungel ansuerde : he gate a wille to goo on | Pilgrimage fol. 77 a
oute of his contree, leuyng his goodes and his frendes, visiting

holy places with many labours. And thise he fulfilled in dede.
He arraied him also in suche wyse that he was worthy to
resceyue indulgence and pardon of holy chirche. And he
desired to plese God, his maker, by the amendement of his
synnes. Wherefor alle thoo causes that thou saist that thou 5
haste write arne foryoue.

The feende ansuerde: yet, at the leest, I moste punische
hym for suche venial synnes that he did, for thay arne not alle
done away by indulgences ; for they arne thousand thousandes
whiche arne writen in my tonge.   1

The aungel aunsuerde: putte oute thi tunge and schewe thy
wryting.

The feende ansuerde with grete yellyng, wailyng, and
cryeng, and saide: allas and woo vn-to mee, for I haue not oo
worde to speke ; for my tunge is cutte a-way by the rootes 1,
with all his strengthes.

The aungel aunsuerd : that hath his modir do with hir besy
prayers and labour. For sche loued his soule with alle hir
herte. And ther-for, for hir charitee, it hath plesed God to
foryeue alle his veniall synnes that he did from his childehode 2c
vn-to his dethe. And therefore thy tonge is withouten
strengthe.

The fende aunsuerd: yet haue I oo thinge bisely kepte in
my herte that may not be done a-way. And that is that he
gate thinges vnrightfully, not takyng hede to restore thaim.   2 5

The aungel aunsuerde : his modir dide satisfaccion for suche
thinges with almes and prayeris and dedes of mercy, so that
the rigour of rightwisnesse bowed it vn-to the softnesse of
mercye. For God yaue him a parfyte wille, with-oute sparing
of alle his goodes, to doo full satisfaccion aftir his power to 30
thaim fro whom he had take ony thinge vnrightfully. And
this wille God acceptith for theffecte of dede, for he myght
lyue no lenger. And there-fore his heires most do satisfaccion
for suche thinges to thair power.

The feende aunsuerd : than, yf I may not punysshe hym for 35
fol. 77 b his synnes, yet | me behoueth to chastice hym ; for he did not
goode workes and vertuos aftir his power, whan he hadde full
witte and hoole bodye. For vertues and good workes arne
that tresour that he schulde bere with hym to suche a king-

dome; that is, the gloriouse kingdome of God. Suffre me
therfore to fulfille with payne that that faileth hym in vertuose
workes.

The aungele ansuerde: it is I-write that to the asker it schall
5 be youe and to the knocker with perseueraunce it schall be
opened. Here, therfore, thou fende. His modir knocked for
him at the yate of mercy perseuerantly with prayers of charitee
and dedes of pitee more than thritty yere, weping many thousand teres that God scholde vouche sauf to yeue the holy goost
10 in-to his herte, so that he schulde with glad wille yeue his
goodes, his body, and his soule to the seruyce of God. And so
God did. For this knyght was made so feruent in charitee
that it pleasid him to lyve for none othir thinge but for to folue
and to doo the wille of God. For God was prayed so longe
15 that he yaue his blessid spirit in-to his herte. Also the virgyn
Mary, modir of God, yaue him of hir vertue alle that failed
hym in goostly armure and clothing þat longen vn-to kynghtes
whiche schullen entre in-to þe kyngdome of heuen vn-to þe hye
and soueraigne Emperour. Saintes also þat bene in þe kyng-
20 dome of heuen, whiche this Knyght loued leuyng in the
worlde, haue youen hym comforte of thair merites. For he
gadred tresour as thoo pilgrymes that chaungen euery day
temporal goodes into euerelasting richesses. And for he did
soo, therfor he schall haue ioye and worschip euerelasting;
25 and specially for that feruent desyre þat he had to goo on pil-
grimage to the holy citee of Jherusalem; and for he desired
feruently to haue yofe his lyf in bataile that the holy lande
myght be reduced vn-to þe lordeschip of cristen men, so þat
the glorious sepulcre of God myght be had in due reuerence, End of
30 yf he had be sufficient to haue brought it aboute. And | fol. 77 b

British Museum MS.
Julius F. II, f. 238 b, 1. 14 ff.

[And] þerfore, þou deule, þu has none right to fulfelle tho
thinges þe whech personally he did nat. Than þe deul hering
35 þat cried impaciently and rorid: wo to me! for all myn
memory is ablat fro me. For I have for-getyn his name.

The aungel ansuerd: his name is callid in heuen 'the son of
teeres'.

The deul cried and seide : O cursid be þat modir of him þat had so gret a wombe þat so meche wat*er* was in.   And cursid be she of me and all my*n* felaschep.

The aungil ansued : Thin curs is the Hono*ur* of God and blissing of all his frendis.   5

Than Crist the iuge spac thus, seinge : Thou deule, go thin way. Furdermore he seide to þe knight : Come, myn wel belouyd.

And so a-noon the deule fled.

Than the spowse seeing [1] these thing*es*, she seyd : O ever- 1 lasting v*er*tu and in-comp*r*ehensibil, þu my*n* lord Ih*es*u Crist, thou yet*es* all good thought*es* to h*er*tis w*ith* preyours and teeris.   Therefore honour and grace be to þe of all thing*es* þat thou has creat.   O þu my*n* suete God, þu art mo*st* deere to me and truely derer to me þan my*n* body or my*n* soule.   1

And þan the angel seid to þe spowse : thou owis to knowe þat this vision is nat only shewid of God to þe for thin com- fort, but also þat þe frendis of God may vndirstonde what he wil doo for the pr*ay*ours, weping*es*, and laboure*s* of his frendis, fol. 239 a þe whech pr*ay*ours cheritefully for | odir men and laboris w*ith* 2(perseuerans and good wil.   Thou may knowe þat þis knight thin sone shuld [2] not have had soche gr*ac*e but that he had wil fro his youþe to love God and his frendis and to eschewe gladly fall of synne.

1 MS. seing*es*.   2 MS. sh shuld.

NOTES

1/1. The chapter headings in the Garrett MS. usually differ from the Latin text; these differences are not usually mentioned in the notes, as the headings do not form an integral part of the revelations. References to the Latin text are always to the 1628 edition of the Durantus (see Table of Abbreviations).

The literary independence and originality of Birgitta, mentioned in the Introduction, pp. xxvii–xxviii, is more fully discussed in a letter written by Knutt B. Westman to Bishop Wordsworth, and printed by him (John Wordsworth, *The National Church of Sweden*, A. R. Mowbray & Co., 1911):

'Unfortunately the notices in this regard [about the books Birgitta studied or owned] are very few and not very significant. She has surely known the following books : The Bible ; Historiae Scholasticae (which I suppose to be the Historia Scholastica by Petrus Comestor); Diologus Gregorii ; Vitae patrum ; Pseudo-Bernhard, Liber de modo bene vivendi, and Speculum Virginum (an ascetic book, later on translated into Swedish, now edited by Geete, Stockholm, 1897-8).

'There is scarcely anything more to mention, if not some Italian heretical and apocalyptic books—no doubt emanating from the Fratelli—which she disapproves (Bk. III, ch. 33 ; Bk. VI, ch. 67, ch. 68).

'So there is no explicit trace of any literary influence from any of the earlier female mystics. To the question whether any such influence on the text of the revelations—for instance, from Gertrude, or either of the two Mechthild's—is, on inner reasons, to be supposed, I would personally answer in the negative. At least, no such influence is needed to explain those rather unliterary writings of Birgitta. If there can be found any detail, a thought or parable or something like that, that could be best explained by supposing such an influence (a possibility which I do not deny, though I have not found any), it must always be remembered that Birgitta and the above-named mystics are religious types of a very different kind. They are ecstatic, with their visions centred around a bridal mysticism on the lines of Bernhard's Sermones in Canticum, partly (Mechthild of Magdeburg) also devoted to the metaphysical trend of Dionysius Areopagita and the Victorines. She, even in her visions, is prophetical and practical, intent on finding and interpreting the intensely active and world-reforming will of God. To this type belongs, for instance, Savanarola, and, in some degree also, Hildegard of Bingen.'

6/10. enmy : Latin, immitior, more harsh. Immitior was mistaken for inimicior by a Latin transcriber or by the translator.

8/29. accipiunt : Latin, recipiunt.

11/32. and while he that : Latin, qui. The translation is awkward, since this clause and the preceding one are correlative.

14/3. enim is not in the Latin text.

14/17. fowle : Latin adds 'ei', which clarifies the sense.

27/2. profetying : Latin, perfectio erit.

27/34. seke : Latin adds, id est verba consolatoria cum charitate Dei.

31/5. goyng abowte seketh : Latin, circumiens monticulos inquirit.

34/23. **apostata**: Latin, apostata. The form in the MS. is probably due to the Latin.

35/4. **for he yafe Ioyfully himself**: Latin, Nam ipsa gaudenter dedit seipsam mihi. Marie and Martha are feminine throughout in the Latin; but the translator evidently felt that as long as the two were considered abstractly, as typifying the contemplative life and the active life, they should have the masculine gender. But in the following passage (35/5–24), where the Bible story is retold and the two sisters are individualized, the translator uses *she* and *hyr*. The symbolization of the lives of Mary and Martha (vita contemplativa et vita activa) began very early in Biblical exegesis. Augustine (ser. civ. 4, Migne, *Patrologia Latina* xxxviii, col. 617) writes: Duae vitae in Martha et Maria figuratae ... quae ambae fuerant Domino gratae ... duas vitas esse figuratas, presentem et futuram, laboriosam et quietam, aerumnosam et beatam, temporatem et aeternam.

42/1. **What are thes, &c.**: Latin, Quid est Domini mei. Cumque Domini circumstantes quaererent. The translator or transcriber misunderstood the passage. Julius F. II. 226 b has 'What is it, myn lordes?'

42/23. **ethiope**: see 47/27: **The ethiope betokeneth the fende.** In medieval allegorical literature an Ethiopian often represents a devil or some particular sin. It is described in Birgitta's Life how, during a period of fasting and asceticism, an Ethiopian, Castramargia, the devil of gluttony, sorely tempted Birgitta (S.R.S. iii, p. 201). Palladius (*Paladii Helenopolitani episcopi Historia Lausiaca*, ed. J. Meursius, iii, p. 427) narrates a vision of Saint Antonius which is probably the earliest medieval vision in which the judgement of souls is seen by an onlooker (*Die lateinischen Visionen des Mittelalters bis zur Mitte des 12. Jahrhundrets*, C. Fritzsche, *Romanische Forschungen*, iii, p. 264). Antonius, while praying to God, sees two souls, the one of a just and the other of a wicked man, stand before a black giant. The soul of the just man flies upward and becomes an angel, but that of the wicked man is struck down by the black giant into the sea (hell). Rabanus Maurus, archbishop of Mainz (*Allegoriae in universam sacram scripturam*, Migne, *Patrologia Latina*, cxii, col. 918), gives the following definition: Ethiopes sunt peccatores. Original as Birgitta is in her numerous descriptions of hell and purgatory, she undoubtedly owes much to the rich store of such visions which were so popular in the Middle Ages.

44/9. **lie, MS. be**: Latin, Scriptura dicit, quae mentiri non potest. *lie* and *be* are written very much alike; the scribe probably read incorrectly.

44/24. **mych lasse, &c.**; i. e. they are of much less avail in doing away his sins.

45/1–3. **hauynge . . . with-oute þe.** A difficult passage: Latin, nihil habens diminutum in te, nec transmutabile, sicut decet Deum, extra te nihil absque te, quod gaudium habeat.

48/2. **limbus.** Cf. Durantus i, p. 324, note 5: subtus terram esse quattuor sinus, siue vnum in quattuor partes divisum, quorum omnium in praesenti Capite mentio sit: primus quidem & infimus Infernus dicitur, & locus est pro damnatis constitutus; secundus est Limbus puerorum, ad quem decedentes sine Baptismo paruuli cum solo originali peccato eunt, ibique morantur ; tertius Purgatorium vocatur, in quo tandiu manent animae quamdiu pro commissis culpis diuinae iustitiae satisfecerint, & postmodum ad Dei visionem assumuntur; quartus locus dicitur Limbus Patrum, seu Abrahae sinus, qui erat constitus pro iustis, qui ante Christi Domini Passionem moriebantur.

50/3-4. The English translation incorporates in its chapter heading part of the revelation itself. The Latin text begins : Item loquitur Angelus, dicens.

50/22. moste = especially : Latin, maxime.

50/28. after this. . . . In the Latin text, Bk. IV. 9 begins here.

51/17. There is no break in the Latin text at this point ; the chapter heading and the following chapter of the English translation form the remaining part of Bk. IV. 9.

59/1. my frende, thy fader : Father Matthias, Birgitta's confessor and adviser (Durantus i, p. 115, note 2). Birger died in 1328 (S.R.S. iii, p. 188, note *e*), long before this was written.

60/9. the mynde on his werkes : Latin, recordatio operum eius.

60/25. fullfylly[ng] : praeter eius expletionem. According to N.E.D., *fulfilment* does not occur until 1775, nor does the form *fullfylly* occur ; the form *fulfyllyng* is common in the 15th cent. (cf. 60/13).

63/11. the yate of hell. The Latin adds : & eripuit amicos suos. Aperuit & Coelum laetificans Angelos, introduxit in eum ereptos de Inferno.

65/3. and of ane one he makyth a secunde : Latin, & de inimico facit amicum.

66/8. they : Latin, prothoplasti, the first created beings.

71/18. of the realme. The Latin adds : Si ergo talis homo sustineatur, & toleretur, damnabitur respublica, invalescet discordia, & intestina mala adaugebuntur in Regno.

73/1. for þer is not, &c. The translation is not clear ; Latin, nec est aliquis, qui non visitatur a Deo quamdiu viuit.

76/20. for this sowle hath l[o]ved þat is voyde : Latin, Quia ista illud quod vacuum est dilexit.

90/30. verteu, trowth, & rightwysnes. There is an influence here of the widely spread allegory of the Four Daughters of God, Misericordia, Veritas, Justitia, and Pax (Hope Traver, *The Four Daughters of God*, Bryn Mawr, 1907 ; and an article with the same title, P.M.L.A., 1925, xl, pp. 44–92). The *virgyn* here represents Misericordia (180. 16) ; *verteu* takes the place of Pax. The allegory usually concerns itself with the redemption of mankind, which is discussed by God, the Four Daughters, and sometimes by the Virgin Mary and the devil. An interesting variation of this theme is found in a story by Cesarius of Heisterbach : *Exemplum de quodam homine per multa mala opera a diabolo ducto ad iudicium dei, quem sancta Maria, Veritas, et Justitia a diabolo acceperunt.* A man burdened with sins is carried in a vision before the judgement throne of God, where the devil demands the surrender of the soul to him. Through the active aid of the Blessed Virgin Mary, whose assistance is implored by Veritas and Justitia, the soul is saved. The general similarity of this story to the revelation of

Birgitta is apparent ; but the two differ entirely in detail. The influence of the allegory on Birgitta is not close, and possibly she was not conscious of her indebtedness.

98/12. þat was **brighter** : Latin, quae erat. Refers to the Virgin.

100/10. **kyng Saules doughter.** Birgitta's memory of the Bible here plays her false. Saul's daughter, Michal, was not a widow when David married her (1 Samuel xviii. 27, xxv. 44).

107/23. **doughteris doughter.** The Latin has only *neptis* ; evidently the scribe felt that *nyfte* required explanation. Cf. also 112/26 and Glossary.

111/6. **naughtfull** : Latin, accidiosa, which Du Cange glosses molestus, tristis, taediosus.

116/29. **balaunces.** In medieval depictions of the last judgement the sins and good deeds of the soul are often weighed in a pair of scales. An example of this is in the trance of Piers Toller (*North-English Homily Collection*, G. H. Gerould, 1902, p. 56).

The devil often attempts to make false accusations against the soul, either bringing up sins which he has expiated or fabricating sins which he has not committed.   See 119/3 ff. and Book VII, ch. 13 (Durantus ii, p. 214) : Respondit Diabolus, Nam si ego possem aliquid ad eius imperfectionem fabricare, hoc libenter facerem.   A. Maury (*Recherches sur l'origine des représentations figurées de la Psychostacie ou Pèsement des âmes et sur les croyances qui s'y rattachaient* in *Revue Archéologique*, 1844, vol. i, pp. 235–49, 291–317) makes a study of the origin and widespread use of the scales motive.   He assembles a number of very interesting illustrations in art and literature of the belief in psychostacy and describes the various trickeries to which the devil resorts, only to be defeated in his purpose of capturing the soul by the Blessed Virgin Mary or some saint.

116/27–117/2. Birgitta often told anxious inquirers the condition of their friends or relatives in purgatory, and what means would lighten their punishment. ' Nam sepissime accidit, quod alique persone rogabant eam cum deuocione et caritate, ut ipsa oraret deum pro ceteris animabus aliquorum suorum defunctorum, et si ei videretur, quod essent in purgatorio et loco quo egerunt suffragiis, quod ipsa eisdem viuentibus hoc interrogantibus diceret et notificaret, per quas elimosinas et sacrificia aut per qualia viuorum suffragia ab illis penis poterant liberari' (S.R.S. iii, 196–7).

117/24. The chapter heading in the Latin (Durantus ii, p. 210) is of interest : Haec sequens revelatio facta Dominae Brigittae sponsae Christi incoepit in Neapoli statim post mortem Domini Caroli militis filii sui, & continuebatur visio ista per viagium Hierosolymitanum interpolatim, donec accessit ad Hierusalem, & ibi fuit finita in Ecclesia Sancti Sepulchri Domini. . . . (A summary of contents similar to that in the Garrett MS. follows.)

117/37–118/1. **flesshly loue.** Margaret Clausdotter, abbess of Vadstena (*Chronicon de genere et nepobibus sanctae Birgittae*, S.R.S. iii, p. 212) tells of the circumstances preceding the death of Charles. Birgitta, accompanied by Birger and Charles, her sons, Catherine, her daughter, and other devoted friends, stopped at Naples in February of 1372 on their way to Jerusalem.

Joanna, the beautiful and licentious queen of Naples, received the aged Birgitta and her band at her court. Birger paid the customary ceremonious homage before the queen's throne. When Charles's turn came he also knelt before her; but then, impressed by the queen's beauty, he rose from his knees and kissed her soundly on the lips. Instead of being offended, Joanna immediately became enamoured of the reckless young knight; within a few days she proposed marriage to him. Birgitta was highly indignant, not only because Charles was already married, but because of Joanna's very worldly life. She implored the assistance of heaven with fervent prayers; her request was granted, for Charles suddenly became sick and died after an illness of two weeks. Birgitta had a number of revelations after this, in which she denounced Joanna in no uncertain terms (Bk. VII, ch. 11).

120/28. **wordly pryde.** Margaret Clausdotter (*op. cit.*, S.R.S. iii, p. 211) says that Birgitta presented her two sons to Pope Urban V. Birger was dressed modestly in a long gown; Charles was attired in the costume of a knight, wearing an ermine cloak, skins of animals, and a heavy silver belt. The Pope, looking on them, said to Birger, 'Thou art thy mother's son'. Turning to Charles, he said, 'Thou art a son of the world'. Then Birgitta fell on her knees before the Pope and implored the remission of their sins. The Pope lifted the belt which Charles wore and said, 'It must be sufficient penance for him to wear this great weight'. Birgitta replied quickly, 'O Holy Father, take from him his sins, and I shall take away the belt'.

124/24. **And.** The following leaf, the eighth leaf of the last gathering, has been cut off with some sharp instrument. Since *And*, at the bottom of fol. 77 b, is the beginning of a sentence, and since the remaining part of the revelation could easily have been finished on the next leaf (Durantus ii, p. 214), the revelation was in all probability completed by the scribe. The translation of the remainder of the chapter in Julius F. II, which somewhat abbreviates the Latin, is given in the text.

K

GLOSSARY

(The glossary is selective, and includes only unusual words and abnormal forms of words. Where the word is common or the derivation clear, no etymology is given. The equivalent, *as it appears in the Latin text of the Revelations*, is given when it clarifies the meaning or form of the word. When the designations of mood and tense are omitted, supply pres. ind. ; when the mood only, supply ind.)

A

Abhorable, *adj.*, detestable : 60/31. First example in N.E.D., 1633.

Ablat, *p.*, ablated, taken away : 123/36. First example in N.E.D., 1542.

Accendid, *p. p.*, set on fire, kindled : 116/13.

Accion, *n.*, legal process, the taking of legal steps to obtain judicial remedy : 89/25. Lat. *actori.*

Aggrege, *inf.*, aggrieve : 76/12, 85/6 ; *p. p.*, **aggreged**, 84/11. O.F. *agregier* ; Lat. *aggrauare.*

Alther, *adj.*, of all, gen. pl. ; 58/35 ; **althir**, 104/31.

Alto, *adv.*, wholly, completely : 108/12 ; **allto**, 115/29. See N.E.D. under All, C. 14, 15.

Alyene, *v.*, alienate, estrange, transfer (property or ownership) : 91/37 ; *p. p.*, **alyende**, 2/21.

Anenste, *prep.*, before, regarding, against : 28/33, 51/27, 79/1 ; **anempst**, 103/35, 104/4, 7, 8, 10, 119/33. O.E. *on efen* ; Lat. *coram.*

Arted, 3 *pl. pret.*, restrained, pressed : 115/32. Lat. *arctarent.*

Ascapeth, 3 *s. pres.*, escapeth : 70/2.

Assissours, *n.*, assizers, sworn recognitors : 8/23.

At, *conj.*, that : 26/10, 49/18, 65/27. O.E. *þæt* ; a worn-down form, perhaps from O.N. *at*, used in same senses, or perhaps independently developed in No. dialects (N.E.D.). Lat. *quod, quae.*

Auovterer, *n.*, adulterer : 42/24. O.F. *avoutre.*

Auter, *n.*, altar : 14/2 ; **awter**, 36/36, 94/26. O.F. *auter* ; Lat. *altar.*

Ayane-byer, *n.*, saviour, redeemer : 3/13 ; **ayane-byar**, 78/2 ; **ayayne-byer**, 16/37, 83/9. Lat. *Redemptor.*

B

Baptem, *n.*, baptism : 36/17, 76/36.

Bedell, *n.*, beadle : 94/7. O.E. *bydel.*

Beld, *p. p.*, built : 9/10 ; **beldyng**, *pres. p.*, 9/10 ; **byld**, *inf.*, 67/36. Lat. *aedificare.*

Beldame, *n.*, grandmother : 112/27. Lat. *auiae.*

Besyly, *adv.*, attentively, carefully : 121/5 ; **besily**, 101/18 ; **bysely**, 22/27.

Blesful, *adj.*, full of blessing : 104/35. Lat. *benedictus.*

Bode, *p. p.*, commanded, proclaimed : 3/35, 97/28, 30. O.E. *bēodan.*

Bodely, *adv.*, boldly : 51/9. Lat. *audacter.*

Borione, *inf.*, bud or sprout : 22/9. O.F. v. from *borjon*, a bud ; cf. F. *bourgeonner*. Lat. *germinare.*

Bosn, *n.*, bosom : 72/29, 79/18. O.E. *bōsm.*

Brede, *n.*, breadth : 74/35, 83/33, 85/29. O.E. *brǣdu* ; Lat. *latitudinem.*

Brille, 2 *pl. imper.*, pour out : 105/19. O.E. *byrlian.*

Byshede, *p. p.*, drenched, moistened : 47/6. M.E. from *be* + *shed* ; Lat. *circumfusa.*

C

Caryth, *v.*, carrieth : 3 *pl.*, 22/30; 3 *s.*, 22/31. Lat. *promoveant.*

Cheker, *n.*, ex-chequer : 91/29 ; **escheker**, 72/10. O.F. *eschekier* ; Lat. *Fiscalium.*

Choweth, 3 *s. pres.*, cheweth : 59/26.

Chynes, *n.*, chines, backbones : 108/2.

Clobbed, *p. p.*, knotted, pressed into a confused mass : 76/29. Lat. *conglobata.*

Coluer, *n.*, dove : 8/16. O.E. *culfre.*

Compuncte, *p.p.,* affected with compunction or remorse: 67/28, 74/19.

Comynte, *n.,* commonalty, commonwealth: 91/15; **coméntye,** 93/35. O.F. *comunalte*; Lat. *communitatis.*

Correkke, *inf.,* correct: 91/33.

Cur, *n.,* care: 35/8. MS. *toke kepe and cur*; Lat. *curabit.*

D

Delices, *n.,* pleasures: 19/22. Lat. *delectabilitate.*

Dempte, *p.p.,* judged: 116/21.

Disperplyng, *pres. p.,* dividing, dispersing: 102/22. O.F. *desparpelier*; Lat. *distendentens.*

Dispocion, *n.,* abbreviated form of disposition: 50/5, 50/27, 52/33. Lat. *dispositio.*

Distrowble, *inf.,* disturb, trouble greatly: 71/17; *3 s.,* **distrowbleth,** 18/11. O.F. *destrobler*; Lat. *persecutor, distendit.*

Dolly, *adv.,* sluggishly, slowly: 35/35. The first example in N.E.D., 1591. O.E. *dol*; Lat. *remisse.*

Dredeful, *adj.,* fearful, full of dread: 50/14. Lat. *timorosa.*

Dysperpeler, *n.,* disperser: 5/29. See **disperplying**; Lat. *dispersor.*

E

Elke, *pron.,* each: 21/28, 29. See N.E.D. ilk, *a²*.

Endeles, *n.,* endlessness: 86/18. Only citation in N.E.D. is *endlesse,* used by Trevisa in 1398 as a quasi-substantive meaning arithmetical infinity. Lat. *aeternitatem.*

Enherite, *v.,* to make heir: 106/14.

Enmye, *n.,* enemy: 50/20; *pl.,* **enmyse,** 50/19; **Enmyes,** 99/16, 20. Lat. *inimicus.*

Entriked, *p.p.,* deceived, entangled: 84/26. O.F. *entriquer*; Lat. *implicati.*

Evyn cristen, *n.,* fellow Christian: 28/35; **evyn crysten,** 36/4; **euyn cristen,** 29/6; **eyn cristen,** 28/12, 28.

F

Farrer, *comp. adj.,* fairer: 22/36. Lat. *pulchrius.*

Fawtoures, *n.,* adherents: 9/6. O.F. *fauteur.*

Felde, *p.p.,* felt: 42/19. Lat. *expertus.*

Fered, *p.p.,* inspired with fear, terrified: 97/10.

Flayn, *p.p.,* flayed, skinned: 76/28. Lat. *decoriatum.*

Fonned, *p.p.,* to be foolish, infatuated: 56/26. M.E. *fonnen*; Lat. *infatuatus.*

Frelte, *n.,* frailty: 18/26; **freltee,** 21/2; **freelte,** 18/34.

(F)rosses, *n.,* frogs: 82/18. For MS. *throsses,* see article on **frosh** in N.E.D. No example of *throsses* for thrushes is given in N.E.D. Lat. *ranae.*

Fruyte, *v.,* bear fruit, fructify: 22/19.

G

Gameful, *adj.,* jesting, sportive: 111/6.

Glorifie, *n.,* glory: 55/35. Not in N.E.D. Lat. *Benedictum sit.*

Good, *n.,* God: 38/14; **Gode,** 50/33; **Godd,** 61/32, 64/29.

Goodely, *adj.,* Godly: 24/25; **gudely,** 24/36. Lat. *divinus.*

Goodhed, *n.,* Godhead: 86/23; **godhod,** 55/35.

Grinted, *3 pl.pret.,* ground or gnashed the teeth: 107/28; *3 pl.,* **grintith,** 111/8. Lat. *collidebatur.*

Gurched, *p.p.,* murmured, grumbled: 28/16; *pres. p.,* **gurching,** 42/26; **grucchyng,** 110/3. O.F. *grouchier*; Lat. *murmurare.*

Gurcher, *n.,* grumbler: 33/8.

H

Happes, *pl. n.,* hap, fortune: in happes, perchance: 67/28, 102/7. O.N. *happ*; Lat. *forte.*

Heleth, *n.,* health: 76/10.

Helen, *inf.,* conceal, cover: 13/18; *3 s.,* **heleth,** 17/37. O.E. *helian*; Lat. *restiant.*

Hely, *n.,* Elijah; his translation is described in 4 Kings ii. 1–11: 56/14, 19. Lat. *Helias, Elias.*

Hetee, *n.,* heat: 15/12.

Hevy, *v.,* make heavy, trouble;

3 *pl.*, 28/22. O.E. *hefigian* ; Lat. *molestantibus*.

Hooles, *n.,* holes : 65/11 ; howles, 65/9.

Horred, 3 *pl. pret.,* trembled, quaked : 95/2. 'To abhor' is the only definition given in N.E.D., which has three quotations. Lat. *horrebant.*

Hossebond, *n.,* husband : 1/22 ; hosbounde, 4/11.

Hungorie, *n.,* 49/14.

Hylle, *inf.,* cover, conceal : 19/9 ; hille, 113/15 ; 3 *s.,* hilleth, 53/18. M.E. *hulen.*

Hyued, *p. p.,* raised, exalted : 87/14 ; heved, 58/2.

I

I-now, *adj.,* enough : 25/24 ; I-noght, 27/14 ; I-neught, 71/1.

Irn, *n.,* iron : 43/2, 47/1, 79/31 ; irne, 72/1, 30, 79/11, 107/35 ; iren, 111/4 ; yren, 110/39.

J

Iaper, *n.,* jester : 93/12. Lat. *ioculatori.*

K

Kitte, *v.,* cut ; 3 *s.,* kitte, 22/16 ; kitteth, 112/13 ; *pres. p.,* kittyng, 107/35 ; *p.p.,* kytt, 79/35, 80/2 ; kutte, 112/17 ; cutte, 111/5. Lat. *abscindere.*

Knawe, *imper. s.,* know : 117/17.

L

Lake, *n.,* lack : 48/7. Lat. *defectus.*

Lefte, 3 *s. pret.,* neglected or omitted to perform (some action, duty, &c.) : 104/1.

Lepe, *n.,* hamper, basket : 27/29. O.E. *leap* ; Lat. *sporta.*

Lett, *inf.,* impede : 32/30.

Lettruer, *n.,* literature : 7/24 ; letruer, 15/32 ; lettrur, 16/16. O.F. *lettreure.*

Leuennyng, *pres. p.,* levining, lightning : 115/23. Lat. *fulminans.*

Leving, *pres. p.,* living : 115/31.

Love-drede, *n.,* the fear that proceeds from love : 24/28.

Lowsed, *p. p.,* loosed : 49/23. O.E. *losian* ; Lat. *solui.*

Lyvelod, *n.,* means of living :

66/27 ; lyfelod (Lat. *obventio,* revenue), 91/29. Lat. *victus.*

M

Maly[t]e, *n.,* stomach : 77/28. MS. *malyce* ; see Godefroy, mailleite, mulete, *estomac.* Not listed in N.E.D. Lat. *visceribus.*

Maughtes, *n.,* moths : 82/15.

Medeled, *p.p.,* mixed, mingled in conflict : 86/17. Lat. *confusum.*

Merowth, *n.,* marrow : 83/33. O.E. *mearh* ; Lat. *medulla.*

Morede, *p.p.,* increased : 30/35.

Morentyde, *n.,* morning time, dawn : 53/32 ; mornetyde, 49/36. O.E. *morgentīd* ; Lat. *aurora.*

Mowe, *inf.,* be able : 49/27, 74/25, 115/6 ; *inf.,* mow, 59/17, 115/5 ; 3 *pl.,* mowe, 104/2 ; mowen, 105/11. Lat. *posse.*

N

Naughtfull, *adj.,* possessed of no value, useless : 111/6. Lat. *pigra.*

Negh, *v.,* approach, come near to : *inf.,* negh, 4/2, 57/29 ; 3 *s.,* neghe, 99/2 ; neght, 4/3 ; neghis, 89/1 ; 3 *s. pret.,* neyght, 57/24 ; *p.p.,* neghed, 88/36. From O.E. adv. *neāh.*

Neghtburr, *n.,* neighbour : 14/35 ; neighburgh, 102/1.

Norsshyng, *pres. p.,* nourishing : 106/18.

Nowe, *n.,* that which is new : of nowe, with some change or alteration : 32/37.

Noyous, *adj.,* troublesome, injurious : 102/27. See nye.

Nye, *inf.,* annoy, injure : 89/7, 90/18, 92/15 ; 3 *s.,* noyse, 14/20. O.F. *annoier, ennuier* ; Lat. *nocere.*

Nyfte, *n.,* granddaughter : 107/22, 112/26. 'A niece' is the only definition given by the N.E.D. ; but here nyfte = *doughtres doughter* : 107/23, 112/26. O.E. *nift* ; Lat. *neptis.*

O

Oned, *n.,* onehead, unity : 86/13. See onehead in N.E.D. Lat. *vnitatem.*

Oost, *n.,* host : 65/34.

Or, *conj.* and *adv.,* ere, before : 14/33, 87/24. O.N. *ār.*

Ordinate, *adj.*, well-ordered : 26/26.
Orelege, *n.*, sun-dial : 69/1. Lat. *horologio.*
Owch, *n.*, necklace : 62/22. O.F. *nouche.*
Ower, *n.*, owner, possessor : 48/23. Lat. *possessori.*

P

Peronell, *n.*, St. Petronilla : 41/29. There is a M.E. *Legende of St. Petronilla* (*Lydgate Canon*, E.E.T.S., E.S., cvii, p. 266 ff.) in which the forms *Parnell* (l. 130) and *Pernell* (l. 157) occur.
Picke, *n.*, pitch : 111/28, 36, 112/4.
Poynte, *n.*, an instant of time : in a poynte, in a moment : 84/20. Lat. *in vnico puncto.*
Precypitacion, *n.*, action of hurling down : 65/33. Earliest definite example given in N.E.D., 1502 (1477 example questionable) ; earliest recorded use in this sense, 1607.
Pyght, *n.*, pith : 73/16. O.E. *piþa.* Lat. *medulla.*

Q

Queres, *n.*, choir : 56/17 ; quers, 56/33 ; quores, 56/7. Lat. *choros.*
Quyke, *adj.*, living : 20/21 ; whykke, 20/22 ; qwhik, 68/28 ; whyke, 77/1. O.E. *cwic* ; Lat. *viva.*

R

Reicetter, *n.*, resetter, harbourer of thieves : 5/29. O.F. *recetour*, derived from Lat. *receptorem.* Lat. *lacerator.*
Releefs, *n.*, leavings, remains of a meal : 114/4, 10. O.F. *relief.* Lat. *reliquas.*
Reperell, *inf.*, repair : 22/22. O.F. *repareiller* ; Lat. *repararet.*
Reynyng, *pres. p.*, running : 10/21. Lat. *currens.*
Roten, *p. p.*, root : 58/4 ; roted, 58/12. O.N. *rōta* ; Lat. *radicor.*
Rowned, *v.*, whispered : 3 *pl. pret.*, 89/34. O.E. *rūnian* ; Lat. *sibilaverunt.*

S

Sacrede, *p. p.*, consecrated : 78/29. O.F. *sacrer* ; Lat. *consecratus.*
Saffren, *n.*, saffron ; used as an aromatic, pungent drug and spice

in the Middle Ages : 39/5. Lat. *insipidus.*
Sake, *n.*, sack : 10/20.
Seriously, *adv.*, in order, in a series : 84/19. Lat. *seriatim.*
Seth, *conj.*, seeing that : 20/2.
Sewed, 3 *s. pret.*, petitioned, sued, made application before a court for some grant : 67/1. Lat. *insonuit.*
Singlarte, *n.*, singleness : 33/1. Lat. *singularitatem.*
Skyll, *n.*, skill, reason : 29/37. Lat. *ratione.*
Sleuth, *adj.*, slothful, slow : 91/17. Earliest example given in N.E.D., 1567. Lat. *remissior.*
Sliper, *adj.*, slippery : 68/3 ; sleper, 114/20. O.E. *slipur* ; Lat. *labilis.*
Slouthe, *n.*, sloth : 121/31 ; slewth, 16/12 ; slouþe, 121/30 ; s[l]awth, 27/37 ; slewth, from O.E. *slǣwþ* ; slouthe and slawth from M.E. *slǣwþ*, from O.E. *slǣw.* Lat. *segnities.*
Sowlle, *n.*, food, any kind of food eaten with bread : 13/21, 28 ; sowle, 16/1. O.E. *sufol* ; Lat. *edulium.*
Sparr, *inf.*, close, bar : 5/25, 24/35 : 3 *s.*, speryth, 25/1 ; *p. p.*, sperrede, 24/12 ; sperde, 101/24 ; sperd, 112/9 ; spered, 114/14. O.E. *sparrian* ; Lat. *claudere.*
Sprenkle, *n.*, sprinkler, especially one for sprinkling holy water : 106/38.
Styede, 3 *s. pret.*, rose, ascended : 1/18. O.E. *stīgan.*
Sueth, 3 *s.*, followeth : 106/23. O.F. *suer* ; Lat. *sequitur.*
Superflew, *adj.*, superfluous : 34/37.
Swaged, *p. p.*, appeased : 52/13. O.F. *suager.*
Sweth, *n.*, Sweden : 86/36. Lat. *Suetiae.*

T

Thiresty, *adj.*, thirsty : 50/15 ; thirsty, 49/15.
Thrilled, *p. p.*, pierced, penetrated : 79/10.
Thruste, *n.*, thirst : 63/1.
Trauelowse, *adj.*, laborious : 22/24.
Tremeleth, *v.*, trembleth : 50/13 ; tremlith, 111/12 ; *pres. p.*, tremelyng, 111/8 ; *past ind.*, tremeled, 107/27.

Tristyng, *pres. p.*, confiding : 4/11.
Troblesse, *adj.*, troubled, disturbed: 20/31. First example in N.E.D., c. 1. 449. Lat. *turbidam.*
Trusty, *adj.*, trustworthy : 4/14.
Trystely, *adv.*, confidently : 3/9.
Tyll man, *n.*, farmer, ploughman : 22/7 ; **tylle man,** 22/21. Lat. *excolentis, rustici.*

U

Vnlikely, *adj.*, dissimilar : 60/16. Not listed in this sense in N.E.D. Lat. *incomparabilis.*
Vnneth, *adv.*, with difficulty, scarcely : 11/4 ; **vneth,** 15/31. O.E. *unēāþe* ; Lat. *vix.*
Vnspectable, *adj.*, not able to be regarded, incomprehensible : 43/13, 45/8. Lat. *incomprehensibilem.*
Vsshe, *n.*, issue : 30/25 ; **yshew,** 31/13.

V

Venym, *n.*, venom : 72/25, 80/6, 80/8, 105/10 ; **venem,** 72/22 ; **venum,** 38/8.
Veyleable, *adj.*, beneficial, advantageous, efficacious : 14/31. Lat. *bona.*
Vowterer, *n.*, 4/11 ; *see* auovterer.
Vyce, *n.*, voice : 44/34. Lat. *voce.*
Vykked, *n.*, wicked : 21/25.

W

Wakernesse, *n.*, watchfulness : 25/8. Not in N.E.D. ; formed from the adjective *waker.* Lat. *vigilantiam.*

Warnes, *n.*, cautiousness, vigilance : 117/15. O.E. *wœrnes.*
Warr, *adj.*, cautious, ware : 27/13 ; **war,** 28/21, 32/21 ; **whar,** 23/12. O.E. *wœr.*
Wery, *adv.*, very : 98/4.
Wessell, *n.*, vessel : 72/24.
Weyte, *p. p.*, wet, moistened : 80/17. O.E. *wǣtan* ; Lat. *intinxisset.*
Whele, *n.*, wheel : 70/10, 80/30 ; **wheel,** 108/8. Lat. *rota.*
Whenched, *p.p.*, quenched : 8/24.
Whiter, *n.*, quitter, pus ; 47/8. Lat. *sanies.*
Whykke, *see* quyke.
Whyt, *prep.*, with : 58/12.
Worde, *n.*, world : 28/33.
Wordely, *adj.*, worldly : 18/7, 23/20, 47/19 ; **wordly,** 101/21, 102/33, 120/28.
Worschip, *n.*, worship : 106/21 ; **wyrshuppe,** 7/34.
Woyce, *n.*, voice : 62/30.
Wratthe, *n.*, wrath : 113/12 ; **wreth,** 37/28.
Wroth, *adj.*, angry : 89/29.
Wrayste, *v.*, wrest, deflect from the normal state : 95/28.
Wyrschoped, *p. p.*, worshipped : 98/14.
Wyssemen, *n.*, wise men : 3/36. Lat. *sapientibus.*

Y

Yate, *n.*, gate : 63/11, 123/7.
Ympnes, *n.*, hymns : 43/22.
Ysache, *n.*, Hezekiah ; cf. Isaiah, chap. 39 ; the name of the king is in neither Durantus' Latin nor Klemming's Swedish text : 64/15.

PRINTED IN GREAT BRITAIN AT THE UNIVERSITY PRESS, OXFORD
BY JOHN JOHNSON, PRINTER TO THE UNIVERSITY

Early English Text Society.

OFFICERS AND COMMITTEE:

Honorary Director:

SIR I. GOLLANCZ, Litt.D., F.B.A., KING'S COLLEGE, LONDON, W.C. 2.

Assistant Director and Secretary:

Miss MABEL DAY, D.Lit., 15, ELGIN COURT, ELGIN AVENUE, LONDON, W. 9.

Professor R. W. CHAMBERS, D.Lit., F.B.A.

Dr. S. J. CRAWFORD, M.A., B.Litt.

Dr. HENRY LITTLEHALES.

Miss A. C. PAUES, Ph.D.

Professor A. W. POLLARD, C.B., F.B.A.

Mr. ROBERT STEELE.

Sir G. F. WARNER, D.Lit., F.B.A.

American Committee { Chairman: Professor G. L. KITTREDGE, Harvard Coll., Cambr., Mass.

Hon. Sec.: Professor CARLETON BROWN, Bryn Mawr Coll., Penn., U.S.A.

Bankers:

THE NATIONAL PROVINCIAL BANK LIMITED,
2, PRINCES STREET, LONDON, E.C. 2.

The Subscription to the Society, which constitutes membership, is £2 2s. a year for the annual publications, from 1921 onwards, due in advance on the 1st of JANUARY, and should be paid by Cheque, Postal Order, or Money Order, crost 'National Provincial Bank Limited,' to the Secretary, Dr. MABEL DAY, 15, Elgin Court, Elgin Avenue, London, W. 9. The Society's Texts can also be purchased separately through a bookseller at the prices put after them in the Lists.

Any Member could save time and trouble by sending the Secreta an order on the Member's Banker to pay the subscription each Janua until countermanded. A printed form for this purpose would be sent application to the Secretary.

THE EARLY ENGLISH TEXT SOCIETY was started by the la DR. FURNIVALL in 1864 for the purpose of bringing the mass of Ea English Literature within the reach of the ordinary student, and wiping away the reproach under which England had long rested, having felt little interest in the monuments of her early langua and life.

On the starting of the Society, so many Texts of importance were once taken in hand by its Editors, that it became necessary in 1867 open, besides the *Original Series* with which the Society began, an *Ext Series* which should be mainly devoted to fresh editions of all that most valuable in texts already printed and Caxton's and other black-lett books, though first editions of MSS. will not be excluded when t convenience of issuing them demands their inclusion in the Ext Series. From 1921 there will be but one series of publications, mergi the *Original* and *Extra Series*.

During the sixty years of the Society's existence, it has produce with whatever shortcomings, and at a cost of over £35,000, an amount good solid work for which all students of our Language, and some our Literature, must be grateful, and which has rendered possible t beginnings (at least) of proper Histories and Dictionaries of th Language and Literature, and has illustrated the thoughts, the life, t manners and customs of our forefathers and foremothers.

The Society's experience has shown the very small number those inheritors of the speech of Cynewulf, Chaucer, and Shakspe who care two guineas a year for the records of that speech. The Socie has never had money enough to produce the Texts that could easily ha been got ready for it; and Editors are now anxious to send to press t work they have prepared. The necessity has therefore arisen for tryin to increase the number of the Society's members, and to induce its we wishers to help it by gifts of money, either in one sum or by instalmen The Committee trust that all Members will bring before their frien and acquaintances the Society's claims for liberal support. Until Early English MSS. are printed, no proper history of our language social life is possible.

3

ORIGINAL SERIES. *(One guinea each year up to 1920.)*

Early English Alliterative Poems, ab. 1360 A.D., ed. Rev. Dr. R. Morris. 16s.   1864
Arthur, ab. 1440. ed. F. J. Furnivall, M.A. 4s.   ,,
Lauder on the Dewtie of Kyngis, &c., 1556, ed. F. Hall, D.C.L. 4s.   ,,
Sir Gawayne and the Green Knight, ab. 1360, ed. Rev. Dr. R. Morris. 3s. 6d.   ,,
Hume's Orthographie and Congruitie of the Britan Tongue, ab. 1617, ed. H. B. Wheatley. 4s.   1865
Lancelot of the Laik, ab. 1500, ed. Rev. W. W. Skeat. 8s.   ,,
Genesis & Exodus, ab. 1250, ed. Rev. Dr. R. Morris. 8s.   ,,
Morte Arthure, ab. 1440, ed. E. Brock. 7s.   ,,
Thynne on Speght's ed. of Chaucer, A.D. 1599, ed. Dr. G. Kingsley and Dr. F. J. Furnivall. 10s.   ,,
Merlin, ab. 1440, Part I., ed. H. B. Wheatley. 2s. 6d.   ,,
Lyndesay's Monarche, &c., 1552, Part I., ed. J. Small, M.A. 3s.   ,,
Wright's Chaste Wife, ab. 1462, ed. F. J. Furnivall, M.A. 1s.   ,,
Seinte Marherete, 1200-1330, ed. Rev. O. Cockayne.   1866
Kyng Horn, Floris and Blancheflour, &c., ed. Rev. J. R. Lumby, D.D., re-ed. Dr. G. H. McKnight. 5s.   ,,
Political, Religious, and Love Poems, ed. F. J. Furnivall. 7s. 6d.   ,,
The Book of Quinte Essence, ab. 1460-70, ed. F. J. Furnivall. 1s.   ,,
Parallel Extracts from 45 MSS. of Piers the Plowman, ed. Rev. W. W. Skeat. 1s.   ,,
Hali Meidenhad, ab. 1200, ed. Rev. O. Cockayne, re-edited by Dr. F. J. Furnivall. (*v.* under 1920.)   ,,
Lyndesay's Monarche, &c., Part II., ed. J. Small, M.A. 3s. 6d.   ,,
Richard Rolle de Hampole, English Prose Treatises of, ed. Rev. G. G. Perry. (*v.* under 1920.)   ,,
Merlin, Part II., ed. H. B. Wheatley. 4s.   ,,
Partenay or Lusignen, ed. Rev. W. W. Skeat. 6s.   ,,
Dan Michel's Ayenbite of Inwyt, 1340, ed. Rev. Dr. R. Morris. 10s. 6d.   ,,
Hymns to the Virgin and Christ; the Parliament of Devils, &c., ab. 1430, ed. F. J. Furnivall. 3s.   1867
The Stacions of Rome, the Pilgrims' Sea-voyage, with Clene Maydenhod, ed. F. J. Furnivall. 1s.   ,,
Religious Pieces in Prose and Verse, from R. Thornton's MS., ed. Rev. G. G. Perry. 5s. [1913.]   ,,
Levins's Manipulus Vocabulorum, a ryming Dictionary, 1570, ed. H. B. Wheatley. 12s.   ,,
William's Vision of Piers the Plowman, 1362 A.D. : Text A, Part I., ed. Rev. W. W. Skeat. 6s.   ,,
Old English Homilies (ab. 1220-30 A.D.). Series I, Part I. Edited by Rev. Dr. R. Morris. 7s.   ,,
Pierce the Ploughmans Crede, ed. Rev. W. W. Skeat. 2s.   ,,
Myrc's Duties of a Parish Priest, in Verse, ab. 1420 A.D., ed. E. Peacock. 4s.   1868
Early English Meals and Manners: the Boke of Norture of John Russell, the Bokes of Keruynge, Curtasye, and Demeanor, the Babees Book, Urbanitatis, &c., ed. F. J. Furnivall. 12s.   ,,
The Knight de la Tour Landry, ab. 1440 A.D. A Book for Daughters, ed. T. Wright, M.A. 8s.   ,,
Old English Homilies (before 1300 A.D.). Series I, Part II., ed. R. Morris, LL.D. 8s.   ,,
Lyndesay's Works, Part III. : The Historie and Testament of Squyer Meldrum, ed. F. Hall. 2s.   ,,
Merlin, Part III. Ed. H. B. Wheatley. On Arthurian Localities, by J. S. Stuart Glennie. 12s.   1869
Sir David Lyndesay's Works, Part IV., Ane Satyre of the Three Estaits. Ed. F. Hall, D.C.L. 4s.   ,,
William's Vision of Piers the Plowman, Part II. Text B. Ed. Rev. W. W. Skeat, M.A. 10s. 6d.   ,,
Alliterative Romance of the Destruction of Troy. Ed. D. Donaldson & G. A. Panton. Pt. I. 10s. 6d.   ,,
English Gilds, their Statutes and Customs, 1389 A.D. Edit. Toulmin Smith and Lucy T. Smith, with an Essay on Gilds and Trades-Unions, by Dr. L. Brentano (reprinted 1924). 30s.   1870
William Lauder's Minor Poems. Ed. F. J. Furnivall. 3s.   ,,
Bernardus De Cura Rei Famuliaris, Early Scottish Prophecies, &c. Ed. J. R. Lumby, M.A. 2s.   ,,
Ratis Raving, and other Moral and Religious Pieces. Ed. J. R Lumby, M.A. 3s.   ,,
The Alliterative Romance of Joseph of Arimathie, or The Holy Grail: from the Vernon MS.; with W. de Worde's and Pynson's Lives of Joseph : ed. Rev. W. W. Skeat, M.A. 5s.   1871
King Alfred's West-Saxon Version of Gregory's Pastoral Care, edited from 2 MSS., with an English translation, by Henry Sweet, Esq., B.A., Balliol College, Oxford. Part I. 10s.   ,,
Legends of the Holy Rood, Symbols of the Passion and Cross Poems, ed. Rev. Dr. R. Morris. 10s.   ,,
Sir David Lyndesay's Works, Part V., ed. Dr. J. A. H. Murray. 3s.   ,,
The Times' Whistle, and other Poems, by R. C., 1616 ; ed. by J. M. Cowper, Esq. 6s.   ,,
An Old English Miscellany, containing a Bestiary, Kentish Sermons, Proverbs of Alfred, and Religious Poems of the 13th cent., ed. from the MSS. by the Rev. R. Morris, LL.D. 10s.   1872
King Alfred's West-Saxon Version of Gregory's Pastoral Care, ed. H. Sweet, M.A. Part II. 10s.   ,,
The Life of St Juliana, 2 versions, A.D. 1230, with translations; ed. T. O. Cockayne & E. Brock. 2s.   ,,
Palladius on Husbondrie, englisht (ab. 1420 A.D.), ed. Rev. Barton Lodge, M.A. Part I. 10s.   ,,
Old-English Homilies, Series II., and three Hymns to the Virgin and God, 13th-century, with the music to two of them, in old and modern notation ; ed. Rev. R. Morris, LL.D. 8s.   1873
The Vision of Piers Plowman, Text C: Richard the Redeles (by William, the author of the *Vision*) and **The Crowned King**; Part III., ed. Rev. W. W. Skeat, M.A. 18s.   ,,
Generydes, a Romance, ab. 1440 A.D. ed. W. Aldis Wright, M.A. Part I. 3s.   ,,
The Gest Hystoriale of the Destruction of Troy, in alliterative verse ; ed. by D. Donaldson, Esq., and the late Rev. G. A. Panton. Part II. 10s. 6d.   1874
The Early English Version of the "Cursor Mundi"; in four Texts, edited by the Rev. R. Morris, M.A., LL.D. Part I, with 2 photolithographic facsimiles. 10s. 6d.   ,,

58. **The Blickling Homilies,** 971 A.D., ed. Rev. R. Morris, LL.D.   Part I.   8s.
59. **The " Cursor Mundi "** in four Texts, ed. Rev. Dr. R. Morris.   Part II.   15s.
60. **Meditacyuns on the Soper of our Lorde** (by Robert of Brunne), edited by J. M. Cowper.   2s. 6d.
61. **The Romance and Prophecies of Thomas of Erceldoune,** from 5 MSS.; ed. Dr. J. A. H. Murray.   10s. 6d.
62. **The "Cursor Mundi,"** in four Texts, ed. Rev. Dr. R. Morris.   Part III.   15s.
63. **The Blickling Homilies,** 971 A.D., ed. Rev. Dr. R. Morris.   Part II.   7s.
64. **Francis Thynne's Embleames and Epigrams,** A.D. 1600, ed. F. J. Furnivall.   7s.
65. **Be Domes Dæge** (Bede's *De Die Judicii*), &c., ed. J. R. Lumby, B.D.   2s.
66. **The " Cursor Mundi,"** in four Texts, ed. Rev. Dr. R. Morris.   Part IV., with 2 autotypes.   10s.
67. **Notes on Piers Plowman,** by the Rev. W. W. Skeat, M.A.   Part I.   21s.
68. **The "Cursor Mundi,"** in 4 Texts, ed. Rev. Dr. R. Morris.   Part V.   25s.
69. **Adam Davie's 5 Dreams about Edward II., &c.,** ed. F. J. Furnivall, M.A.   5s.
70. **Generydes,** a Romance, ed. W. Aldis Wright, M.A.   Part I.   4s.
71. **The Lay Folks Mass-Book,** four texts, ed. Rev. Canon Simmons.   25s.
72. **Palladius on Husbondrie,** englisht (ab. 1420 A.D.).   Part II.   Ed. S. J. Herrtage, B.A.   15s.
73. **The Blickling Homilies,** 971 A.D., ed. Rev. Dr. R. Morris.   Part III.   10s.
74. **English Works of Wyclif,** hitherto unprinted, ed. F. D. Matthew, Esq.   20s.
75. **Catholicon Anglicum,** an early English Dictionary, from Lord Monson's MS. A.D. 1483, ed., with Introduction & Notes, by S. J. Herrtage, B.A.; and with a Preface by H. B. Wheatley.   20s.
76. **Aelfric's Metrical Lives of Saints,** in MS. Cott. Jul. E 7., ed. Rev. Prof. Skeat, M.A.   Part I.   10s.
77. **Beowulf,** the unique MS. autotyped and transliterated, edited by Prof. Zupitza, Ph.D.   25s.
78. **The Fifty Earliest English Wills,** in the Court of Probate, 1387-1439, ed. by F. J. Furnivall, M.A.   7s.
79. **King Alfred's Orosius,** from Lord Tollemache's 9th century MS., Part I. ed. H. Sweet, M.A.   13s.
79 b.   *Extra Volume.*   Facsimile of the Epinal Glossary, ed. H. Sweet, M.A.   15s.
80. **The Early-English Life of St. Katherine** and its Latin Original, ed. Dr. Einenkel.   12s.
81. **Piers Plowman :** Notes, Glossary, &c.   Part IV, completing the work, ed. Rev. Prof. Skeat, M.A.   18s.
82. **Aelfric's Metrical Lives of Saints,** MS. Cott. Jul. E 7., ed. Rev. Prof. Skeat, M.A., LL.D.   Part II.   12s.
83. **The Oldest English Texts, Charters, &c.,** ed. H. Sweet, M.A.   20s.
84. **Additional Analogs to ' The Wright's Chaste Wife,'** No. 12, by W. A. Clouston.   1s.
85. **The Three Kings of Cologne.**   2 English Texts, and 1 Latin, ed. Dr. C. Horstmann.   17s.
86. **Prose Lives of Women Saints,** ab. 1610 A.D., ed. from the unique MS. by Dr. C. Horstmann.   12s.
87. **The Early South-English Legendary** (earliest version), Laud MS. 108, ed. Dr. C. Horstmann.   20s.
88. **Hy. Bradshaw's Life of St. Werburghe** (Pynson, 1521), ed. Dr. C. Horstmann.   10s.
89. **Vices and Virtues,** from the unique MS., ab. 1200 A.D., ed. Dr. F. Holthausen.   Part I.   8s.
90. **Anglo-Saxon and Latin Rule of St. Benet,** interlinear Glosses, ed. Dr. H. Logeman.   12s.
91. **Two Fifteenth-Century Cookery-Books,** ab. 1430-1450, edited by Mr. T. Austin.   10s.
92. **Eadwine's Canterbury Psalter,** from the Trin. Cambr. MS., ab. 1150 A.D., ed. F. Harsley, B.A. Pt. I. 12s.
93. **Defensor's Liber Scintillarum,** edited from the MSS. by Ernest Rhodes, B.A.   12s.
94. **Aelfric's Metrical Lives of Saints,** MS. Cott. Jul. E 7, Part III., ed. Prof. Skeat, Litt.D., LL.D.   15s.
95. **The Old-English version of Bede's Ecclesiastical History,** re-ed. by Dr. Thomas Miller.   Part I, § 1.   18s.
96. **The Old-English version of Bede's Ecclesiastical History,** re-ed. by Dr. Thomas Miller.   Pt. I, § 2.   15s.
97. **The Earliest English Prose Psalter,** edited from its 2 MSS. by Dr. K. D. Buelbring.   Part I.   15s.
98. **Minor Poems of the Vernon MS.,** Part I., ed. Dr. C. Horstmann.   20s.
99. **Cursor Mundi.**   Part VI.   Preface, Notes, and Glossary, ed. Rev. Dr. R. Morris.   10s.
100. **Capgrave's Life of St. Katharine,** ed. Dr. C. Horstmann, with Forewords by Dr. Furnivall.   20s.
101. **Cursor Mundi.**   Part VII.   Essay on the MSS., their Dialects, &c., by Dr. H. Hupe.   10s.
102. **Lanfranc's Cirurgie,** ab. 1400 A.D., ed. Dr. R. von Fleischhacker.   Part I.   20s.
103. **The Legend of the Cross,** from a 12th century MS., &c., ed. Prof. A. S. Napier, M.A., Ph.D.   7s. 6d.
104. **The Exeter Book** (Ang.-Saxon Poems), re-edited from the unique MS. by I. Gollancz, M.A.   Part I.   20s.
105. **The Prymer or Lay-Folks' Prayer-Book,** Camb. Univ. MS., ab. 1420, ed. Henry Littlehales.   Part I.   10s.
106. **R. Misyn's Fire of Love and Mending of Life** (Hampole), 1434, 1435, ed. Rev. R. Harvey, M.A.   15s.
107. **The English Conquest of Ireland,** A.D. 1166-1185, 2 Texts, 1425, 1440, Pt. I, ed. Dr. Furnivall.   15s.
108. **Child-Marriages and -Divorces, Trothplights, &c.**   Chester Depositions, 1561-6, ed. Dr. Furnivall.   15s.
109. **The Prymer or Lay-Folks Prayer-Book,** ab. 1420, ed. Henry Littlehales.   Part II.   10s.
110. **The Old-English Version of Bede's Ecclesiastical History,** ed. Dr. T. Miller.   Part II, § 1.   15s.
111. **The Old-English Version of Bede's Ecclesiastical History,** ed. Dr. T. Miller.   Part II, § 2.   15s.
112. **Merlin,** Part IV : Outlines of the Legend of Merlin, by Prof. W. E. Mead, Ph.D.   15s.
113. **Queen Elizabeth's Englishings of Boethius, Plutarch &c. &c.,** ed. Miss C. Pemberton.   15s.
114. **Aelfric's Metrical Lives of Saints,** Part IV and last, ed. Prof. Skeat, Litt.D., LL.D.   10s.
115. **Jacob's Well,** edited from the unique Salisbury Cathedral MS. by Dr. A. Brandeis.   Part I.   10s.
116. **An Old-English Martyrology,** re-edited by Dr. G. Herzfeld.   10s.
117. **Minor Poems of the Vernon MS.,** edited by Dr. F. J. Furnivall.   Part II.   15s.
118. **The Lay Folks' Catechism,** ed. by Canon Simmons and Rev. H. E. Nolloth, M.A.   5s.
119. **Robert of Brunne's Handlyng Synne** (1303), and its French original, re-ed. by Dr. Furnivall.   Pt. I.   10s.
120. **The Rule of St. Benet in Northern Prose and Verse, & Caxton's Summary,** ed. by E. A. Kock.   15s.
121. **The Laud MS. Troy-Book,** ed. from the unique Laud MS. 595, by Dr. J. E. Wülfing.   Part I.   15s.
122. **The Laud MS. Troy-Book,** ed. from the unique Laud MS. 595, by Dr. J. E. Wülfing.   Part II.   20s.
123. **Robert of Brunne's Handlyng Synne** (1303), and its French original, re-ed. by Dr. Furnivall.   Pt. II. 10s.
124. **Twenty-six Political and other Poems** from Digby MS. 102 &c., ed. by Dr. J. Kail.   Part I.   10s.

Medieval Records of a London City Church, ed. Henry Littlehales. Part I. 10s.   1904
An Alphabet of Tales, in Northern English, from the Latin, ed. Mrs. M. M. Banks. Part I. 10s.   ,,
An Alphabet of Tales, in Northern English, from the Latin, ed. Mrs. M. M. Banks. Part II. 10s.   1905
Medieval Records of a London City Church, ed. Henry Littlehales. Part II. 10s.   ,,
The English Register of Godstow Nunnery, ed. from the MSS. by the Rev. Dr. Andrew Clark. Pt. I. 10s.   ,,
The English Register of Godstow Nunnery, ed. from the MSS. by the Rev. Dr. A. Clark. Pt. II. 15s.   1906
The Brut, or The Chronicle of England, edited from the best MSS. by Dr. F. Brie. Part I. 10s.   ,,
John Metham's Works, edited from the unique MS. by Dr. Hardin Craig. 15s.   ,,
The English Register of Oseney Abbey, by Oxford, ed. by the Rev. Dr. A. Clark. Part I. 15s.   1907
The Coventry Leet Book, edited from the unique MS. by Miss M. Dormer Harris. Part I. 15s.   ,,
The Coventry Leet Book, edited from the unique MS. by Miss M. Dormer Harris. Part II. 15s.   1908
. *Extra Issue.* Prof. Manly's **Piers Plowman & its Sequence,** urging the fivefold authorship of the *Vision.*
   5s. [*On sale to Members only.*]
The Brut, or The Chronicle of England, edited from the best MSS. by Dr. F. Brie. Part II. 15s.   ,,
Twelfth-Century Homilies in MS. Bodley 343, ed. by A. O. Belfour, M.A. Part I, the Text. 15s.   1909
The Coventry Leet Book, edited from the unique MS. by Miss M. Dormer Harris. Part III. 15s.   ,,
John Arderne's Treatises on Fistula in Ano, &c., ed. by D'Arcy Power, M.D. 15s.   1910
b, c, d, e, f, Extra Issue. **The Piers Plowman Controversy:** *b.* **Dr. Jusserand's 1st Reply to Prof.**
   Manly; *c.* Prof. Manly's Answer to Dr. Jusserand; *d.* Dr. Jusserand's 2nd Reply to Prof. Manly;
   e. Mr. R. W. Chambers's Article; *f.* Dr. Henry Bradley's Rejoinder to Mr. R. W. Chambers
   (issued separately). 10s. [*On sale to Members only.*]   ,,
Capgrave's Lives of St. Augustine and St. Gilbert of Sempringham, A.D. 1451, ed. by John Munro. 10s. ,,
Earth upon Earth, all the known texts, ed., with an Introduction, by Miss Hilda Murray, M.A. 10s.   1911
The English Register of Godstow Nunnery, edited by the Rev. Dr. Andrew Clark. Part III. 10s.   ,,
The Wars of Alexander the Great, Thornton MS., ed. J. S. Westlake, M.A. 10s.   ,,
The English Register of Oseney Abbey, by Oxford, edited by the Rev. Dr. Andrew Clark. Part II. 10s.   1912
The Northern Passion, ed. by Miss F. A. Foster, Ph.D. Part I, the four parallel texts. 15s.   ,,
The Coventry Leet Book, ed. Miss M. Dormer Harris. Introduction, Indexes, etc. Part IV. 10s.   1913
. The Northern Passion, ed. Miss F. A. Foster, Ph.D., Introduction, French Text, Variants and
   Fragments, Glossary. Part II. 15s.   ,,
   [An enlarged re-print of No. 26, **Religious Pieces in Prose and Verse,** from the Thornton MS.,
   edited by Rev. G. G. Perry. 5s.]
. A Fifteenth-Century Courtesy Book and Two Franciscan Rules, edited by R. W. Chambers, M.A.,
   Litt.D., and W. W. Seton, M.A. 7s. 6d.   1914
. Sixty-three Lincoln Diocese Documents, ed. by the Rev. Dr. Andrew Clark. 15s.   ,,
. The Old-English Rule of Bp. Chrodegang, and the Capitula of Bp. Theodulf, ed. Prof. Napier, Ph.D.
   7s. 6d.   ,,
. The Lanterne of Light, ed. by Miss Lilian M. Swinburn, M.A. 15s.   1915
. Early English Homilies, from Vesp. D. XIV., ed. by Miss Rubie D.-N. Warner. Part I, Text. 15s.   ,,
. Mandeville's Travels, ed. by Professor Paul Hamelius. Part I, Text. 15s.   1916
. Mandeville's Travels (Notes and Introduction). 15s.   ,,
. The Wheatley MS., ed. by Miss Mabel Day, M.A. 30s.   1917
. Reginald Pecock's Donet, from Bodl. MS. 916; ed. by Miss E. Vaughan Hitchcock. 35s.   1918
'. Harmony of the Life of Christ, from MS. Pepys 2498, ed. by Miss Margery Goates. 15s.   1919
3. Meditations on the Life and Passion of Christ, from MS. Addit. 11307, ed. by Miss Charlotte
   D'Evelyn. 20s.   ,,
). Vices and Virtues, Part II., ed. Prof. F. Holthausen. 12s.   1920
   [A re-print of No. 20, **English Prose Treatises** of Richard Rolle de Hampole, ed. Rev. G. G. Perry.
   5s.]   ,,
   [A re-edition of No. 18, **Hali Meidenhad,** ed. O. Cockayne, with a variant MS., Bodl. 34, hitherto
   unprinted, ed. Dr. Furnivall. 12s.]   ,,
0. The Old English Heptateuch, MS. Cott. Claud. B. IV., ed. S. J. Crawford, M.A. 42s.   1921
1. Three O.E. Prose Texts, MS. Cott. Vit. A. XV., ed. Dr. S. Rypins. 25s.   ,,
2. Facsimile of MS. Cotton Nero A. x (Pearl, Cleanness, Patience and Sir Gawain), Introduction by
   Sir I. Gollancz. 63s.   1922
3. Book of the Foundation of St. Bartholomew's, Smithfield, ed. the late Sir Norman Moore. 10s.   1923
'4. Pecock's Folewer to the Donet, ed. by Miss E. Vaughan Hitchcock. 30s.   ,,
'5. Middleton's Chinon of England, with Leland's Assertio Arturii and Robinson's translation, ed. Prof.
   W. E. Mead, Ph.D. 25s.   ,,
'6. Stanzaic Life of Christ, ed. Dr. Frances A. Foster. 35s.   1924
'7. Trevisa's Dialogus inter Militem et Clericum, Sermon by FitzRalph, and Bygynnyng of the World,
   ed. A. J. Perry, M.A. 25s.   ,,
'8. Caxton's Ordre of Chyualry, ed. A. T. P. Byles, M.A. 15s.   1925
39. The Southern Passion, ed. Dr. Beatrice Brown. 15s.   ,,
'0. Walton's Boethius, ed. Dr. M. Science. 30s.   ,,
'1. Pecock's Reule of Cristen Religioun, ed. Dr. W. C. Greet. 35s.   1926
72. The Seege or Batayle of Troy, ed. Miss M. E. Barnicle. 25s.   ,,
73. Hawes' Pastime of Pleasure, ed. Prof. W. E. Mead. 15s.   1927
74. The Life of St. Anne, ed. R. E. Parker. 10s.   ,,
75. Barclay's Eclogues, ed. Miss Beatrice White, M.A. 25s.
76. Caxton's Prologues and Epilogues, ed. W. J. B. Crotch, M.A. 15s.   ,,

EXTRA SERIES. *(One guinea each year up to 1920.)*

The Publications for 1867-1919 (one guinea each year) are :—

I. **William of Palerne**; or, **William and the Werwolf**. Re-edited by Rev. W. W. Skeat, M.A. 13*s.*

II. **Early English Pronunciation** with especial Reference to Shakspere and Chaucer, by A. J. Ellis, F.R.S. Part I. 10*s.*

III. **Caxton's Book of Curtesye**, in Three Versions. Ed. F. J. Furnivall. 5*s.*

IV. **Havelok the Dane**. Re-edited by the Rev. W. W. Skeat, M.A. 10*s.*

V. **Chaucer's Boethius**. Edited from the two best MSS. by Rev. Dr. R. Morris. 12*s.*

VI. **Chevelere Assigne**. Re-edited from the unique MS. by Lord Aldenham, M.A. 3*s.*

VII. **Early English Pronunciation**, by A. J. Ellis, F.R.S. Part II. 10*s.*

VIII. **Queene Elizabethes Achademy, &c.** Ed. F. J. Furnivall. Essays on early Italian and German Books of Courtesy, by W. M. Rossetti and Dr. E. Oswald. 13*s.*

IX. **Awdeley's Fraternitye of Vacabondes, Harman's Caveat, &c.** Ed. E. Viles & F. J. Furnivall. 7*s.* 6*d.*

X. **Andrew Boorde's Introduction of Knowledge, 1547, Dyetary of Helth, 1542, Barnes in Defence of the Berde, 1542-3.** Ed. F. J. Furnivall. 18*s.*

XI. **Barbour's Bruce**, Part I. Ed. from MSS. and editions, by Rev. W. W. Skeat, M.A. 12*s.*

XII. **England in Henry VIII.'s Time** : a Dialogue between Cardinal Pole & Lupset, by Thom. Starkey, Chaplain to Henry VIII. Ed. J. M. Cowper. Part II. 12*s.* (Part I. is No. XXXII, 1878, 8*s.*)

XIII. **A Supplicacyon of the Beggers**, by Simon Fish, 1528-9 A.D., ed. F. J. Furnivall ; with **A Supplication to our Moste Soueraigne Lorde ; A Supplication of the Poore Commons ;** and **The Decaye of England by the Great Multitude of Sheep**, ed. by J. M. Cowper, Esq. 6*s.*

XIV. **Early English Pronunciation**, by A. J. Ellis, Esq., F.R.S. Part III. 10*s.*

XV. **Robert Crowley's Thirty-One Epigrams, Voyce of the Last Trumpet, Way to Wealth, &c.**, A.D. 1550-1, edited by J. M. Cowper, Esq. 12*s.*

XVI. **Chaucer's Treatise on the Astrolabe**. Ed. Rev. W. W. Skeat, M.A. 6*s.*

XVII. **The Complaynt of Scotlande**, 1549 A.D., with 4 Tracts (1542-48), ed. Dr. Murray. Part I. 10*s.*

XVIII. **The Complaynt of Scotlande**, 1549 A.D., ed. Dr. Murray. Part II. 8*s.*

XIX. **Oure Ladyes Myroure**, A.D. 1530, ed. Rev. J. H. Blunt, M.A. 24*s.*

XX. **Lovelich's History of the Holy Grail** (ab. 1450 A.D.), ed. F. J. Furnivall, M.A., Ph.D. Part I. 8*s.*

XXI. **Barbour's Bruce**, Part II., ed. Rev. W. W. Skeat, M.A. 4*s.*

XXII. **Henry Brinklow's Complaynt of Roderyck Mors** (ab. 1542) : and **The Lamentacion of a Christian against the Citie of London**, made by Roderigo Mors, A.D. 1545. Ed. J. M. Cowper. 9*s.*

XXIII. **Early English Pronunciation**, by A. J. Ellis, F.R.S. Part IV. 10*s.*

XXIV. **Lovelich's History of the Holy Grail**, ed. F. J. Furnivall, M.A., Ph.D. Part II. 10*s.*

XXV. **Guy of Warwick**, 15th-century Version, ed. Prof. Zupitza. Part I. 20*s.*

XXVI. **Guy of Warwick**, 15th-century Version, ed. Prof. Zupitza. Part II. 14*s.*

XXVII. **Bp. Fisher's English Works** (died 1535), ed. by Prof. J. E. B. Mayor. Part I, the Text. 16*s.*

XXVIII. **Lovelich's Holy Grail**, ed. F. J. Furnivall, M.A., Ph.D. Part III. 10*s.*

XXIX. **Barbour's Bruce**. Part III., ed. Rev. W. W. Skeat, M.A. 21*s.*

XXX. **Lovelich's Holy Grail**, ed. F. J. Furnivall, M.A., Ph.D. Part IV. 15*s.*

XXXI. **The Alliterative Romance of Alexander and Dindimus**, ed. Rev. W. W. Skeat. 6*s.*

XXXII. **Starkey's "England in Henry VIII's time."** Pt. I. Starkey's Life and Letters, ed. S. J. Herrtage. 8*s.*

XXXIII. **Gesta Romanorum** (englisht ab. 1440), ed. S. J. Herrtage, B.A. 15*s.*

XXXIV. **The Charlemagne Romances :—1. Sir Ferumbras**, from Ashm. MS. 33, ed. S. J. Herrtage. 15*s.*

XXXV. **Charlemagne Romances :—2. The Sege off Melayne, Sir Otuell**, &c., ed. S. J. Herrtage. 12*s.*

XXXVI. **Charlemagne Romances :—3. Lyf of Charles the Grete**, Pt. I., ed. S. J. Herrtage. 16*s.*

XXXVII. **Charlemagne Romances :—4. Lyf of Charles the Grete**, Pt. II., ed. S. J. Herrtage. 15*s.*

XXXVIII. **Charlemagne Romances :—5. The Sowdone of Babylone**, ed. Dr. Hausknecht. 15*s.*

XXXIX. **Charlemagne Romances :—6. Rauf Colyear, Roland, Otuel**, &c., ed. S. J. Herrtage, B.A. 15*s.*

XL. **Charlemagne Romances :—7. Huon of Burdeux**, by Lord Berners, ed. S. L. Lee, B.A. Part I. 15*s.*

XLI. **Charlemagne Romances :—8. Huon of Burdeux**, by Lord Berners, ed. S. L. Lee, B.A. Pt. II. 15*s.*

XLII. **Guy of Warwick** : 2 texts (Auchinleck MS. and Caius MS.), ed. Prof. Zupitza. Part I. 15*s.*

XLIII. **Charlemagne Romances :—9. Huon of Burdeux**, by Lord Berners, ed. S. L. Lee, B.A. Pt. III. 15*s.*

XLIV. **Charlemagne Romances :—10. The Four Sons of Aymon**, ed. Miss Octavia Richardson. Pt. I. 15*s.*

XLV. **Charlemagne Romances :—11. The Four Sons of Aymon**, ed. Miss O. Richardson. Pt. II. 20*s.*

XLVI. **Sir Bevis of Hamton**, from the Auchinleck and other MSS., ed. Prof. E. Kölbing, Ph.D. Part I. 10*s.*

XLVII. **The Wars of Alexander**, ed. Rev. Prof. Skeat, Litt.D., LL.D. 20*s.*

XLVIII. **Sir Bevis of Hamton**, ed. Prof. E. Kölbing, Ph.D. Part II. 10*s.*

XLIX. **Guy of Warwick**, 2 texts (Auchinleck and Caius MSS.), Pt. II., ed. Prof. J. Zupitza, Ph.D. 15*s.*

L. **Charlemagne Romances :—12. Huon of Burdeux**, by Lord Berners, ed. S. L. Lee, B.A. Part IV. 5*s.*

LI. **Torrent of Portyngale**, from the unique MS. in the Chetham Library, ed. E. Adam, Ph.D. 10*s.*

LII. **Bullein's Dialogue against the Feuer Pestilence, 1578** (ed. 1, 1564). Ed. M. & A. H. Bullen. 10*s.*

LIII. **Vicary's Anatomie of the Body of Man, 1548**, ed. 1577, ed. F. J. & Percy Furnivall. Part I. 15*s.*

LIV. **Caxton's Englishing of Alain Chartier's Curial**, ed. Dr. F. J. Furnivall & Prof. P. Meyer. 5*s.*

LV. **Barbour's Bruce**, ed. Rev. Prof. Skeat, Litt.D., LL.D. Part IV. 5*s.*

LVI. **Early English Pronunciation**, by A. J. Ellis, Esq., F.R.S. Pt. V., the present English Dialects. 25*s.*

LVII. **Caxton's Eneydos**, A.D. 1490, coll. with its French, ed. M. T. Culley, M.A. & Dr. F. J. Furnivall. 13*s.* 18

LVIII. **Caxton's Blanchardyn & Eglantine, c. 1489**, extracts from ed. 1595, & French, ed. Dr. L. Kellner. 17*s.*

LIX. **Guy of Warwick**, 2 texts (Auchinleck and Caius MSS.), Part III., ed. Prof. J. Zupitza, Ph.D. 15*s.* 18

Forthcoming issues will be chosen from the following, and will be issued as complete

Byrhtferth's Manual, ed. S. J. Crawford. [*At Press.*
Sir Firumbras, ed. Miss M. I. O'Sullivan. [*At Press.*
The Alliterative Siege of Jerusalem, ed. the late Prof. E. Kölbing, Ph.D. [*At Press.*
The Earliest English Apocalypse with a Commentary, ed. Dr. Anna C. Paues. [*At Press.*
Piers Plowman, the A Text, ed. Prof. R. W. Chambers and J. H. G. Grattan. [*At Press.*
Lydgate's Minor Poems, ed. Dr. H. N. MacCracken. Part II, Secular Poems. [*At Press.*
Lydgate's Troy Book, ed. Dr. Hy. Bergen. Part IV, Introduction, Notes, &c. [*At Press.*
Lydgate's Siege of Thebes, ed. the late Prof. A. Erdmann and Prof. Ekwall. Part II, Notes, &c.
Sir Thomas More's Apology, ed. A. M. Taft.
English Poems of Charles of Orleans, ed. R. Steele. [*At Press.*
Tudor English Lives of Sir Thomas More, by Roper, Harpsfield and Ro. Ba., ed. Prof. R. W. Chambers
    Dr. E. V. Hitchcock. [*At Press.*
The Mirror of Life, ed. D. Irwin Price.
Seinte Marherete, re-ed. Miss F. Mack.
The Dance of Death, ed. the late Miss Florence Warren.
Caxton's Faits of Armes and Chiualry, ed. A. T. Byles.
Revelations of St. Birgitta, ed. Prof. W. P. Cumming. [*At Press.*
The Castle of Pleasure, ed. Miss R. Cornelius. [*At Press.*
Bokenham's Lives of Holy Women (Lives of the Saints), ed. Dr. Mary Sergeantson.
Harleian MS. 2253 (English Poems), ed. Miss Hilda Murray.

Other texts are under consideration.

November 1928.

_____

PUBLISHER:

LONDON: HUMPHREY MILFORD, OXFORD UNIV. PRESS, Amen House, E.C.